Outsourcing and Human Resource Management

Outsourcing is an increasingly popular strategy deployed by a variety of institutions, including banks, multinational companies and small and medium-sized enterprises (SMEs). However, the literature on outsourcing does not reflect this increasingly complex and important practice in the global economy, having considered it largely from the narrow perspective of cost-saving analysis. Other important dimensions of outsourcing, including human resources, legal and insurance aspects have been neglected. This unique book examines outsourcing in a wide range of countries, including Japan, Europe and the United States, from a broad standpoint – with particular emphasis on the role of human resource management – that goes beyond the traditional view of outsourcing as simply a search for cheaper labour, as happened in the phase of globalization prior to outsourcing.

The book assesses the problems and solutions for those attempting to outsource through an analysis of human resource management, insourcing, lifecycles of the project, insurance requirements, operational management and recruitment within the context of the financial services industry, and automotive and IT industries of Japan, North and South Korea, South Africa, Mexico, Eastern Europe, China and India.

Ruth Taplin is Director of the Centre for Japanese and East Asian Studies, London, which won Exporter of the Year in Partnership in Trading/Pathfinder for the UK in 2000. She received her doctorate from the London School of Economics and is the author/editor of 14 books and over 200 articles. She has been Editor of the *Journal of Interdisciplinary Economics* for 12 years. Currently she is a Research Fellow at Birkbeck College, University of London, the University of Leicester and a number of universities globally. She is Visiting Professor at the School of International Business and Management, University of Warsaw, Poland, and was a Visiting Fellow at the University of Mumbai Economics Department in January 2007.

Routledge Studies in the Growth Economies of Asia

1 **The Changing Capital Markets of East Asia**
Edited by Ky Cao

2 **Financial Reform in China**
Edited by On Kit Tam

3 **Women and Industrialization in Asia**
Edited by Susan Horton

4 **Japan's Trade Policy**
Action or reaction?
Yumiko Mikanagi

5 **The Japanese Election System**
Three analaytical perspectives
Junichiro Wada

6 **The Economics of the Latecomers**
Catching-up, technology transfer and institutions in Germany, Japan and South Korea
Jang-Sup Shin

7 **Industrialization in Malaysia**
Import substitution and infant industry performance
Rokiah Alavi

8 **Economic Development in Twentieth Century East Asia**
The international context
Edited by Aiko Ikeo

9 **The Politics of Economic Development in Indonesia**
Contending perspectives
Edited by Ian Chalmers and Vedi R. Hadiz

10 **Studies in the Economic History of the Pacific Rim**
Edited by Sally M. Miller, A. J. H. Latham and Dennis O. Flynn

11 **Workers and the State in New Order Indonesia**
Vedi R. Hadiz

12 **The Japanese Foreign Exchange Market**
Beate Reszat

13 **Exchange Rate Policies in Emerging Asian Countries**
Edited by Stefan Collignon, Jean Pisani-Ferry and Yung Chul Park

14 **Chinese Firms and Technology in the Reform Era**
Yizheng Shi

15 **Japanese Views on Economic Development**
Diverse paths to the market
Kenichi Ohno and Izumi Ohno

16 **Technological Capabilities and Export Success in Asia**
Edited by Dieter Ernst, Tom Ganiatsos and Lynn Mytelka

17 **Trade and Investment in China**
The European experience
Edited by Roger Strange, Jim Slater and Limin Wang

18 **Technology and Innovation in Japan**
Policy and management for the twenty-first century
Edited by Martin Hemmert and Christian Oberländer

19 **Trade Policy Issues in Asian Development**
Prema-chandra Athukorala

20 **Economic Integration in the Asia Pacific Region**
Ippei Yamazawa

21 **Japan's War Economy**
Edited by Erich Pauer

22 **Industrial Technology Development in Malaysia**
Industry and firm studies
Edited by Jomo K. S., Greg Felker and Rajah Rasiah

23 **Technology, Competitiveness and the State**
Malaysia's industrial technology policies
Edited by Jomo K. S. and Greg Felker

24 **Corporatism and Korean Capitalism**
Edited by Dennis L. McNamara

25 **Japanese Science**
Samuel Coleman

26 **Capital and Labour in Japan**
The functions of two factor markets
Toshiaki Tachibanaki and Atsuhiro Taki

27 **Asia Pacific Dynamism 1550–2000**
Edited by A. J. H. Latham and Heita Kawakatsu

28 **The Political Economy of Development and Environment in Korea**
Jae-Yong Chung and Richard J. Kirkby

29 **Japanese Economics and Economists since 1945**
Edited by Aiko Ikeo

30 **China's Entry into the World Trade Organization**
Edited by Peter Drysdale and Ligang Song

31 **Hong Kong as an International Financial Centre**
Emergence and development 1945–1965
Catherine R. Schenk

32 **Impediments to Trade in Services**
Measurement and policy implication
Edited by Christoper Findlay and Tony Warren

33 **The Japanese Industrial Economy**
Late development and cultural causation
Ian Inkster

34 **China and the Long March to Global Trade**
The accession of China to the World Trade Organization
Edited by Alan S. Alexandroff, Sylvia Ostry and Rafael Gomez

35 **Capitalist Development and Economism in East Asia**
The rise of Hong Kong, Singapore, Taiwan, and South Korea
Kui-Wai Li

36 **Women and Work in Globalizing Asia**
Edited by Dong-Sook S. Gills and Nicola Piper

37 **Financial Markets and Policies in East Asia**
Gordon de Brouwer

38 **Developmentalism and Dependency in Southeast Asia**
The case of the automotive industry
Jason P. Abbott

39 **Law and Labour Market Regulation in East Asia**
Edited by Sean Cooney, Tim Lindsey, Richard Mitchell and Ying Zhu

40 **The Economy of the Philippines**
Elites, inequalities and economic restructuring
Peter Krinks

41 **China's Third Economic Transformation**
The rise of the private economy
Edited by Ross Garnaut and Ligang Song

42 **The Vietnamese Economy**
Awakening the dormant dragon
Edited by Binh Tran-Nam and Chi Do Pham

43 **Restructuring Korea Inc.**
Jang-Sup Shin and Ha-Joon Chang

44 **Development and Structural Change in the Asia-Pacific**
Globalising miracles or end of a model?
Edited by Martin Andersson and Christer Gunnarsson

45 **State Collaboration and Development Strategies in China**
The case of the China–Singapore Suzhou Industrial Park (1992–2002)
Alexius Pereira

46 **Capital and Knowledge in Asia**
Changing power relations
Edited by Heidi Dahles and Otto van den Muijzenberg

47 **Southeast Asian Paper Tigers?**
From miracle to debacle and beyond
Edited by Jomo K. S.

48 **Manufacturing Competitiveness in Asia**
How internationally competitive national firms and industries developed in East Asia
Edited by Jomo K. S.

49 **The Korean Economy at the Crossroads**
Edited by MoonJoong Tcha and Chung-Sok Suh

50 **Ethnic Business**
Chinese capitalism in Southeast Asia
Edited by Jomo K. S. and Brian C. Folk

51 **Exchange Rate Regimes in East Asia**
Edited by Gordon de Brouwer and Masahiro Kawai

52 **Financial Governance in East Asia**
Policy dialogue, surveillance and cooperation
Edited by Gordon de Brouwer and Yunjong Wang

53 **Designing Financial Systems in East Asia and Japan**
Edited by Joseph P. H. Fan, Masaharu Hanazaki and Juro Teranishi

54 **State Competence and Economic Growth in Japan**
Yoshiro Miwa

55 **Understanding Japanese Saving**
Does population aging matter?
Robert Dekle

56 **The Rise and Fall of the East Asian Growth System, 1951–2000**
Institutional competitiveness and rapid economic growth
Xiaoming Huang

57 **Service Industries and Asia-Pacific Cities**
New development trajectories
Edited by P. W. Daniels, K. C. Ho and T. A. Hutton

58 **Unemployment in Asia**
Edited by John Benson and Ying Zhu

59 **Risk Management and Innovation in Japan, Britain and the United States**
Edited by Ruth Taplin

60 **Japan's Development Aid to China**
The long-running foreign policy of engagement
Tsukasa Takamine

61 **Chinese Capitalism and the Modernist Vision**
Satyananda J. Gabriel

62 **Japanese Telecommunications**
Market and policy in transition
Edited by Ruth Taplin and Masako Wakui

63 **East Asia, Globalization and the New Economy**
F. Gerard Adams

64 **China as a World Factory**
Edited by Kevin Honglin Zhang

65 **China's State-Owned Enterprise Reforms**
An industrial and CEO approach
Juan Antonio Fernández and Leila Fernández-Stembridge

66 **China and India**
A tale of two economies
Dilip K. Das

67 **Innovation and Business Partnering in Japan, Europe and the United States**
Edited by Ruth Taplin

68 **Asian Informal Workers**
Global risks, local protection
Santosh Mehrotra and Mario Biggeri

69 **The Rise of the Corporate Economy in Southeast Asia**
Rajeswary Ampalavanar Brown

70 **The Singapore Economy**
An econometric perspective
Tilak Abeyshinge and Keen Meng Choy

71 **A Basket Currency for Asia**
Edited by Takatoshi Ito

72 **Private Enterprises and China's Economic Development**
Edited by Shuanglin Lin and Xiaodong Zhu

73 **The Korean Developmental State**
From dirigisme to neo-liberalism
Iain Pirie

74 **Accelerating Japan's Economic Growth**
Resolving Japan's growth controversy
Edited by F. Gerard Adams, Lawrence R. Klein, Yuzo Kumasaka and Akihiko Shinozaki

75 **China's Emergent Political Economy**
Capitalism in the dragon's lair
Edited by Christopher A. McNally

76 **The Political Economy of the SARS Epidemic**
The impact on human resources in East Asia
Grace O. M. Lee and Malcolm Warner

77 **India's Emerging Financial Market**
A flow of funds model
Tomoe Moore

78 **Outsourcing and Human Resource Management**
An international survey
Edited by Ruth Taplin

Outsourcing and Human Resource Management

An international survey

Edited by
Ruth Taplin

Routledge
Taylor & Francis Group
LONDON AND NEW YORK

First published 2008
by Routledge
2 Park Square, Milton Park, Abingdon, Oxon OX14 4RN

Simultaneously published in the USA and Canada
by Routledge
270 Madison Ave, New York, NY 10016

Routledge is an imprint of the Taylor & Francis Group, an Informa business

Transferred to Digital Printing 2009

Typeset in Times New Roman by
Florence Production Ltd, Stoodleigh, Devon

British Library Cataloguing in Publication Data
A catalogue record for this book is available
from the British Library

Library of Congress Cataloging in Publication Data
Outsourcing and human resource management: an international survey/edited by Ruth Taplin.
p. cm. – (Routledge studies in the growth economies of Asia series)
Includes bibliographical references and index.
1. Contracting out – Cross-cultural studies. 2. Personnel management – Cross-cultural studies. I. Taplin, Ruth.
HD2381.O98 2007
658.3 – dc22 2007015399

ISBN10: 0–415–42891–2 (hbk)
ISBN10: 0–203–93395–8 (ebk)

ISBN13: 978–0–415–42891–0 (hbk)
ISBN13: 978–0–203–93395–4 (ebk)

Contents

Illustrations

Figures

Tables

Contributors

Bernard Arogyaswamy is Madden Professor of Business and Director at the Madden Institute, New York. Prior to this, he was Chair and Professor at LeMoyne College, Department of Business Administration, Syracuse, New York, and a consultant to SMEs on quality and international business. He was a Fulbright Professor, 2002–03, at the School of Management, University of Warsaw, Poland, and was awarded MBA Teacher of the Year. His first degree and industrial experience was in Madras, India.

Graeme Fry is an engineer by background and holds a degree in Electronic Engineering from Liverpool University. The early part of his career was spent as a design engineer working in the UK and US. He has extensive overseas experience, having worked in North America, the Far East and the Caribbean region. His sector experience in engineering includes industrial controls, power generation, marine electrical systems and instrumentation.

As an entrepreneur Graeme has been involved in a technology start-up for which he led the team raising venture capital, and he was a founding director of OEE Consulting Ltd. His current role is as Commercial Director for OEE, with responsibility for contract negotiation, business development and marketing. He is a major shareholder and member of the company's management board. OEE is a management consulting firm specializing in operational excellence and lean service. It is the UK market leader in transferring the improvement tools and techniques developed in industry into the service sector. The company is particularly strong in financial services, counting many of the major UK banks and insurance companies as clients.

Wonchang Hur received a Ph.D. in Industrial Engineering from Seoul National University in 2004. He is currently an Assistant Professor of Management Information Systems at the College of Business Administration, Inha University, Korea. His research interests include business process management, intelligent systems, business intelligence and IT in the health care industry. His research has been published in a number of journals, including *Concurrent Engineering*, *IEEE Internet Computing*, *Computers in Industry* and the *Journal of Digital Imaging*.

Hyun Jeong Kim is Assistant Professor of Human Resource Management and Organization at the College of Business Administration, Inha University, Korea. Her primary research focuses on the recursive interaction and integration of organizations and human resources, with particular emphasis on issues such as transformation, human resource management, learning and technology in the organization. She has published articles in the *Journal of Government Information Quarterly*, the *Korean Journal of Personnel Administration*, and the *Journal of Training and Development*. She has also written several book chapters and government reports.

H. J. H. J. M. (Cint) Kortmann has been global president of Talent&Pro International Holding – a company he founded – since 1998, and holds the majority of the shares. The company deals with the development and insourcing of Bachelors and Masters in the insurance, pension and banking sectors. Talent&Pro employs them in their first two to five years after graduation and has offices in Leusden (the Netherlands), London, Frankfurt and now Shanghai. In the Netherlands, Talent&Pro also owns the company 'Arrange', an insourcer for facility management and purchasing. At the time of writing, 2007, Talent&Pro employs 350 people and has a turnover of about 25 million euros. Over the last few years the company has had an annual growth of around 30 per cent.

Cint is an entrepreneur who also holds shares in other companies that are focused on the development of young Talents. He is also a member of some advice councils at various Dutch universities.

Royston Morgan is currently Head of Health Services at Manpower Software Ltd, and Director of Crosslight Management Ltd, a company offering a range of programme, research and change management consulting services. His background is in senior management and consultancy. Previous roles include Improvement Planning Manager for Philips, European IT Manager, and Director Transformation Consulting within the Benelux area for Atos-Origin; he also managed international consulting and programme practice in the Netherlands.

Royston has delivered organizational improvements and restructuring of operations within major companies covering all functions, and has implemented high-level consultative change in many industry and public sector organizations. He also led successful change management initiatives that included a large cost-reduction programme involving outsourcing and restructuring, which delivered the cost reduction target of 25 per cent. Particular skills include group facilitation and thinking 'outside the box'. His research interests include political processes in organizational change, and IT-related change management. He has presented a number of papers and spoken at a number of industry conferences.

Stephanie J. Morgan, who has a Ph.D. in Occupational Psychology, is Director of Crosslight Management Ltd, and is consultant to a range of companies on various aspects including outsourcing, staff motivation, customer-service relationships, technology-related change, business planning and managing diversity. Crosslight specializes in bringing academic theory into practical use and underpins all its interventions with solid research. Stephanie is a non-executive Director of Surrey and Sussex Healthcare NHS Trust, and Associate Lecturer at Birkbeck College, University of London.

Stephanie's early career was in the IT industry, and she has many years' experience as a manager and consultant, including a number of international assignments. Her roles have included National Sales and Marketing Manager for desktop systems for Philips Telecommunications and Data Systems, UK, and International Commercial Manager for a major systems house, based in Brussels. At that time Stephanie was a Fellow of the Institute of Sales and Marketing, and had gained qualifications in both IT and marketing management. Managing international teams and negotiations in a constantly changing environment triggered Stephanie's interest in psychology, and led to a dual-track academic and consultancy career.

Ian Pogson is a Chartered Engineer with 26 years' experience in manufacturing, engineering and logistics in the automotive industry. He joined the Institution of Production Engineers and was elected a Chartered Engineer in 1986. He is a Fellow of the Institution of Engineering and Technology.

He was born in Lytham St Annes, Lancashire and lived in Blackpool until the age of 11, surrounded by the ghosts of aircraft projects such as the TSR2 and the Hawker factory in the town, where engineering first made an impression. He moved to Southport where he indulged in his passion for mechanical science through steam engine preservation until he began his degree in Rugby. Lanchester Polytechnic (another famous name from the past) gave a further taste for a career in engineering and he joined Land Rover in 1980.

Through various career moves in automotives, Ian has headed Competitor Analysis and Benchmarking, been involved in selling powertrain to third-party customers such as Morgan and TVR, studied Technical Research for new products, run Manufacturing Engineering projects, and managed contracts in Logistics. He was the Powertrain Project Manager for two V8 programmes many years apart: the MGRV8 and the more recent Rover 75 V8 auto. He has worked with BMW at a high level during their tenure of Rover and set strategic goals for his function, linking with German colleagues, and set targets for the Hams Hall engine plant, recruiting and developing many of the engineers who worked there.

Ian recently lived and worked in China for 15 months on a large-scale outsourcing project that began under MG Rover. He has a keen interest in the practical and human aspects of outsourcing, such as the effects on the original manufacturer and its society and on the outsourced employees. He kept a detailed daily diary of life in China, which is to be published by Brewin Books in 2007, logging events and the cultural observations of himself and others.

Oliver Prior commenced work as a Lloyd's Insurance Broker in 1963 with Lambert Brothers and then joined Bland Welch Ltd in 1970 and there began to specialize in insurance for financial institutions. In 1975 Sedgwick and Bland Welch merged to form Sedgwick Group (now Marsh & McLennan) and he was appointed Managing Director of the Financial Services subsidiary.

In 1986, Oliver joined Alexander & Alexander (now Aon) as a Director of Alexander Howden Ltd and was also Chairman of Holmes Johnson Lessiter Ltd and Halford Shead Ltd (specialist financial institution and fine art insurance brokers). In 1990, he joined Willis Faber and Dumas (now Willis) as Chairman of the Financial Institution & Specie Division, which in 1992 was awarded the Queen's Award for Export Achievement. In 1999, he was appointed a Research & Development Director for Willis Limited, in which role he served until retirement in 2004. During this time, he gave over 40 external presentations on such topics as alternative risk transfer and capital insurance companies, and developed the Willis Internal ART Training Manual and training strategy. Oliver now works part-time as a Senior Consultant to The FirstCity Partnership Ltd.

Garel Rhys CBE held the SMMT Chair in Motor Industry Economics at the Cardiff Business School, Cardiff University, until 2005. He also headed the Economics Section at the School until 1999. Garel was Director of the Centre for Automotive Industry Research (CAIR) at the University, also until 2005. He is now Emeritus Professor at the Cardiff University Business School and Centre for Automotive Industry Research.

Garel first became interested in the economics of the motor industry when preparing a thesis on the 'Economics of the British commercial vehicle industry' while at the University of Birmingham in 1963–65. This was followed by a book, *The Motor Industry: An Economic Survey* (1972), and numerous articles on a wide variety of economic topics, including the motor industry and transport economics. His first academic post was at the University of Hull, but he subsequently moved to University College, Cardiff. He is a Fellow of both the Institute of Transport Administration, and the Institute of The Motor Industry. In addition, he advised the House of Commons select committees on trade and industry for over 20 years, and also advised the select committees on defence and Welsh affairs. He has also advised select committees in the House of Lords, the National Audit Office, and a number of companies and organizations. He has been a member of the Board of the Welsh Development Agency, and is now Special Adviser to the Agency. In addition, he has produced reports on the motor industry for various UK government departments. He holds a number of non-executive directorships.

In 1989, Garel won the Castrol/IMI Motor Industry Gold Medal Award for his contribution to the motor industry, and, in June 1989, he was awarded the OBE for services to the motor industry and education. In 1993 he was made Welsh Communicator of the Year, and he has been

Lead Adviser to the United Nations Industrial Development Organization on the place of the motor industry in developing countries. In 2001, Garel was appointed a member of the DTI's Motor Racing Industry Competitiveness Panel, and in 2003 the Motor Racing Board. In 2004, he was appointed President of the Institute of the Motor Industry. He is Chairman of the Welsh Automotive Forum. In 2007 he was advanced to a CBE for services to economic research in Wales.

Ivan Schouker is Managing Partner of Astwood Partners LLP, his advisory and investment firm. He is a board member and adviser of several entrepreneurial companies as well as charities. He was previously Chief Executive Officer of American Express Financial Services Europe Ltd, and former Head of American Express group international business development and strategic planning. Prior to this, he was a Principal at Booz Allen & Hamilton and started his career at Banque Paribas in New York and Taipei. He holds Masters degrees from Columbia University, the London School of Economics, and the Institut d'Etudes Politiques de Paris.

Sean S. Stuttaford is the Managing Director of a division of a South African listed IT services organization in Johannesburg. He is also Chairman of a non-profit housing company in Cape Town. He attained a Mechanical Engineering diploma before qualifying for a BComm, and recently received a Masters in Business Leadership from Unisa's Graduate SBL. His final-year research project investigated outsourcing success from the perspective of the transferred employee. Sean's career started in manufacturing, and he then moved into the IT services sector, where he has filled a number of management positions, including taking responsibility for outsource engagements.

Ruth Taplin is Director of the Centre for Japanese and East Asian Studies, which won Exporter of the Year in Partnership in Trading/Pathfinder for the UK in 2000. Ruth received her doctorate from the London School of Economics and is the author/editor of 14 books and over 200 articles. The most recent are: *Exploiting Patent Rights and a New Climate for Innovation in Japan* (2003), published by the Intellectual Property Institute; and *Valuing Intellectual Property in Japan, Britain and the United States* (2004); *Risk Management and Innovation in Japan, Britain and the United States* (2005); *Japanese Telecommunications: Market and Policy in Transition* (2006); and *Innovation and Business Partnering in Japan, Europe and the United States* (2006), all published by Routledge.

Ruth has been Editor of the *Journal of Interdisciplinary Economics* for 12 years. Currently she is a Research Fellow at Birkbeck College, University of London, the University of Leicester and a number of universities globally. She is Visiting Professor at the School of International Business and Management, University of Warsaw, Poland, and was a Visiting Fellow at the University of Mumbai Economics Department for their 150th Anniversary in January 2007.

Foreword

Outsourcing is a topic that the wider business community is increasingly discussing and it is timely that recognition is being given to such an important subject in this broad based book that goes beyond cost saving analysis.

The NOA recently celebrated its twentieth birthday. Over the years we have observed several significant developments in the way companies contract and work together, but one of the most dramatic changes and opportunities has been the globalisation of services and the growth of offshoring. This book addresses the paradigm shift from old forms of industrialisation and globalisation to that of outsourcing and the value of human talent.

The arrival of the internet in the 1990s, the subsequent reduction in international communication costs and the arrival of the millennium bug all converged to create an environment in which companies started embracing the offshore option, whether by outsourcing to a partner or by going it alone. This has now developed to such an extent globally that, for example, most analysts believe that India has the highest quality software industry anywhere in the world, regardless of cost.

Professor Taplin's book assesses the problems and solutions for those attempting to outsource from a wide range of perspectives including analysis of human resource management, service level agreements, lifecycles of the project, insurance requirements, operational management and recruitment within the context of the financial services industry (both banking and insurance), automotive, IT and other sectors. This breadth of enquiry accesses absolutely key issues concerning any outsourcing project and another topic that this book addresses is the issue of insourcing. One might consider the NOA to be vehemently opposed to insourcing, but the reality is contrary to this – we understand the need to insource – provided of course one establishes this "source" in the same way one would an external supplier (NOA best practices might be useful here).

This book is a valuable contribution to our understanding of the international outsourcing marketplace today and I offer my congratulations to Professor Taplin for publishing another book that helps us all understand this important subject in all its complexity and through the case studies from a cross border perspective.

Martyn Hart
Chairman and Founder, The National Outsourcing Association
www.noa.co.uk

Acknowledgements

I would like to thank the sponsors of this book: Oliver Prior of FirstCity Partnership Ltd for his insightful suggestions; and Cint Kortmann of Talent&Pro and Graeme Fry of OEE Consulting Ltd for their dynamic input. Michael Barrett OBE and Professor Peter Mathias, President of the Great Britain Sasakawa Foundation, must also be thanked for their continuing support over the whole current series of books that I have edited for Routledge.

Abbreviations

ABC	activity-based costing
ASP	application service provision
BPO	business process outsourcing
BPR	business process re-engineering
BR	business re-engineering
CAD	computer-aided design
CAPP	Centre for Applied Positive Psychology
CEO	chief executive officer
CFO	chief financial officer
CIO	chief information officer
CMM	coordinate measuring machine
CPI	corruption perception index
CRO	chief resource officer
CZK	Czechoslovakian koruna
ERM	enterprise risk management
ERP	enterprise resource planning
EU	European Union
FDI	foreign direct investment
FMEA	failure mode and effect analysis
FSA	Financial Services Authority
GDM	Global Delivery Model
GDP	gross domestic product
H&S	health and safety
HR	human resources
IDC	International Data Corporation
IIT	Indian Institute of Technology
IPR	intellectual property rights
IS	information system
IT	information technology
ITeS	IT-enabled services
KDB	Korea Development Bank
KITSIA	Korean Information Technology Service Industry Association
KM	knowledge management
LAN	local area network

LRA	Labour Relations Act, South Africa
M&A	mergers and acquisitions
MNC	multinational corporation
MSSP	managed security service provider
NCA	National Computerization Agency, Korea
NIIT	National Institute for Information Technology, India
OECD	Organization for Economic Cooperation and Development
PFI	private finance initiative
PPE	personal protection equipment
PPP	public–private partnership
R&D	research and development
SECOFI	Secretariat of Commerce and Industrial Development, Mexico
SEDUE	Secetariat of Urban Development and Ecology, Mexico
SI	systems integration
SLA	service level agreement
SMEs	small and medium-sized enterprises
SPC	statistical process control
TI	Transparency International
TUPE	transfer of undertaking, protection of employment
WIP	work in progress

1 Outsourcing and human resource management

An introduction and comparative overview

Ruth Taplin

Outsourcing is a growing phenomenon and it needs to be assessed from a broad standpoint as it constitutes a new historical phase in global production and the global division of tasks. Severe teething problems exist with the process of outsourcing and this is reflected in the projection that in the next few years the costs of legal proceedings just in the US for such problems will exceed half a billion dollars. The countries of the world are increasingly becoming less national and more focused on being centres of excellence.[1]

Outsourcing is following this tendency with certain regions such as Bangalore in India developing their own specialities that are preferred by companies throughout the world. The phenomenon of the 1960s, in which companies behaved in a footloose manner, opening and closing semiconductor factories at a ferocious rate and seeking the cheapest labour, are of a bygone era, as today companies seek added value from innovation that affects what they require in outsourcing activities as well. Therefore, most current outsourcing books that concentrate on cost efficiency are out of date. New global production, whether increasingly in services or in manufacturing, needs to be analysed within the context of added value and complexity of service rendered. Not understanding this leads to contracts that are not negotiated properly and a misreading of the dynamics of human resources (HR). Definitions of outsourcing, insourcing and backsourcing, outsourcing lifecycles and the role of HR all require clarification, extending beyond viewing outsourcing as a cost-saving exercise. Outsourcing is assessed in this book in all its dimensions from an interdisciplinary perspective encompassing management, financial services, HR, operational management, organizational and behavioural psychology, and socialization. The second half of the book also provides a cross-cultural, cross-border approach, assessing how outsourcing is manifested within different cultures and sectors. Too often outsourcing is seen as a process that can be universally applied without any regard to country-specific issues or cultural considerations.

Practical and interdisciplinary solutions

In this book both practitioners and academics with practical experience explore and provide case study examples of all different aspects of the outsourcing process, so that a multidimensional, interdisciplinary perspective is gained, thus enabling the reader to see outsourcing from all the different perspectives elaborated below. Also provided are practical solutions based on years of experience by practitioners to make the process of outsourcing proceed smoothly.

Outsourcing is a particular form of externalization of employment involving an outside contractor taking over an in-house function *including* the management of staff. A broad range of activities has been transferred in this way, including catering, cleaning and security – often termed 'secondary' or 'non-core' functions. There has also been an increase in the outsourcing of professional activities, including HR, IT and financial services. When an outsourcing agreement is negotiated a clear target and understanding of responsibilities should be accomplished at the outset but within a flexible context. As Chapter 4 shows, an over-rigid service level agreement (SLA) can only lead to disappointment and conflict. A clear set of aims backed up by some form of insurance, as explained in Chapter 5, will also serve to clarify the risks involved. Risk assessment and an understanding of enterprise risk management (ERM) are vital to successful outsourcing, multi-vendor outsourcing, insourcing, backsourcing or offshoring within an outsourcing context.

According to Professor Gerry Dickinson, enterprise risk is the 'extent to which the outcomes from the corporate strategy of an enterprise may differ from those specified in its corporate objectives, or the extent to which it fails to meet these objectives (using a "downside risk" measure)'. ERM has developed over the years from general management thinking but has been broadened to consider insurable and financial risks together and to develop a more holistic approach to risk management, including the greater role that shareholder value models have been playing in strategic management, which have all been a reaction against the crises in corporate governance in the last decade.[2] We can be sure that such a strategy of enterprise risk and ERM theory will work smoothly if the targets are both realistic and not too ambitious. Yet risk and the management of risk usually entail hidden outcomes that a corporate strategy is unable to foresee or account for. This is especially the case in relation to HR management where the human element itself always carries inherent greater risk as humans, according to organizational behaviour theory, are unpredictable, most especially when they are thrust into an unfamiliar way of working, such as transferring the processes outside the organization, or are perceived to be set adrift in a new situation within the loose context of their original company or a new one as in outsourcing.

HR outsourcing strategy is nowhere weaker than within a rigid rule-based corporate agreement. This is clearly seen in the process of outsourcing in which high attrition rates, resentment at being set adrift from the original company context, insecurity concerning company identity and poorly negotiated SLAs lead to high-risk profiles. Many of the risks taken in outsourcing by corporations are perceived as not being subject to insurance or as unable to be hedged against or securitized, which Chapter 5 exposes as an inaccurate perception.

Often the risks are not even thought of and only become an item on corporate strategy and risk once performance targets remain unmet. Enterprises usually divest a part of their operations because they believe that those to whom they are outsourcing are better equipped and more capable of handling the task and risks.[3] This is the reasoning behind much of the outsourcing of computer and information systems, especially those from financial institutions. Outsourcing is there to deal with the risks of technological obsolescence and systems failure. One dimension that does not seem to be factored into the equation is the unreliability of HR and analysis of how well-placed companies or the companies of the outsourcers are to deal with these risks, whether they are in-house, outsourced, insourced or backsourced. A rigid contract can never cope with elements of organizational behaviour psychology and personal relations, which ultimately affect the outcome of successful outsourcing.

The importance of flexible contracts

Outsourcing arrangements that are poorly executed and that rely on rigid SLAs with little understanding of what ERM constitutes are doomed to fail. As explained in Chapter 4, in 2005 McKinsey carried out a study of 30 outsourcing deals that had occurred four years prior to the study and were worth a total of 20 billion dollars.[4] The conclusion was that up to 50 per cent of outsourcing arrangements did not deliver the anticipated value. These failures were found to be linked to over-reliance on standard procurement approaches and cost/price as the primary consideration. Such rigid procedures all fly in the face of what ERM should constitute. Rigid and detailed rules that are handed down to implementation teams often contain more risks than utilizing an approach that contains fewer detailed, directional procedures. Much like business in East Asia, lesser risks are taken if trust and personal relations are built upon over the long term rather than in distant, proscribed, short-term confrontational business practice. A flexible approach that builds on these relationships by sharing strategic intent, having regular and transparent communications, is essential and needs to occur throughout the lifecycle of the project. Just handing a proscribed set of rules to those implementing the outsourcing and leaving it unattended until problems occur, which is then often too late with extensive damage having occurred with no foundation built between the two parties to resolve the matter, can only lead to disaster. ERM, in relation to outsourcing and HR management, should be more akin to how the Financial Services Authority (FSA) has organized its regulation of the financial services industry in the UK, this being based on high-level principles rather than detailed prescription, accompanied by flexibility to fill in the details as the project proceeds to completion. The preferred method therefore should be a loose framework that is part of a strategic planning agenda, including a lucid assessment of core competencies and skills, particularly in relation to the outsourcing suppliers, that is clear in the SLA.

Also required is a clear mapping for value creation according to new products, innovative design processes and new relationship clusters and where the business partnering model within ERM will create demonstrable results over the lifecycle of the project. In this book we intend to assess some of these potentially useful contractual frameworks within the financial services industry and in relation to insurance and risk, especially in Chapters 4 and 5. In Chapter 6 the operational risks of outsourcing are assessed through a matrix of what to look for and examples of what can go badly wrong if potential operational risks are not factored into the initial contract.

Definitions of outsourcing

Outsourcing may be defined in a number of ways. A concise definition other than contracting out or buying in, which can serve to prevent misunderstanding, is provided in Chapter 3: 'the delegation or handing over to a third party (external supplier) mediated via a contractual agreement, all or part of the technical, process and human resources, including management responsibility for transferred staff . . .'.[5] This serves to differentiate outsourcing from the process of insourcing, which is shown in Chapter 7 to refer to bringing in external contractors to assist with processes that are understaffed in the host company or that the company is trying to expand. Fitting in as part of the team can be a problem for insourcing, which is still not a highly developed variant of outsourcing (see Figure 1.1).

Another major variant of outsourcing is backsourcing. This is when a process that has been outsourced has been brought back in-house. This has been occurring in a number of companies and increasingly so as the outsourcing partners have underperformed or were negligent or engaged in criminal activity, points that will be taken further in Chapters 4 and 5. Most companies do not even consider this as an option and are forced to accept it when performance levels are not reached by outsourcing partners or in the event of criminal activity. Chapter 3 shows how the need to backsource comes to light when the lifecycle of the agreement is not considered right from the beginning. Outsourcing can be defined in a number of ways depending on the type of service and the form of relationship with the supplier. Complete outsourcing occurs when an entire department or function is externalized and can be handled by one vendor or multiple suppliers. Offshoring is another term that is often confused with outsourcing. It is possible to outsource to an offshore destination such as a free trade zone in another country or part of the country but outsourcing does not have to occur in the process of offshoring. It is possible to hire people in a free trade zone without lifting out or externalizing a company department or section. Offshoring was developed many years ago, especially in the IT, semiconductor

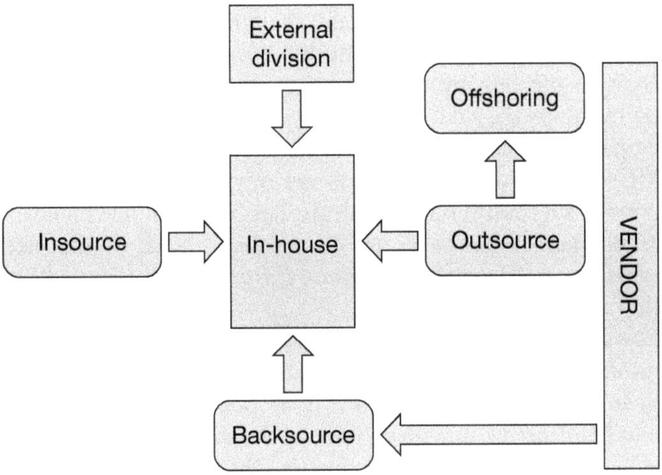

Figure 1.1 Clarifying outsourcing.

Source: S. J. Morgan, 'Is outsourcing the answer for IT & HR functions?', paper presented at the Housing Association National Conference, London, 2002.

sector where there was a constant search for cheap labour that was semi-skilled and pliable in terms of putting together component parts.[6] Tasks undertaken in offshoring are often more akin to selective outsourcing, such as dealing with accounts that are not current in the insurance industry but that require repetitive attention in keeping them open, or payroll activities in HR management, or a limited number of repetitive tasks in component manufacture. However, in the case study section of the book we provide an example of offshoring outsourcing in South and North Korea within the IT sector (Chapter 10).

Reassessing the role of human resources

What is explained in this book is unique and takes the outsourcing paradigm a great step further in that all the chapters in the first half explain both theoretically and through example how the fundamentals are not dealt with properly in the beginning of the outsourcing arrangement and lead to greater problems further down the line. Outsourcing is also viewed from all different perspectives, not just cost efficiency. In Chapter 2 all dimensions of HR are explored, including psychological and human organizational behaviour in relation to employees from the same company being outsourced, outsourcing using the outsourcing partners' staff, feelings of loss and resentment, and problems of retention and attrition and why these occur. Attitudes of employees to employers and HR departments are explained. Chapters 2, 3 and 4 note that the bulk of HR activities are outsourced but not enough attention is paid to the organizational behaviour aspects of HR management or, as shown by the longitudinal studies in Chapter 2, to the thoughts and feelings of those being outsourced. In Chapter 4 it is shown that not enough attention is paid to the basic SLA in the beginning of negotiations about the contract and that trust and partnerships should be the primary forms of relationship between the outsourcing partners. Business partnering in the small and medium-sized enterprise (SME) sector, where companies are relying on mutual trust and cooperation to make successful business deals, has been outlined extensively and comparatively across countries in the previous book of this series, *Innovation and Business Partnering in Japan, Europe and the United States*, edited by Ruth Taplin.[7]

Chapter 7, however, describes how insourcing relies on an acute awareness of what constitutes talent and how HR divisions need to understand the nature of such talent and how to nurture it. If companies that engage in insourcing are to be effective they need to have flexible, thoughtful problem solvers who can enter a company and, no matter what the temporary or long-term company needs, adapt themselves successfully to the particular company they are required to work with. This also requires management skills as the insourced person needs to work with the existing employees as a team. The insourcing company that recruits the talented people who are insourced also needs to understand that such people are part of a movable, elite workforce who are able to work in any metropolis around the world and who will not tolerate being bored, so require extras such as challenging, dynamic work and social networking events.

HR departments in large companies have traditionally acquired a poor reputation in that they have often attracted low-skilled people with little understanding of business or the subjects of the training courses they are supposed to organize for the staff of the company. Often they are seen as interfering, uninterested when there are genuine employee problems or needs, yet quick to involve and assert themselves in a negative manner when disputes arise. They are often seen as arrogant and interfering by the employees and have been traditionally defended by the company hierarchy without much analysis of their function and role.

Outsourcing provides an option to such companies to rid themselves of the problems caused by ineffective HR departments and to put pressure on them to perform in a business context rather than be seen as an extended branch of social work. It could be argued that individual problems of employees, training or career planning issues are too sensitive to be subject to outsourcing. However, the existing HR departments in many large companies are so abysmal that alternative action is required urgently. A possibility in the outsourcing set of alternatives to deal with sensitive HR tasks is to insource. In other words, specialists in the areas of staff relations, career planning or training could be hired into companies, thus avoiding the tendencies of *in situ* HR departments towards protectionism, power-grabbing and justification of their own existence.

Outsourcing in cross-border and regional contexts

Outsourcing and offshoring are processes that by their very nature tend to occur in cross-border contexts. This creates a great deal of variation in implementation of tasks outsourced and can affect level of performance. Language, customs, decision-making and the extent of outsourcing taking place are all affected. As Ruth Taplin notes in a recent publication, both risk-taking and management decision-making are affected by cultural patterns of behaviour.[8]

In *Risk Management and Innovation in Japan, Britain and the United States*[9] Ruth Taplin explains that, in comparing management styles and decision-making methodically across a number of countries, a tendency towards risk-taking can be seen in terms of the process of globalization, placing pressure on different societies to change their attitudes to risk out of necessity, especially in new working relationships such as outsourcing. Analyses in relation to risk and different cultures have been few and far between, mainly deriving from the sociological work of Aaron Wildavsky, in 'Choosing preferences by constructing institutions – a cultural theory of preference formation',[10] or Mary Douglas in 'Witchcraft and leprosy: two strategies of exclusion',[11] and the economic/management analysis of Ruth Taplin in 'The new Silk Road – amalgamating Western and Asian style management'.[12] Wildarsky argues that risk is one of the areas that most strongly reflects cultural predisposition. In the case of business it can be argued that, when operating in a globalized environment, culture most strongly predisposes attitude to risk and management decision-making. Wildarsky and Douglas discuss further the idea that those people who have the most trust in their institutions are risk-accepting and those who have low trust in their institutions are risk-averse. Trust, as we see in Chapter 4 of this book, is essential to creating a successful partnership between the company that wishes to outsource and those undertaking the outsourcing activities. Employees who trust the institution that they are working in will also be more trusting of the organization that they are being lifted into. Those who do not trust will be risk-averse and thus the prognosis for switching to a new outsourced company will not be good.

Culture, therefore, is an essential and often institutional variable that affects how management decisions are made and what degree of risk is to be taken. Business communication can only benefit from clarifying the degree of risk a business partner is willing to take and how this affects management decision-making and outsourcing decisions. A risk-averse culture, such as that in Japan or Germany, will obviously produce great caution, and an aversion to taking high levels of risk that is not conducive to the promotion of entrepreneurship, flexibility and outsourcing. Other cultures, such as the US, Korea, Finland or mainland China, produce managers who are willing to take high risks and to innovate and support high degrees of entrepreneurship and outsourcing activities. Then there are many shades in between, including such countries as Britain, France or Italy, which exercise risk-taking and the promotion of innovation, but show more caution, which is the case in Britain, or tend towards high risk, as in Italy. Risk management, decision-making and innovation also function in different societies through a variety of institutions. In China and India, for example, the management of risk by companies is exercised through the institution of the family. With family support and resources, risk-taking can be high and decisions flexible, which promotes innovation and willingness to be part of an outsourced organization or to be insourced. In the case of the family, consensus is easily reached because the decision-making process is contained in one of the oldest institutions – that of blood-related individuals, where the trust is high and, in the case of patrilineal societies, where the male autocratic head makes most of the decisions, thus expediting the process.

Chen Min, in *Asian Management Systems*,[13] noted that those who follow Confucian ethics have a collective business advantage in that they are able to mobilize more easily their network of relatives, trusted friends and business contacts, which is conducive to outsourcing activities. This is especially true for China, countries that have a preponderance of Chinese citizens such as Singapore, or those with large segments of Chinese traders. In India, which is largely a country of practising Hindus, networks of relatives pool their resources and manage risk flexibly through the family. The Chinese family structure is more authoritarian and less prone to splintering from infighting among inheritors. The Chinese have always practised primogeniture, where the eldest son is the main inheritor, while in Indian culture inheritance is split between siblings, which allows for greater conflict in decision-making. Such conflict can inhibit risk-taking, while decision-making by one senior person from the top down allows the process to be rapid and flexible, thus facilitating risk-taking. If a consensus has to be reached, as in the Japanese system, where company management controls decision-making, speed of the process is retarded. The greater the number of people involved, the more the element of risk becomes gradually eroded with each doubtful input that does not take ultimate responsibility. The Japanese system with its devolved sense of social responsibility and consensus, which leads to slow decision-making, lends itself to a risk-averse management style. These tendencies are reflected in such countries' attitudes to outsourcing and insourcing. Japan, which is risk-averse, does not have as high a level of outsourcing activities or outsourcing employees as other countries. If it does occur it is under Japanese control and is tightly controlled. China, Korea and India, on the other hand, have experience of patrilineal control from within the family that can be drawn upon to organize groups of relatives quickly in order to carry out a particular task. Risk is absorbed largely by the familiar family unit and is therefore safe and something to which Indian and Chinese families are accustomed. China and India in particular have the highest number of companies involved in outsourcing. China's domestic outsourcing market is growing rapidly and even India is using China increasingly for back-office outsourcing.[14]

Global variations in outsourcing arrangements

The Arab Middle East, since its relatively recent finding of oil wealth, has been practising an early form of outsourcing and insourcing for many years. Arab natives in the Gulf States, for example, have insourced every level of employee from top managers to accountants to low-skilled workers to run their companies. Workers from Europe, Egypt, Pakistan, the Philippines and Goa in India, to name a few regions and countries, have been brought in on a prolonged basis to carry out the vast majority of jobs in these countries. The workers are often on temporary work permit visas and can be sent back at any time.

Outsourcing from a comprehensive cross-cultural/cross-sector perspective

One of the reasons why browsing through the current literature on outsourcing increasingly becomes a fruitless exercise is because none of the books written to date takes a comprehensive view and addresses cross-cultural and cross-sector issues. Outsourcing takes many different forms and emphasizes manufacturing, IT, financial services, HR and many more sectors. Different regions and countries both insource and outsource in many different ways.

As mentioned above, the Arab Middle East has been insourcing on a huge scale for decades, bringing in talent from Egypt, Pakistan, the Philippines, Goa and other parts of India to manage a wide variety of projects and business concerns. Bahrain, for example, has insourced expatriate English from the insurance and banking sectors to build its insurance and banking services, while Dubai has brought in merchants, property developers and bankers from around the world.

India, which is the prime destination for outsourcing in the world, is outsourcing to China and China is outsourcing internally. Tata Consulting Services, part of the largest company in India, looks to China to process its back-office activities. Chinese companies are using their domestic market to outsource the processing of data tasks. China in turn, as shown in Chapter 11, is insourcing research and design talent from companies such as the now defunct Rover company in England. British engineers from Rover have lived in Shanghai, for example, assisting with car design and technology.

Japan, when it does outsource, usually looks to Taiwan and to companies such as Garwin, which researches, designs and manufactures global positioning system equipment for cars, bicycles and hand-held devices.

Jamaica has been promoting and winning business for the Caribbean, especially in the area of telemarketing, data entry, reservations and information-processing. Although Jamaica is not attracting outsourcing business on the scale of India or China, the attrition rates are under 5 per cent compared to many Indian call centres in Bangalore, where the attrition rates are quite high. However, with labour costs about 40 per cent lower than those in the US, operating costs 50 to 60 per cent lower than the US, no tax or import duties on inventory, furniture, equipment and machinery and unrestricted repatriation of profits, English-speaking Jamaica is trying hard to take advantage of the booming outsourcing market.

Other emerging markets such as Hungary in Eastern Europe have been involved strongly in outsourcing for at least 15 years. EDS opened its offices in 1991 and has three regional centres, including the EDS Hungary Data Entry and Document Management Centre, the EDS Contact Centre and the Regional Finance Centre. Hungary is very centrally located in Europe, and its workers are well educated and speak many languages fluently. Hungary is also dynamic and there is plentiful office space. These positive characteristics are reflected in the large number of companies around the world that use its outsourcing services, largely in the areas of financial services, administration, accounting, marketing, and back-office and IT support. Economic and political stability within a democratic context also assists Hungary in being one of the top ten destinations for outsourcing in the world.

It must be remembered that outsourcing is not a new phenomenon. The US tested its new technology and, in the late 1990s, established travel reservation centres on an outsourcing basis in Australia and especially New Zealand that proved to be quite successful. Using countries in different time zones means that work can be continued in shifts on a 24-hour basis.

In the second half of this book we have a case studies section, which gives country-specific, insightful analyses of different outsourcing cases around the world from a variety of sectors, including outsourcing/offshoring. Written by experts in the field from both an academic and practitioners' viewpoint, case studies include 'Information technology outsourcing in Korea' (Chapter 10), which provides hitherto largely unknown insight into the outsourcing relationship between South and North Korea. The Indian case study (Chapter 9) looks at HR in particular and the editor of this volume had the good fortune in January 2007, while a Visiting Fellow at the University of Mumbai's Economics Department, to visit Chennai and speak with one of the HR managers interviewed in this insightful chapter. 'Outsourcing in the automotive industry: Japan' (Chapter 8) is written by a world authority on the subject. The other chapters include those by an experienced practitioner who worked with the now defunct Rover company and who assesses outsourcing in the Far East and other parts of the world (Chapter 11), while South Africa, a market relatively new to outsourcing and probably the only successful outsourcing destination in Africa, is analysed in its geopolitical context and in the case of HR (Chapter 12).

Two cases are not covered and ought to be if providing a comprehensive view of outsourcing historically, culturally and from the point of view of sectors. One concerns Latin America, which is home to the oldest outsourcing industry – Mexico with its cross-border maquiladoras – and is very closely aligned to the US. The other is an emerging Eastern European country that arises within the context of being a new state as well as being recently separated from Slovakia – the Czech Republic. These are discussed below.

The oldest outsourcing case of the maquiladoras

The maquiladora is a Mexican corporation that operates under a maquila programme approved for it by the Mexican Secretariat of Commerce and Industrial Development (SECOFI). It is the oldest and nascent form of outsourcing as we know it today and is well developed. Based on manufacturing, it arose out of a need for cheap labour in manufacturing using women in particular. It may be seen as a globalized division of labour based initially on footloose use of the cheapest and most pliable labour pools. It was the precursor to outsourcing because it developed into a stable not footloose form of manufacturing that was outsourced to it from companies in the US. The maquila programme operates in the following manner.

How does the maquila programme operate?

A maquila programme, first, entitles the company to foreign investment participation in the capital – and in management – of up to 100 per cent without need of any special authorization; second, it entitles the company to special customs treatment, allowing duty-free temporary import of machinery, equipment, parts and materials, and administrative equipment such as computers and communications devices, subject only to posting a bond guaranteeing that such goods will not remain in Mexico permanently.

Ordinarily, all of a maquiladora's products are exported, either directly or indirectly, through sale to another maquiladora or exporter. The type of production may be the simple assembly of temporarily imported parts; the manufacture from start to finish of a product using materials from various countries, including Mexico; or any conceivable combination of the various phases involved in manufacturing, or non-industrial operations, such as data-processing (an outsourcing function that is developing), packaging, and sorting coupons.

The basic legislation now governing the industry's operation is the 'Decree for development and operation of the maquiladora industry', published by the Mexican federal Diario Oficial on 22 December 1989. This decree describes application procedures and requirements for obtaining a maquila programme and the special provisions that apply only to a maquiladora.

Foreign owned/controlled maquiladoras are allowed to own and lease real estate in Mexico

There are two kinds of areas in Mexico where land ownership by foreign interests is prohibited: a 100-kilometre strip along the borders and a 50-kilometre strip along the coasts. In these areas, a foreign-owned maquiladora may acquire trust rights to real estate through creation of a trust, with a Mexican bank of its choice as trustee. The trust rights allow full use and enjoyment to the maquiladora as beneficiary of the trust. It may use, dispose of, encumber and sell such rights, and it may receive any income earned from the property. Trusts have a duration of 30 years, renewable at the end of the period for another 30 years.

Leases are unrestricted regarding both location and duration. Outside the restricted border and coastal strips, any foreign-owned Mexican company is free to purchase real estate. Title transfers (whether transfer into trust or direct transfer to the buyer) are subject to a one-time transfer tax, in the border states generally around 3 per cent of the total appraised value. Thereafter, there is an annual property tax, but in relation to US property taxes it is negligible.

Permits and registration

The 1989 maquiladora decree establishes a 'Sole procedure', which simplifies some of the permit and registration requirements – and there are several. The initial permit needed is that to incorporate from the Secretariat of Foreign Relations, a requirement common to all companies that organize in Mexico.

Once permission to incorporate is received, application may be made to SECOFI for a maquila programme. The SECOFI application asks for corporate data, information on processes to be used and products to be manufactured, and a description of the temporary imports to be brought into Mexico. The new company's Articles of Incorporation, and any other relevant documents (such as a Maquila and Technical Assistance Contract, model labour contracts, or trust, lease and purchase agreements) should be submitted with the application. In processing the application, SECOFI will obtain the needed registrations from the National Maquiladora Industry Registry, the National Foreign Investment Registry, Foreign Relations, the Federal Taxpayer Registry, the National Workers Housing Fund Institute, and Social Security. SECOFI will also notify the Customs Bureau of the maquila programme approval.

Once the maquila programme is approved, along with the registrations noted above, the company will need an operating licence from the Secretariat of Urban Development and Ecology (SEDUE), which will mean submitting an environmental impact statement. It will also need special permits if it will discharge waste water, handle hazardous materials, or produce air emissions.

In addition to the above, the following are needed:

- a sanitary licence from the Health Secretariat, as well as registration and licensing with this authority if cafeteria or dining room facilities will be operated;
- import/export registration from the Secretariat of Finance and Public Credit;
- registration with the Department of Statistics within the Secretariat of Planning and Budget;

- authorization from the Secretariat of Labour for operation of mechanical energy transformation machinery, if any;
- authorization from SECOFI for operation of gas furnaces, if any;
- authorization for telecommunications systems from the Secretariat of Communications and Systems from the Secretariat of Communications and Transportation; and
- registration with the federal Safety and Health Commission.

State and local registrations and licences include:

- a land-use licence from local authorities;
- registration of employee training programmes, labour contracts and internal shop rules with the State Labour Authority;
- registration with the Public Registry of Property in the city of corporate domicile; and
- registration with state tax authorities.

Complicated as this sounds, if preliminary preparation is properly done, the process does not take long. Incorporation usually takes about three weeks once the Foreign Relations permit is received, and the remaining permits and registrations involve about another 30 days.

Any product can be manufactured – or assembled, packaged, processed, sorted, produced in whole or in part, transformed, rebuilt. . . . Mexico places no restrictions on what may be made, other than requiring a special prior permit to be obtained from the Secretariat of Defence for production of firearms or from the Mexican Nuclear Regulatory Agency if the product has radioactive content.

What to produce in a maquiladora is dependent on the parent company's business considerations, including available markets and duties assessed on imports into those markets. For example, companies involved in textiles must consider the Multi-fiber Agreement between Mexico and the US, and its amendments. If an export assignment is not obtained for a proposed textile company's production to enter the US, Mexico will not authorize the textile operation. US customs rulings may have an impact on what a company produces, or where its components come from.

One consideration often overlooked by companies setting up maquiladora operations concerns US Customs. There are several benefits available relating to US duties, depending on components and/or type of product the maquiladora is producing. There are harmonized tariff sections 9802.00.60 and 9802.00.40, where duty is assessed only on value added, and there is the US Generalized System of Preferences, where, if 35 per cent or more of the product is deemed Mexican content, it may enter duty free. Before an operation gets under way, any necessary US Customs rulings should be obtained to assure the benefits expected regarding duties.

What can a maquiladora import into Mexico?

In general terms, it may import in bond whatever is needed directly or indirectly to support the production process. This includes line machinery and equipment, raw materials and parts, items for health and safety, boxes, labels, manuals and pamphlets, anti-pollution equipment, tools, spare parts and equipment necessary for administration. As of the December 1989 maquiladora decree, computers and telecommunications equipment are included among the items that can be brought in as temporary imports.

Installed equipment and machinery, and the various types of equipment used to monitor production and attend to administration, may remain in Mexico as long as the maquila programme continues. Materials and parts consumed in the production process, and shipping-related items, are permitted to remain in Mexico for six months, an extension being available as long as the total period does not extend beyond one year. Trailers and trailer parts may remain only three months.

Bringing in professional staff from abroad

Maquiladoras are permitted to bring in whatever professionals or personnel for positions of trust they need to serve as managers and technicians and in other fields requiring specialization. These foreigners may bring their families with them, but must obtain the proper visas from the General Bureau of Immigration Services. Ordinarily, the visas are non-immigrant visas known as FM-3s, good for six months and renewable as often as may be necessary. Visas of this type for foreign hourly wage employees can be obtained but it must be shown that the employee is in truth temporary and is needed for a specific purpose such as training or supply of some technical service.

Foreign personnel in Mexico under an FM-3 visa are not subject to Mexican income tax if they do not spend 183 or more nights in Mexico during the year; otherwise, they must be registered with the Mexican Federal Taxpayer Registry, and are entitled to Social Security and other Mexican labour benefits.

How Mexican labour law affects maquiladoras

The effect of labour law on a maquiladora is the same as for any other Mexican corporation, and it must be recognized that the impact is significant. Labour rights are enshrined in the Mexican Constitution. The Federal Labour Law, which implements the constitutional guarantees, is a comprehensive statute that attempts to regulate all aspects of a labour relationship, whether individual or collective. It is applicable to all Mexican companies, whether foreign or Mexican owned, with or without a maquila programme.

Salary and working conditions in the maquiladoras

Every hourly and salaried employee must have a written employment contract. The permissible obligatory working week is 48 hours, or six eight-hour shifts; wages are based on a daily rate rather than an hourly rate, with pay for the seventh day as well as the six working days. Many companies, however, work a five-day week based on shifts of more than eight hours, permitting two days off per week. Overtime rates are set by law on an ascending schedule, depending on how much overtime per week is worked, and whether holidays or days of rest are worked.

Employees must be enrolled with Social Security, and companies must contribute to the National Workers Housing Fund. Pregnant women are granted leave of absence during pregnancy, and their positions must be held for them if they wish to return after the child is born. Statutory benefits due to all workers include vacation pay and premiums, a defined vacation period, Christmas bonus, and employees' profit-sharing, all of which must be provided to an employee annually, and in a proportional degree if an employee leaves the company.

Without severance pay, employees cannot be fired except for cause, as specifically defined in the Federal Labour Law. If dismissed without cause, an employee is entitled to certain severance benefits. Rights guaranteed to Mexican workers cannot be waived. The way in which these rights are exercised, however, will vary by region and even from city to city depending on industrial history and culture. Further, the form of their exercise can be negotiated, and a consensus agreement between the parties will be respected.

Finally, although the right to unionize is constitutionally guaranteed, the interest in unionization also varies from region to region. The main concern in the union movement in industry has been improvement of working conditions. Since maquiladoras tend to provide benefits over and above those required by law, unless an area has a strong historical tradition of unionization, employees will probably have little interest in unionizing. However, that lack of interest may change if poor personnel policies are implemented and communication with management is so inadequate that a union is viewed as the only option.

Generally, the existing unions tend to work with management, serving as advocates for the workers and participating in tasks such as hiring, benefits distribution, preparation of vacation schedules and the like, often relieving management of certain burdensome administrative chores.

Tax implications in maquiladora operations

There are several federal tax laws that apply to maquiladoras, the most important being the Income Tax Law and the Assets Tax Law. Since they are subject to frequent modification, with an annual readjustment of provisions at the end of each calendar year, the broadest generalizations only are noted here.

The Income Tax Law provides for both assessment on corporate profits and employee withholding, and requires provisional payments to be made monthly, prior to the eleventth day of each month. Overpayments or underpayments of these taxes can be adjusted and refunds or credits claimed, taking deductions similar to those provided under US tax law. Since maquiladoras are usually structured as cost centres, with machinery and equipment, materials, components and spare parts on loan (rent free) from the parent company, their profits are marginal, thus the income tax impact is marginal.

Under the Assets Tax Law, the tax on assets, also payable monthly on a provisional basis, can be offset by income tax paid. Mexico has a value added tax, but the rate on products that maquiladoras buy in Mexico is zero. Services, however, are subject to this tax, but it is always refundable to the maquiladora with respect to exports.

Moving away from cheap labour

Although still largely low cost, with workers earning between $3 and $10 per hour or in very low-skilled work less than this, there is a move towards producing more highly skilled technical workers. Softtek is such a company and hires hundreds of newly trained software engineers as the software sector is developing. The cost for technical and engineering workers is still relatively low in Mexico, even if an increasing number of graduates have been educated in the US.

Contract negotiation, insuring against performance problems and avoiding damaging liabilities

Three major points need to be addressed when negotiating a contract to minimize risk and liability when outsourcing as in Mexico.

First, the allocation of risk needs to be considered in the contract that you are negotiating and signing. It is appropriate to carry out a due diligence review of the service provider, including a risk analysis of the provider's financial strength, reputation, risk management policies and controls and its ability to fulfil its obligations. Risks for exit strategies need to be made clear at the outset in the contract. Responsibilities for overseeing the outsourcing arrangements need to be clearly defined and associated risk management obligations throughout the contract need to be transparent.

Second and third, it is important in the pre-contract stage that a clear strategy for working together productively is outlined, including performance targets and insurance in the event that such agreed performance targets are not met. It is too late to ask for compensation once the performance targets have not been met. Clearly define performance targets at the outset and arrange for insurance cover. Carefully assess and amend if necessary the allocation of insurance provisions on both sides, outlining what liabilities and risks need to be covered by the company and the third party. This needs to be defined and dealt with in the pre-contract. Most contracts are for three years. Theoretically this should leave manufacturing processes and administration in such a good established state that the enterprise can continue.

Again the devil is in the detail provided in the initial contract and depends on whether provision has been made for continuation leaving the terms of agreement for success intact. As seen in the remainder of this book, such prescription is necessary for successful outsourcing contracts that facilitate successful outcomes.[15]

Outsourcing in the newly emerging outsourcing country of the Czech Republic

The Czech Republic (formerly part of Czechoslovakia) is not only a new country but it provides a good example of a recent newly emerging country that offers outsourcing services. Below we assess the benefits and the problems. Some of the problems, such as corruption, emanating from the communist era are shared with other newly emerging Eastern European countries. The leading manufacturing sector is the automotive industry and the engineering industry in general (transport machinery, TV production); and the Republic is financially stable due to foreign investors.

The average wage is about 19,000 Czechoslovakian koruna (CZK), that is, 678 euros (1 euro = 28 CZK), but there are great differences; the initial wage for graduate engineers starts at 14,000 CZK, that is, 5,000 CZK below the average wage in general. Yet, foreign companies such as Robert Bosch or Panasonic are required to pay specialists at least 40,000 CZK per month and provide a new rented flat if they wish to attract high-level engineers.

Foreign companies have their own policies, but Czech manufacturing companies depend on loans entirely (e.g. liability and corporate bonds). Manufacturing comprises 45 per cent of gross domestic product (GDP) and 97 per cent of exports (2005 figures).

The Czech government designated a high number of industrial complexes especially in regions with high unemployment – northern Bohemia and northern Moravia – where Hyundai announced a big investment recently. They decided to invest here because it is close to the Slovak borders, where other related companies produce supplementary goods.

The technical capability of Czech manufacturing companies is of a high standard. Special managerial training courses do not exist at technical universities, so companies set up their own training schemes. For example, Skoda, which is a part of the Volkswagen company and a primary car producer in the Czech Republic, established its own private university to train students according to its needs both technically and in management. This does not occur only in the Czech Republic – HSBC, for example, has its own training programmes in India.

Universities are not ranked, but there are three major technical universities with a long history in Prague, Brno and Ostrava (the Technical University of Ostrava is the best) and one smaller one in Liberec specializing in the past in textile engineering.

Problems of cultural attitude

High expectations were created for foreign company investment but some disappointment occurred because of cultural differences and attitudes to discipline in management. In general, Czechs prefer domestic companies to foreign ones and can be seen as slightly xenophobic and antagonistic towards other cultures. Their language is very difficult, like Polish, but the Polish people are perceived to be a much more hospitable people. For example, they are more willing to change their working practices to accommodate foreign requests, while the Czechs are not so willing to be flexible.

Evolution economically into an outsourcing nation

At the beginning of the 1990s the initial conditions in the Czech Republic (then part of Czechoslovakia), which have given rise to the situation today, were conflicting economically. On the one hand, there was a relatively advanced economy with strong industrial and agricultural potential, with a qualified workforce, and with low domestic and foreign debt. On the other hand, there was hardly any private business sector in existence and there were extremely distorted prices under state control. Heavy industry was overdeveloped, while services were extremely underdeveloped. These and other factors contributed to the low effectiveness on the part of the economy generally.

After the 1990s' recessionary period, in 2000 economic growth began once again with the GDP rising by 2.9 per cent and by 3.6 per cent in the year 2001. Economic growth was a result of domestic demand and within that area household consumption in particular. The gross production of fixed capital grew from 4.2 per cent in the year 2000 to 7 per cent in the year 2001 (see Table 1.1).

Uneven growth and the rise of the manufacturing industry for outsourcing

While economic resurgence is taking place on the basis of intensified restructuring and modernization of production, the transformation of certain large companies in traditional sectors has not been completely dealt with. Segments of the economy with high growth have, up until this point, only made up for other segments where production is stagnating or has even dropped significantly. The processing industry, as well as certain service branches, trade, telecommunications and commercial services in particular, has led to the turnround on the supply side. Industrial production in the year 2000 increased in aggregate by 5.1 per cent. The growth rate fluctuated between 10 and 20 per cent in the most dynamic branches of the manufacturing industry (production of transport vehicles, machinery and equipment, wood processing, and the rubber and plastic industries) and this was due to a great

Table 1.1 Macro-economic indicators, Czech Republic, 1995–2001

Variable		*1995*	*1996*	*1997*	*1998*	*1999*	*2000*	*2001*
Gross domestic product	Mld/CZK, current prices	1381.1	1567.0	1679.9	1837.1	1887.3	1959.6	2146.1
Gross domestic product	Previous year = 100, constant price	106.4	104.3	99.2	98.8	99.6	102.9	103.6
Consumption of households	Previous year = 100, constant price	106.0	107.9	102.4	98.0	101.9	101.9	103.7
Consumption of government	Previous year = 100, constant price	96.6	103.6	95.6	97.6	99.9	98.7	99.0
Fixed capital formation	Previous year = 100, constant price	119.9	108.2	97.1	100.1	99.4	104.2	107.0
Inflation rate	Per cent	9.1	8.8	8.5	10.7	2.1	3.9	
Unemployment rate[a]	Average in per cent	2.99	3.05	4.29	6.04	8.54	9.02	8.54
Current account (balance of payments)	Mld/USD	−1.37	−4.29	−3.21	−1.05			
Trade balance	Mld/CZK		−100.4	−100.0	−26.1	−27.7	−69.8	−65.0
Macroeconomic labour productivity[b]	Previous year = 100	105.2	104.1	99.9	100.2	101.7	103.6	103.2

Source: *Czech Republic – Macroeconomic Forecast* (Prague: Ministry of Finance and Czech Statistical Office, 2002; available online at www.mfcr.cz, in Czech).

Notes:
a Registered unemployment.
b GDP in current prices per employed person.

extent to direct foreign investment. At the same time, however, other production areas decreased interannually (the shoe industry, metal production and food processing). The construction industry was also showing recovery.

This growth tendency in the economy was supported by a significant growth in work productivity. The number of employees continued to decrease, even though the gradual economic recovery slowed down this tendency gradually.

In 2000 the GDP for a worker grew by 3.9 per cent while employment decreased by 0.7 per cent. The growth in work productivity in industry, measured by the index of industrial production, reached as high as 8 per cent.

On the side of demand the economic growth was brought about first and foremost by the gross production of fixed capital. Its recovery was accompanied by a high inflow of direct foreign investment. The domestic demand, however, grew more rapidly than the domestic supply. In the end the growth in consumption was moderate (1.4 per cent) even though it was supported by a small decrease in the level of saving in connection with the increased use of consumer loans. While in the first half of 2000 the contribution to the growth in the GDP was still evenly divided between investment, household consumption and exports of goods and services, in the second half of the year exports slowed, widening the gap between imports and exports.

Available labour

Out of the ten million inhabitants of the Czech Republic, five million make up the number of the economically active population. Unemployment, from a rate of practically zero, increased very rapidly to around 3 per cent in 1992 and remained at this level up until the beginning of 1997, that is to say, at the beginning of the economic recession. The surprisingly low level of unemployment had a number of causes and was connected with the rapid expansion of the private sector, the development of the entrepreneurial sector and the structural changes connected with it. On the one hand, employment in agriculture decreased from 14.9 per cent in 1990 to 5.4 per cent in 2000. On the other hand, employment in the service industry increased from 42.6 per cent to 56.6 per cent over the same time period.

Relatively strict conditions for obtaining unemployment benefits had a positive influence on the activities of those looking for work (even though the generous social benefits were devalued in the second half of the 1990s). Growing participation in the grey economy and a widening wages gap contributed to people looking for work abroad. Overemployment emerged, which was finally removed after the recession in 1997 (see Figure 1.2). Unemployment fluctuated between 3 and 4 per cent until the economic downturn in 1997, when unemployment rose to 8 per cent. Yet, because industry in the Czech Republic had a higher proportion of smaller firms offering greater opportunities for entrepreneurial activities that could draw workers away from larger industries, the proximity of the Czech Republic to Germany and the markets of the European Union (EU) also eased some of their labour market pressures and encouraged the inflow of foreign direct investment into the economy.

Starting in 1991, the Czech government privatized industries faster, completing the task by 1995, by which time 75 per cent of productive capacity had been transferred into private hands. Regional disparities in employment rates and the types of employment are high. Prague dominates the Czech

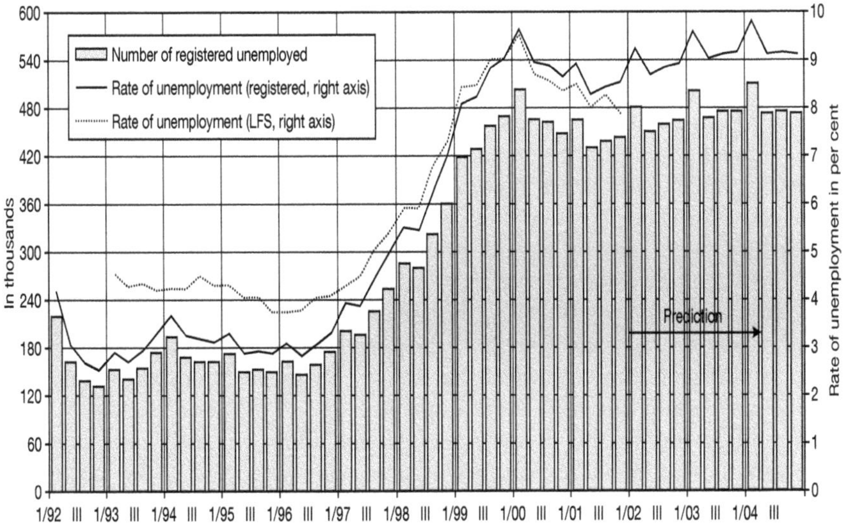

Figure 1.2 Unemployment trends, Czech Republic.

Source: *Czech Republic – Macroeconomic Forecast* (Prague: Ministry of Finance, 2002; available online at www.mfcr.cz, in Czech).

economy, while specialist regions such as northern Moravia (steel and coal) and northern Bohemia are unemployment black spots. Labour mobility is low, which is also indicative of a skills mismatch in the labour market. The Czechs have traditionally perceived their workforce as being highly skilled, particularly given the high proportion of those with secondary vocational education. However, comparative international indicators show that the quality of Czech human capital may not be as high as the educational attainment measures suggest. Indeed the share of people with tertiary-level education, although growing, remains very low compared to other members of the Organization for Economic Cooperation and Development (OECD). Poor vocational education and training, which fail to meet the needs of the labour market, are also reported in Slovakia. Thus there is a growing sense that the education system needs to adapt to meet the needs of a modern 'market' economy.

Notwithstanding these differences, by any standard, both countries have undergone significant changes in their employment structure. In both countries, service sector employment has increased during transition at the expense of agriculture, mining and other heavy industry. Czech rates have converged to the EU average.

Cheap and reliable labour

Although for many workers wage determination is now free from many of the shackles of the communist era, explicit wage regulation has been applied sporadically in both countries to prevent excessive wage growth. During the first stages of transition (1991–95) in the Czech Republic prohibitive taxes were imposed on firms that raised wages substantially above the prevailing rate of inflation. However, their application was not widespread and exemptions were numerous, implying that their role was rather a psychological one and indirect. Another imperfection stems from the blurred boundaries between public and private ownership in the Czech economy. Through the state National Property Fund, which effectively controls an estimated 75 per cent of the book value of almost 400 major private firms, it has been argued that the Czech government has been able to exert some degree of influence over private sector pay. Further, there exists the legal right for trade unions or employer associations to apply to the Ministry of Labour to make industry-level agreements binding on all enterprises in a sector, although this has rarely been applied in the Czech Republic.

Rigidities within the functioning of the labour markets may also be substantial. The heavy tax burden, which, with taxes and social insurance payments, comprises 47 per cent in the Czech Republic, acts to suppress labour demand and encourages tax evasion. What this means is that foreign potential investors who wish to hire Czechs are pleased with low unemployment benefits, which encourage Czechs to be available for work, but the high minimum wage guaranteed by the state puts such foreign investors off, as wage levels become too high to remain competitive. In addition, employee protection regulations still reflect their socialist heritage. Strict criteria exist regarding layoffs, including a statutory two-month period for redundancies or notice.

Education and training in the Czech Republic

Since transition, return to education has continued to grow across groups. While the growing shortage of graduates suggests higher levels of return for these individuals, there is evidence of a skills mismatch among less-qualified workers. Changes in education have not kept pace with the structural changes occurring in the country, pointing to lower future returns for these individuals. Changes may also have distorted the link between experience and pay. Traditionally, experience was well rewarded in the communist era, but has been found to be in decline in the immediate post-communist years, possibly indicating that recent labour market experience is more valuable than experience acquired under central planning. However, this was before the privatization programme was complete and large-scale structural change had occurred.

The training of graduates and the lack of practical skills

The best-trained individuals for the manufacturing sector and those with some knowledge of English are graduates from technical universities. The share of technically orientated graduates is traditionally high in the Czech Republic – about 30 per cent of the total number, compared to Poland or Hungary, where it is about 15–20 per cent. The graduates have a very solid theoretical technical background, but they lack 'soft' skills: the social, language and often practical skills so desired by companies seeking to outsource.

Companies usually invest huge amounts of money in on-the-job training to train a graduate for a specific job and some of the firms have serious problems in shouldering such extra costs. The larger companies, often multinational companies, have their own trainers, while the others hire private consultants and management trainers available on the market. Today technical graduates do not have trouble in finding a worthwhile job, but technical studies are not as popular as social studies, law or economics and a lot of young people still prefer the latter occupations. The point is that evaluation of the universities is not based on the number of successful students capable of finding a job and in general there is a weak link between universities and the labour market.

Other variables that influence the workforce

In the newly liberalized economy of the Czech Republic the relationship between gender and pay is also not well established. Inequality of pay and opportunity according to gender is largely legislated against in the Western world, although pay disparities still persist. Given the lack of legislative provision, the wage gap between men and women in the private sector will widen. However, under the more regulated system in the public sector, pay disparities should be fewer and may help explain the large proportion of women employed in the public sector.

Central planners devalued 'mental' work as opposed to 'physical' work – a philosophy that also influenced their approach to education. Thus, as an indicator of individuals' abilities, skills and level of responsibilities, there is evidence of movement towards a complete turnaround in the relative valuation of different occupations. Particularly in the private sector, a widening gap is occurring between the wages of senior or professional occupations and those of the semi-skilled and unskilled. While some remnants of the communist approach may still exist in the public sector, a similar if less pronounced trend has been occurring.

What about the likely impact of establishment size and workplace location on wage levels? Before transition, employees in larger firms were given higher wages due to their stronger political and bargaining situation. While some vestiges of this system may remain, this effect is diminishing in line with the decline in size of the public sector. Conversely, larger firms in the private sector will pay more, as is the case in many Western economies. Workers in Prague, the capital of the Czech Republic, have always earned a more than their fellow nationals. With the inflow of foreign capital and as Prague is the centre of entrepreneurial activity these differentials will increase further.

These effects will be accentuated by tighter labour market conditions driven by the lower levels of unemployment and labour mobility in these areas.

Fewer workers are now covered by collective agreements and these are less likely to be 'imposed' on other workers in the same industry.

Corruption

Corruption is endemic to most Central and Eastern European countries. Former Czechslovakia used to be notorious for corrupt practices, which continue to exist. According to *Mladá Fronta Dnes* (*MFD*) (22 February 2005), 67 per cent of Czechs believe that corruption is an alarming problem in need of a thorough solution. In addition, 20 per cent of Czechs admit to giving a bribe in order to speed up procedures at local offices (*MFD*, 10 December 2004). In light of these numbers, it is hardly comforting that in 2004 the Czech Republic, after years of downward slides, finally managed to move slightly up in the corruption perception index (CPI) rankings reported annually by Transparency International (TI): specifically, it moved from being ranked fifty-fourth (out of 149 countries) in 2003, with a CPI value of 3.93, to being ranked fifty-first (out of 146 countries) in 2004, with a CPI value of 4.2. For comparison, Finland had a 2004 CPI of 9.7.

According to a new corruption assessment instrument, the V4 City Corruption Propensity Index, which was conceived by the local branch of TI and implemented in the capitals of the four Visegrad countries (Prague, Bratislava, Budapest and Warsaw) during the winter and spring of 2004, Prague City Hall has severe problems in all five areas investigated: how public procurement tenders are processed, internal audit and audit control mechanisms, codes of ethics, conflict-of-interest regulations and open-information policies. These are assessed objectively in terms of insufficient rules and regulations as well as subjectively in terms of the perceptions of various respondent groups (members of civic associations, businessmen, journalists) of the level of anticorruption efforts. Clearly, the Czech Republic and Prague City Hall have a lot of catching up to do.

The public's view of corruption as an alarming problem, apart from doubtlessly pervasive personal experiences, was reinforced by several high-visibility affairs. Among them was the apparently widespread, and not just recent, bribery of soccer referees documented during the spring of 2004. The two first league teams were fined 500,000 CZK and deductions of six points were imposed on them. Police also charged at least 25 league officials, using phone-tapping extensively in order to gather evidence. The scandal caused severe damage to the credibility of the game (and did not make sponsors happy).[16]

Conclusion

As shown in the above case studies on Mexico and the Czech Republic, outsourcing needs to be seen within the comparative context of culture, the industrial sector that predominates in a particular country, and the level of economic development. The overall picture becomes even more complex when other economic and cultural variables are taken into consideration, such as country-specific rules and legislation (e.g. import restrictions, and labour and immigration laws), labour availability and mobility, cultural attitudes, corruption, education and training, and the variable that is usually least taken into account – the need for insurance against risk. In this book, we assess all these variables and, in the case studies, within a wide variety of cultural and sector contexts.

Notes

1 See Ruth Taplin, 'Can Europe make it? SME innovation business partnering – the missing links', in Ruth Taplin (ed.) *Innovation and Business Partnering in Japan, Europe and the United States* (Abingdon: Routledge, 2007), pp. 9–40.
2 See Gerry Dickinson, 'The evolution of enterprise risk management', in Ruth Taplin (ed.) *Risk Management and Innovation in Japan, Britain and the United States* (Abingdon: Routledge, 2005), pp. 150–62.
3 Ibid.
4 See Ivan Schouker, Chapter 4, this volume.
5 See Stephanie Morgan's 'Is outsourcing right for IT and HR functions', a white paper prepared for Crosslight Consulting, and Chapter 3, this volume.
6 See Ruth Taplin, *Economic Development and the Role of Women: An Interdisciplinary Approach* (Aldershot: Gower, 1989).
7 See Ruth Taplin (ed.) *Innovation and Business Partnering in Japan, Europe and the United States* (Abingdon: Routledge, 2007).
8 See Ruth Taplin and Nick Schymyck, 'Introduction: an interdisciplinary and cross-cultural approach', in Ruth Taplin (ed.) *Risk Management and Innovation in Japan, Britain and the United States* (Abingdon: Routledge, 2005), pp. 1–21.
9 Ibid.
10 Aaron Wildarsky, 'Choosing preferences by constructing institutions – a cultural theory of preference formation', *American Political Science Review*, 81(1) (March 1987): 3–22.
11 Mary Douglas, 'Witchcraft and leprosy: two strategies of exclusion', *Man*, New Series, 26(4) (December 1999): 723–36.
12 Ruth Taplin, 'The new Silk Road – amalgamating Western and Asian style management'. presentation to Managing Asia Pacific Business into the Twenty-first Century, International Management Conference, Westin Stamford, Singapore, 6–8 November 1995,.
13 Chen Min, *Asian Management Systems* (London: Routledge, 1995).
14 A good deal of the material comes from the author's time in India as a Visiting Fellow at the University of Mumbai, December /January 2006/07, and a visit to Chennai.
15 The material on the maquiladoras derives from early research by the author over the years, beginning with the footloose patterns of production as mentioned above in the IT/semiconductor industries.
16 I would like to thank Dr Jana Drastikova, Department of European Integration, Faculty of Economics, Technical University of Ostrava, Czech Republic, for her invaluable assistance with this material and translation from Czech. Other sources include the Czech Statistical Office (CSO), the Ministry of Finance and the World Bank.

2 Human resource management and employee engagement

Stephanie J. Morgan

Introduction

Although a substantial amount of outsourcing research has been carried out at the senior management level, particularly concerning the cost-benefits of outsourcing and vendor selection, little is known about the impact of the outsourcing process upon the staff concerned. Literature sometimes briefly suggests that the transition (logistical and contractual aspects of transferring the staff from one employer to another) should be managed carefully because of the potential impact on human and performance aspects. However, very little is known about how the process is experienced by the staff, the role of HR, and whether some interventions may be more helpful than others in facilitating a more positive experience.

Outsourcing is a particular form of externalization of employment, and, as highlighted in Chapter 1, involves an outside contractor taking over an in-house function, *including* the management of staff. A broad range of activities has been transferred in this way, including catering, cleaning and security, often termed 'secondary' or 'non-core' functions. However, there has also been an increase in the outsourcing of professional[1] activities, including HR and IT. The management literature suggests that these may not be 'core competencies' for many organizations. This chapter deals with the challenges involved in transferring staff during outsourcing, raising issues that have been fundamentally neglected in the literature.

There have been discussions in the literature concerning the implications for outsourced staff of shifting to contingent working, sometimes linked to the concept of 'employability'. However, not all employees transferred under an outsourcing agreement can be classed as 'contingent'; they are likely to be core workers for their new employer. Particularly for professional staff, an argument often put forward is that transfer offers them the potential to enhance their career by moving to an organization dedicated to their area of specialization. However, professional staff are also more likely to have enjoyed or expected a career future within their employing organization, and less likely to accept the vulnerability and lack of control inherent in forced transfers. There is potentially more chance that they will leave before the transfer, in good market conditions. In this chapter I will focus on an example of professional-level outsourcing; however, many of the issues will be similar for other levels of staff; those who stay on and are transferred, whatever the level of their work, are likely to share many concerns. Although the sample here is predominantly UK based, some participants were based in other parts of Europe, and cultural differences are discussed in more detail in the chapter on outsourcing in South Africa. In our view, the main cultural issues are around differences in negotiating and communication styles, rather than the fundamental experience of the transfer. To highlight issues around staff experience and aid understanding I will apply theory and concepts linked to justice perceptions, career transitions, socialization and identification. Practical aspects surrounding the transfer, HR and line management will be considered.

As discussed in Chapter 1, outsourcing transfers can occur in many forms, with many different factors influencing the process. In particular, the length of time taken to agree contracts, whether internal bidding has been allowed,[2] whether the entire department or one section is involved, and which organization gains the contract are all aspects that may affect how staff experience the transfer. In many ways outsourcing can be viewed as a breaking of the psychological contract.[3] Justice perceptions have been linked to psychological contract shifts,[4] although due to lack of research it is unclear whether the increased prevalence of outsourcing has resulted in a change of standards for the contract or related perceptions of fairness. A key issue with outsourcing is that staff are generally expected to continue carrying out the same work for their old employer, and ex-colleagues become representatives of the 'client'. All of these transition processes are likely to impact upon perceptions of justice. Most importantly, poor justice perceptions during the transfer may lead to poor working relationships later. There is also increasing evidence of impact on performance, and even the health of the staff concerned.[5]

In an outsourcing transfer, much of the process may be managed by HR, with some assistance from senior management. Yet the practitioner literature suggests that the HR dimensions are often overlooked or mismanaged. There are also many assumptions of resistance, and staff are viewed as awkward and against any change.[6] Possibly, the focus on strategic issues is partly to blame. Willcocks *et al.*[7] discuss the importance of dealing with employee concerns during the change process, and also highlight the problems that an organization may experience if it needs to bring the systems back in-house (referred to in this book as 'backsourcing'), if they have previously transferred all their people. Lacity and Willcocks[8] outline a range of stakeholder groups involved in outsourcing, including client management, vendor management, end-users and the IT staff. They suggest that the transferred IT staff form the stakeholder group most profoundly affected by outsourcing evaluations, and may feel that senior managers are making life-choices for them. These studies suggest that transfers may be viewed as unfair by staff. However, almost all of the literature is based on interviews and case study research with *senior* management; the employees concerned are given little voice, and little is really understood regarding the experience of the change. This chapter aims to increase our understanding of the issues and concerns experienced by staff, and offer ideas for best practice.

Much of the management literature focuses on IT outsourcing, which is particularly popular as an area to transfer out. Yet from the staff point of view, Martinsons and Cheung[9] found that IT outsourcing received the least support of a range of emerging practices; staff with less than five years' experience were particularly against the practice. They suggest that the dislike of new practices was based on the desire to follow a traditional IT career path. However, they used a broad definition of outsourcing, and, although they highlighted that outsourcing may signal a belief that management is dissatisfied with the performance of the internal function, they did *not* consider transfer situations specifically. Instead they focused on different skills staff may need to monitor contracted work and deal with outsourcing vendors, implying that the existing staff would remain. The need for different skills for those remaining has been discussed more recently, and is outlined in Chapter 3 on the outsourcing lifecycle. In this chapter we focus on those who are transferred to the new organization. In Martinson and Cheung's study, it is possible that respondents *did* consider transfer situations when indicating their attitude to outsourcing. Staff with the least experience may have felt that they would be of little value to an outsourcing company, as these tend to emphasize the importance of experience. Literature in the IT journals supports the idea that outsourcing is particularly unpopular with staff. Glass[10] outlines a range of problems that organizations could face in the future due to wholesale outsourcing of IT, particularly emphasizing the loss of skilled staff. It is suggested that companies that have chosen to outsource in the past will be unable to attract staff when trying to backsource. His suggestion that the staff now owe an allegiance to the outsourcing company is supported by evidence that the best staff are moved on to other clients after outsourcing. However, there has been no research to date assessing the strength or quality of this new 'allegiance'. We suggest that these relationships may be influenced by the management of the transfer and in particular perceptions of justice. If correct, HR and management involved in managing transfers will need to ensure that perceived justice is high and reduce the impact of the break in the psychological contract.

Justice and the psychological contract

Performance during and after an organizational change can be affected by perceptions of justice and changes in the psychological contract. Extant literature tends to focus on three specific forms of justice perceptions: *distributive justice* considers perceptions of fairness of outcomes (equity, equality and needs); *procedural justice* emphasizes the importance of fairness of the methods or procedures used (decision criteria, voice and control of the process); and *interactional justice* is based on the perceived fairness of the interpersonal treatment received, whether those involved are treated with sensitivity, dignity and respect, and also the nature of the explanations given. Although there have been concerns regarding the distinctions between different forms of justice, a recent meta-analysis suggests that the distinction between these three forms is merited.[11] Justice perceptions have been related to a range of work outcomes, including performance, turnover, commitment and cooperative behaviours.[12] It is not the purpose of this chapter to review the justice literature, which has been extensively discussed in recent years. However, of specific interest to this research is the repeated finding that good attention to procedural justice concerns can increase perceptions of fairness even if the outcomes are unfavourable.[13] If we assume that, at least initially, staff will view the likely outcome of being forcibly transferred to another organization as unfair, it may be possible that procedural justice will reduce their perceptions of unfairness.

As research on justice in outsourcing transitions is minimal, we should look to related change literature, such as that on downsizing and mergers, to increase understanding. Survivor expressions of organizational resentment have been linked to procedural justice aspects,[14] supporting the view that the management of the transfer process may be crucial. In mergers and acquisitions, employee reactions are frequently claimed to be responsible for lack of success.[15] Although clear evidence is often lacking, it seems logical that the widespread disruption, employee resistance, job insecurity and stress reported will impact upon performance. Although outsourcing may share some similarities with mergers, care should be taken in assuming that justice concerns will be the same, due to the ongoing relationship with the ex-employer. The break in the psychological contract may be an important aspect.

Studies have shown that a perceived breach of the psychological contract is linked to reduced commitment, trust and performance and a decline in citizenship behaviour.[16] In principle, this concept could be of use in assessing organizational change processes, as the changing or breaking of contracts is perhaps more likely to occur. The psychological contract has been used to understand outsourcing in terms of the relationship between customers and vendors,[17] but little research has been carried out on staff in this area.

Rousseau[18] claims that organizational attachments, and particularly relational contracts, evolve, to a certain extent, by length of tenure and extent of security, although there is little evidence of a direct link between relational contracts and formal contract type. In their study, team spirit and identity were considered to be a predictor of relational psychological contracts, although this finding was based on regression analysis with a cross-sectional study, which limits the validity of causal findings. Rousseau suggests that two factors are critical to the formation of contracts: external messages, including observations of the treatment of others with the same deal, and personal interpretations and dispositions. The recruitment process and early socialization is considered key, although much of the research focuses on MBA graduates, for whom organizational recruitment and socialization may be particularly new and crucial. Alternatively, graduates may find it easier to accept more transactional contracts. In outsourcing, the initial presentations and early socialization practices may be influential in developing a 'new' psychological contract, but most of the staff involved have a substantial career behind them. We therefore need to consider the implications for careers and how this aspect of the change will be viewed by staff.

Career transitions

Outsourcing transfers could be viewed as a new form of work transition. Certainly the relationship between staff and the two organizations concerned is likely to be influenced by the nature of the initial transfer. Indeed Nicholson[19] argues that the outcomes of work transitions will depend substantially upon prior influences. In a similar way to mergers and acquisitions, the literature on work transitions tends to emphasize stages, viewing role transitions as discrete steps between fixed states. Weiss[20] suggests that change or transition that involves loss of relationships (which may include distancing from co-workers) may trigger a form of grieving. Recovery stages are similar to those proposed by Kubler-Ross[21]: disbelief and denial, anger, emotional bargaining and depression, followed by acceptance.[22] It is proposed that employees may become fixated at an early stage, leading to unproductive behaviour. Whilst there are some problems with stage models, in particular the tendency to focus on 'states' rather than processes, the acceptance of the emotional aspects of the change process may be useful, particularly where uncertainty and loss of control are experienced, such as in outsourcing. However, Weiss also discusses recovery *processes*; these include cognitive acceptance, emotional acceptance and identity change. However, often in transition research little attention is paid to the nature of the transition process. Bullis and Wackernagel Bach[23] assessed the importance of *turning points* and events or episodes during role transitions, and there is evidence that these may be perceived differently at different times in the transition process. It may be helpful, therefore, to assess the specific events and any perceived phases of work transitions that are relevant to outsourcing transfers, to ensure that the context and the temporal nature of the experience is understood. Outsourcing is often seen as a straightforward one-off transaction; however, the research discussed here indicates the need to consider the various impacts on staff across the lifecycle (see Chapter 3).

Transitions can be analysed across a range of dimensions, including the speed at which they occur and the extent of change involved. The literature offers different terms and types of factors that impact upon the transition experience and some are likely to be more important than others in an outsourcing transition. In terms of key attributes, outsourcing is likely to be a high magnitude, involuntary, unpredictable and collective form of transition; these aspects are discussed further below. It is also likely that the duration and extent to which the transfer is viewed as socially desirable varies a great deal. Temporally there may be substantial differences. The research discussed below shows that outsourcing transitions can take place within days of an announcement, or can take years. Similarly, the nature and reputation of the company taking over the staff, and the individual perceptions of the desirability of working for that company, will vary.

Although research on outsourcing transitions is in its infancy, some studies do focus on changes after an outsourcing transition. Kessler *et al.*[24] specifically focused on *employee* reactions to an outsourcing transfer. They found slight increases in attitudinal measures, including organizational commitment and perceived organizational support, although due to the small sample size no firm statistical conclusions could be drawn. They emphasize the context within which the outsourcing takes place, particularly how employees feel they have been treated by their existing employer. Other research indicates a less positive view, including difficult relations with the original employer and negative long-term impact.[25] Studies in related areas demonstrate increased work-related injury and illness as a result of similar organizational changes.[26] The ongoing relationship with this 'client' (the previous employer) was not investigated in these studies and the authors did not consider the links between socialization in the new organization and these variables.

Socialization and identification – engaging staff

Staff being transferred in an outsourcing situation are likely to want to know something about their new employer. Socialization processes are argued to be key to enabling newcomers to become effective members of the organization. Individuals need to learn about their organization and their role within it to be effective. Organizations may facilitate this learning in a number of ways, including inductions, training and mentoring. Theory development in this area is still fragmented. However, Saks and Ashforth[27] present a multi-level process model that emphasizes the role of learning, uncertainty reduction and cognitive sense-making. In this model, contextual and individual variables at a number of levels influence socialization outcomes. However, there are some aspects of outsourcing that are not fully accounted for in this model.

First, the transition is not voluntary, which may lead to individuals resisting organizational socialization tactics.[28] Although the employees do have a choice in principle, in that they can look for alternative employment, this is a strategy likely to be taken up only by the most confident members of staff. Research suggests that expectations are crucial to socialization outcomes.[29] These expectations may also be affected by the nature of employees' initial contact with the new organization and their perceptions of the handling of the change by their previous employer. Furthermore, some staff have also been through downsizing, often during the transfer, which has been argued to make them less easy to socialize into a new organization.[30] Whilst this suggests that there may be some similarity between outsourcing and mergers and acquisitions, a key difference is the continued, long-term exposure to the old organization, which may further complicate the situation. Louis[31] suggested that part of the process of becoming socialized to a new organization was the turning away from old role relationships and experiences – this may be particularly difficult in outsourcing. Conversely, staff may often feel that their psychological contract has been violated, and turn against their old organization.[32] It is unclear, therefore, whether staff will be easier or more difficult to socialize into the new organization in these circumstances.

Furthermore, staff are likely to have little exposure to the new organization, and to remain in their original grouping, at least initially. Research suggests that it is particularly difficult to socialize staff from a distance,[33] with lack of understanding of organizational goals and values being a key issue. It has been argued that it is more effective to use an existing group to socialize a new individual than to apply organizational socialization tactics.[34] However, in outsourcing the group usually moves across together, and will therefore consist only of outsiders, making group socialization difficult. These factors suggest that socialization might be extremely difficult in outsourcing.

Organizational identification has been proposed as a key outcome of successful socialization.[35] Definitions of identification vary substantially. Some suggest that identification occurs when one adopts values and behaviours in order to be associated with someone or something. Rousseau[36] describes identification as a psychological state where the individual perceives the 'self' to be part of a larger whole. Both identification and commitment have been shown to be important concepts linked to performance, and both are influenced by socialization. There is also a clear link to understanding one's role in the organization – individuals going through outsourcing transitions are likely to feel uncertain about their future roles. Although they are in principle continuing the same work, they are moving from being members of the organization to being outsiders, needing to treat colleagues as 'clients', and there may be a lack of clarity about their precise role in the new organization. There are some known negative effects from experiencing weak role identification, including absenteeism, lack of enthusiasm, and resistance to change.[37] This lack of role identification also has implications for commitment and motivation. For HR practitioners, these aspects are often included in the concept of 'employee engagement', a concept increasingly viewed as useful in explaining employee performance.[38] Research on employee engagement itself is increasing, including that by the Employee Engagement Forum at the Centre for Applied Positive Psychology (CAPP) – a much-needed move as there is little quality academic research to date, and even less on how to manage this during outsourcing. Academics argue that engagement may be a new name for existing concepts of identification and commitment, but the term is increasingly used in the HR world. Many measures of engagement could be argued to assess little more than job satisfaction, although Konrad[39] argues that engagement taps the actionable facets of the more general theoretical construct of job satisfaction. Stairs[40] suggests that this 're-branding' may be useful as the concept embraces a range of facets that are particularly important in HR. Yates[41] highlights the importance of communication in engaging employees; however, justice during communication is not included. The research discussed below suggests that this may be vital. Some outsourcing companies are taking the concept of engagement seriously, but how well they help employees to develop relationships and engage with *both* organizations is uncertain. The actual practice of HR needs careful consideration.

Practitioner/HR research on outsourcing

Much of the practitioner research on outsourcing retains very positive views of transfers. Even when resistance is outlined, rather simplistic arguments are given regarding the management of transfers. Contract arrangements remain a core focus. Even in the IT industry, it is rare to see much consideration for staff motivation. The weekly magazines are full of discussions around contract negotiations. Although occasional articles suggest that outsourcing is problematic, emphasizing the need for flexibility and for retention of skills, and the recruitment drives of IT systems houses, they still tend to ignore the implications for staff. Even when discussing how outsourcing suppliers are now steering away from large staff transfers,[42] the emphasis is on having a better opportunity with the outsourcer if you have the right skills, rather than the potential worry and implications for performance that this situation may bring.

Brown and Wilson[43] suggest that managers should consider staff motivation and retention, but offer little advice or detail. A short chapter is dedicated to highlighting new career opportunities in outsourcing management (although this is primarily aimed at very high-level managers) – the effect on organizational performance of staff insecurity and changes in motivation are not really explored. Corbett[44] highlights the need for effective communication, and emphasizes the opportunities for career advancement for staff. He does suggest that HR planning should begin 12 months before the transition (not always possible), but indicates that the provider should take over completely after the integration of new employees. This may be a risky strategy, according to Khanna and Randolph.[45] They emphasize the importance of managing staff even after transfer, and the need for a high-quality team remaining on the client site to manage the relationships. However, they also suggest a phased approach to the transition, whilst acknowledging that this may cause more pain to the employees. The impact of this on staff and performance is not really discussed. Although most outsourcing organizations have clear processes in place for taking on staff, this still tends to emphasize the contractual aspects. A few organizations are starting to highlight the broader role of HR,[46] but many companies arranging outsourcing seem happy to leave all of this to the vendor.

To summarize, theoretically the reactions of staff to an outsourcing transfer can be understood by considering the breach in the psychological contract, perceptions of justice, the nature of the transition cycle, and the impact of socialization (and resultant identification and engagement) into the new organization. From a practitioner point of view staff reactions do receive some consideration, but little clear advice is given regarding how to manage the change and reduce the impact on staff (and performance). In practice, very few seem to treat this as an important element of outsourcing. To help increase our understanding of how staff experience outsourcing, I now discuss specific research on the topic.

Our research on the experience of outsourcing[47]

The main study was of a longitudinal design based on face-to-face interviews. An interview guide was drawn up to ensure that all main areas relating to the research were discussed, but the questions were not asked in strict order, and care was taken to follow the flow of the participants' comments. The questions covered the transfer process and their experience during that time, but no direct reference was made to justice or fairness. This ensured that any discussions of these aspects arose because they were concerns of the participants and not the researcher.

The interviews were carried out at two time-points, the first being shortly after the outsourcing transfer (between one and six months from the transfer date) and the second being carried out six to eight months after the first. This enabled an understanding of changes over time, and potential impacts on longer-term relationships. The total number of participants involved in the first stage from a UK sample was 33, and a total of 18 UK participants agreed to take part in the second-stage interviews. All of these were held face to face. Additional electronic interviews[48] were held with 20 English-speaking employees from Germany, Belgium, Spain and Italy. Although the small samples meant no generalizations could be made, the organization found it helpful to see the similarities in response. The high attrition rate was caused primarily by major restructuring taking place in the systems houses involved. This is not unusual in the IT industry and was anticipated; hence the relatively high number in the first sample. Both managers and staff were interviewed, as research suggests that employee level in the organization can impact upon perceptions, with, for example, higher-level managers less likely to perceive injustice.[49]

The sample at both stages is uneven, with more public sector participants and more males. At the first-stage interviews there were 18 from the public sector and 15 from the private (the pilots were all private sector). Of these, 23 were male and 10 female. In the second stage there were 12 public sector and 6 private sector participants, 14 males and only 4 females. From the international sample, 12 were male and 8 female. It is noticeable also that all of the managers were male. These differences are partly a reflection of the IT industry, and of the facts that more public sector organizations are involved in outsourcing, while management is male dominated. Due to the low numbers involved in qualitative research, a 'representative' sample is not a key quality criterion, and the sample differences can be used as part of the contextual analysis, rather than controlled for.[50] Ethical considerations were continually assessed, according to British Psychological Society guidelines.

Analysis was based on a hermeneutic interpretive approach,[51] to assess meaning and experience. This included repeated readings of each of the transcripts, at both time-points; writing a summary 'story' for each participant; developing key theme charts for each; and compiling a change chart to assess differences between the first and second interviews. A number of themes were developed and a range of notes and diagrams, including detailed time-charts, were also drawn up with generalized notes on the experiences discussed, linked to notes regarding individual context. To enhance quality, the second interviews were analysed completely separately from the first, and comparisons between the two made only after completion. Interpretations were also discussed with colleagues, and a sample of the transcripts was given to another colleague to analyse. One small difference was found, regarding the emphasis on HR, possibly due to the additional expertise this colleague had in the area. This was incorporated into the final analysis.

Results

Participants raised a number of issues during the interviews that were clearly linked to problems with the transfer. For this chapter we focus on key areas: poor communication or lack of voice; the blame culture; lack of control; future relationships and performance; and the role of HR departments. For each participant quoted details are given of whether they work in the public or private sector, whether they are male or female and whether they are staff or management. As the focus here is on individual meaning, the quotes from participants are given in full, without editing, enabling the reader some access to hesitations in the discussions. The original company is referred to as 'Oldco' and the outsourcing organization as 'Newco'. Many of these quotations are from the first interviews (shown as p. [number]-1) as this is where the initial transfer experience was discussed in detail; however, the second interviews allowed us to assess the longer-term implications, which will be discussed later.

Poor communication and lack of voice

There were many discussions regarding how badly the outsourcing process was managed, with poor communication and an apparent lack of understanding by management. People quickly began to feel that they were just a number, and that nobody cared about them as individuals. Although there was a sense of injustice and unfairness in many of the discussions, this was rarely expressed directly. Perhaps the interview situation made people careful not to sound too hard done by (although in most of the transcripts participants can clearly be seen to be expressing dissatisfaction). The following excerpt indicates this general blaming, and takes place after a discussion about poor communication:

> *Interviewer*: Right, how did you feel about all that?
> *Participant*: Oh, terrible really, we just felt that we were being, well the wool was being pulled over our eyes although it wasn't because we knew exactly what was going on, but we felt, well let down, basically just completely let down by the Oldco to be honest, erm, not only on the fact, by the fact they wouldn't listen to what we were trying to say, but erm, by the fact that, y'know the way they were treating us and the way they were sort of y'know saying what was happening, you just didn't trust them to be honest, we just thought there was a hidden agenda.
>
> (p. 11-1, public/staff/male)

In this example the loss of trust is evident, and this is discussed in a number of cases. Although loss of trust is discussed in downsizing and justice literature, the links to blame and poor communication indicate that procedural justice may be of *particular* importance in these situations. The focus seems to be very much on poor management and in particular on lack of communication. There was also a feeling that, once a decision had been made, it would be railroaded through whatever else happened. In justice terms there is a lack of explanation and little voice allowed – factors that are likely to increase perceptions of injustice. Some participants highlighted that everything suddenly became very secretive around the organization:

> They went into secret squirrel mode and nobody knew what was going on, and er, nobody knew really.
>
> (p. 08-1, public/staff/female)

For some, this was clearly viewed as a deliberate attempt to hide facts:

> And . . . Well, erm, yeah, you could say that, that's the sort of erm, attitude they had, pretend that it wasn't happening, as far as the staff were concerned, although, they could see it happening erm, with what was going on around them, the meetings that they were having, it was definitely happening, but the feedback to staff was quite poor.
>
> (p. 19-1, public/staff/male)

Problems with lack of communication are highlighted in the justice literature, and related to this for many was the timing of announcements, which could be classed as interactional justice (showing a lack of sensitivity), for example:

> I actually remember erm, when we actually found out, and we had a visit from a Director, the day before Christmas Eve, to tell us that er, they were going to shut down the mainframe stuff at the Oldco and get rid of it, and find jobs for us, so that was quite nice er, nice timing. And the way the Oldco handled it was actually I think, quite poor, all along really, and I think that is an important point.
>
> (p. 19-1, public/staff/male)

Also noticeable in many of the transcripts is a form of counterfactual talking – where participants discussed what could or should have been if events had transpired differently.[52] This form of understanding can be useful, both to the individual and in positioning themselves to the interviewer. The discussions suggest that, *if* things had been managed better, the people would have been more positive. Justice literature does highlight that, in many cases, good procedural justice can reduce reactions to poor outcomes. In some cases, it is clear that the participants had expected better treatment, and look to formal procedures or standard views of fairness to demonstrate what should be happening, and illustrate the exchange relationship highlighted by the justice literature:

> Y'know, I mean I, I was the one that said we must, we must do this this way, y'know, this can't be right, this just can't happen. If you really think about this, it will not happen, it's not sensible, if they would only listen to us like this, and y'know, they can't do that, they must be telling us this, and they must be, giving us information about what's happening.
>
> (p. 11-1, public/staff/male)

Here the participant was trying to articulate the view that the company should have been keeping them informed and following specific procedures, and that the staff would therefore do the right things in return. This demonstrates the exchange concept upon which justice theory has been developed. HR and line managers are expected to keep people informed about such major change, yet communication in this case was poor.

The blame culture

Talk of poor management tended to lead to discussions of blame, which were often very focused on an individual or specific department. The loss of trust, and linked to this the sense of resentment, led to very strong feelings and a need to pinpoint the blame as being on those who had been expected to communicate the change. Most of the attributions of blame were aimed at very senior managers, none of whom had been included in the outsourcing transfers:

> Well I mean, a lot of the staff involved, the senior staff in the technology department involved in the whole outsourcing business, have either retired,

> or have taken early retirement. So, it, there has certainly been a lot of changes in the senior posts within the Oldco, but I mean I think, I think there was a lot of resentment towards the erm, the former IT Director, (name), I mean, he wasn't really held in high regard by the staff, particularly the way he was handling the whole business of outsourcing.
> (p. 19-1, public/staff/male)

Comments were made regarding the golden goodbyes these people were thought to have received – how they arranged the outsourcing and then retired on a good package. It appeared that the only people who lost out in all this was the group being outsourced. In other cases the senior people or departments involved were still working for the old company, managing the contracts. It was clear that participants felt that this led to further problems, continuing the atmosphere of secrecy and covert control. Blame and resentment are key outcomes of perceptions of injustice, and are linked to judgements of responsibility.[53] Blame is only placed on those viewed as involved with, and responsible for, the outsourcing decision. The blame in this study was often justified with supporting evidence, including examples of further unfair behaviour. In one case a particular individual was cited as having 'got through seven PAs in 18 months' (p. 08-1, public/staff/female) as evidence of her poor interpersonal skills. This need to cite evidence to support their claims suggests that participants were very aware of potential counter-arguments, that perhaps they were exaggerating their claims due to ill-feeling, or that they might be partly to blame for what had happened to them. Whilst this laying of blame may be helpful in enabling people to accept the situation, it may be dangerous in the long term. If people continue to blame those who have now become 'clients', the relationships are likely to be adversely affected.

There were a number of disclaimers, as if people could really not understand why outsourcing was happening to them, including comments regarding length of service and how it 'obviously means nothing really' (p. 06-1, public/mgr/male). People showed surprise that they were ever involved in such a process, the sense of rejection was acute: 'I'm supposed to be one of the good guys' (p. 13-1, public/mgr/male), and for some the idea that it was nothing personal was very important: 'you are just a cog in the wheel' or 'I was just in the wrong seat at the wrong time' (p. 06-1, public/mgr/male). Although the recognition that it was not personal helped in some ways (they could not be found lacking themselves, it's just the way the system works), it also generated ill-feeling. The idea that 'you are just a body, a number, you are going whether you want to or not' (p. 09-1, public/staff/female) generated discussions about the uncaring attitudes of those responsible for the decisions. A number explained that their entire attitude to work and organizational relationships had been changed since the transfer.

Some sadness was shown, in that there was an awareness that it was the poor management that made things so difficult: 'it doesn't need to be that painful' (p. 17-1, private/staff/male). The difference between rational concepts and personal experience was also highlighted:

> You move beyond the intellectual broad picture view to the 'what about me' concerns.
>
> (p. 25-1, private/mgr/male)

The view that thinking rationally still did not protect one fully from emotional turmoil was also discussed:

> It was, basically I was okay with the idea, but it was all the mucking about, changing, really, really just, it just strips you emotionally really.
>
> (p. 10-1, public/staff/male)

The difficulties discussed often highlighted the emotional aspects of the process, as in the example above. It seemed that, in some way, disclosing the emotional aspects of a transfer may be helping people to make sense of their past experience and link them to their present. Feelings of injustice have been linked to blame, resentment and retaliation in the literature, although the underlying emotions inherent in these are rarely discussed. Certainly there was evidence of a strong sense of rejection, and of transferred staff being the 'losers' in the process, and little evidence of anyone helping them through the process. The later interviews indicated that the emotional scars remained, even two years after the process. These emotions may have been made even stronger by the apparent low levels of control that the interviewees had during the process.

Lack of control

Participants felt that one of the greatest problems for them was the lack of control they had over events. This seemed to be exacerbated by the apparent control some other people in the organization had. This may be a key difference compared to mergers and acquisitions – in outsourcing some are chosen to be transferred whilst others stay. It was stressed that groups and/or individuals were ring-fenced and then prevented from applying for jobs elsewhere in the organization. Conversely other groups or individuals were allowed to do just that, or were pronounced 'safe' almost immediately. The unfairness of this was stressed, but in general the main concern was the lack of control over any aspect of the transfer:

> What I particularly didn't like was that I felt out of control, I didn't feel as I had any say in the matter, and I didn't like that, I like to feel I have at least, some sort of say, in some direction, with my career, and, some choice at least, there was no choice, erm, and that was quite worrying, y'know, and that was sort of, you think, y'know, well okay perhaps it

> will be better, with the organization that we are going to, is pretty clued up, y'know, done loads and loads of outsourcing deals, and, y'know perhaps there will be good opportunities, so you try to be positive about it.
>
> (p.33-1, private/staff/female)

Note how this participant moves from discussing the negative aspects to trying to consider the positives. She tries to develop a positive attitude by thinking through to the future.

The fairness of outcomes often seemed linked to the control aspects:

> And there was a lot of er, voluntary redundancies going on, but we weren't even eligible for the voluntary redundancies, see, they would just turn us down, once you had been ring-fenced, that was it really.
>
> (p. 33-1, private/staff/female)

As outlined in the justice literature, employees were possibly more interested in the *process* of decision-making than in the actual outcomes themselves:

> And you could almost pick the ones who you would think, they'll stay, or they'll go, they'll go, you could name them.
>
> (p. 09-1, public/staff/female)

This choosing of who should stay or go was considered quite unfair, and discussed by management and staff across both the public and private sectors:

> There was definitely anomalies in who was chosen to go and who wasn't.
>
> (p. 33-1, private/staff/female)

Other people not understanding the situation also seemed to make things worse:

> But one of the difficult things is, I speak to people about it and they say 'well you wanna get out then' and I say, 'I can't get out' and they say 'don't be stupid', and I know it sounds stupid, until you get embroiled in it all.
>
> (p. 09-1, public/staff/female)

This was made particularly salient in circumstances where decisions were made about dates or choice of outsourcing company, and then changed, leading to an even greater awareness that someone else was organizing the individual's future. This participant discussed how he and his colleagues were originally told they would join one company, then another, and then the first company again:

Participant: . . . we were told by the bosses, that lasted about a month, and then they came back to us, 'you're going to (the original) Newco after all' (sighs) and we said, actually, have you made up your minds this time(?) (laughs).
Interviewer: Do you mean it this time?
Participant: Yeah, do you mean it, what the hell are you doing, what are you playing at?

(p. 18-1, public/staff/male)

Other participants who had experienced this process of changing suppliers explained how they had just started to become adjusted to the idea of being forced to join one company when they had been told they were going to another. If the decision had been explained as 'not final' they would have held their internal transfer processes in abeyance. Cognitive dissonance theory indicates that people will at least try to adjust their feelings and attitudes to match their actual situation. To put them through this process two or three times in a matter of weeks is extremely unfair. Justice literature suggests that it is important to show some sensitivity during change and treat people with dignity and respect. Most participants felt that the type of decision-making outlined above completely neglected these aspects. They had been rejected, they were the group who 'lost out', and they had little control over their own future. Yet no one seemed to be helping; indeed management actions seemed to be making things worse.

It is likely that some participants genuinely had more choice in the matter than others; as with all forms of change some people may be in a better position than others for many different reasons. Generally managers emphasized the unfair process as something done to themselves and their staff, confirming the view that they have dual concerns, for themselves and for their people. Although all of the managers interviewed had been included in the transfer, and therefore their judgements are based on this, some had not realized that they were going to be part of the transfer until very late in the process. This in itself could be viewed as an unfair process; even those who knew from the start still suggested that the entire process was unfair.

Time was also a key element in the control process, as some participants stressed that things happened so quickly they had no time to think, and this seemed to cause much concern. Others emphasized the long timescales (sometimes years) from initial rumour to final transfer, and discussed the adverse effect this had on morale. This very long timescale may actually have made understanding more difficult and increased anxiety. A number of participants discussed medical problems and the need for time off with 'stress' and/or for long-term medication. These were all from long-drawn-out outsourcing transfers, suggesting that there may be a specific issue in the more protracted outsourcing situations. Those involved may feel unable to take appropriate action for long periods, leading to physiological as well as psychological changes.[54] It is clear that drawn-out procedures have an adverse impact on staff, and that HR and line managers should take steps to reduce this problem. In Japan, for example, there is enhanced support during this type of change, with genuine consultation, teamworking and HR actively supporting the staff during the change in a meaningful way. The failure of HR and management to support staff during the process is likely to have severe implications for performance.

Future relationships and performance

At both sets of interviews, the majority of participants said they felt that their relationship with their previous employer had been adversely affected. Blame was a key focus – the laying of blame may be helpful in enabling people to accept the situation, but it may be dangerous in the long term. If people continue to blame those who have now become 'clients', relationships are likely to be poor. Indeed justice research suggests that there may be retaliation. Some participants discussed this explicitly:

> *Participant*: . . . it made you sort of feel y'know, Oh well, they haven't done any favours for us so why should we do any favours for them? I know that seems wrong, to think like that.
> *Interviewer*: But some people do.
> *Participant*: But some people went, really that way, if you hear them speak about Oldco now, you wouldn't believe some of the things that people actually come out with, y'know.
> *Interviewer*: Yes, some people get very . . .
> *Participant*: They took a really hard line, y'know. Oh they can wait for that, y'know (laughs) but, where's your customer service?
> (p. 32-2, UK/private/staff/female)

For some the recognition that it was not personal seemed to help (they could not be found lacking in themselves, it's just the way the system works), but it also generated ill-feeling. The idea that 'you are just a body, a number, you are going whether you want to or not' (p. 09-1, UK/public/staff/female) generated discussions about the uncaring attitudes of those responsible for the decisions. A number explained that their entire attitude to work and organizational relationships had changed since the transfer.

The perceptions of poor treatment could also be seen to help some people disassociate themselves from the previous organization. Things had got so bad that 'I didn't want to be left at the Oldco at that stage, I was quite happy to be outsourced' (p. 19-1, UK/public/staff/male). But later, the reality that they were still actually working for that company hit home. Some explicitly linked the lack of justice and control to motivation:

> *Participant*: Yes, you are trapped, that's what it is about isn't it, . . .
> *Interviewer*: yes, interesting . . .

Participant: I mean how can people give their best if they feel that they are trapped? That's not a motivation is it really.

(p. 33-2, UK/private/staff/female)

Although some stressed that they felt their relationships with colleagues and their attitude to their ex-employer had impacted a great deal on performance, and a few openly discussed being awkward, some used the commercial aspect of their relationship to assist in 'getting their own back', even when stressing that they were not being vindictive:

Participant: I am not saying we are turning it around now, we not, not in a vindictive way at all.
Interviewer: No.
Participant: We are now in a commercial environment, and so if the Oldco Department require something, that is not part of the contract, we say fine, we will do it, here is the bill.
Interviewer: Yes, do you enjoy that? (Note, body language from participant prompted the question.)
Participant: Yes, I do!

(p. 07-2, UK/public/mgrr/male)

Note the impact that rational discourses can have on people, particularly regarding something they feel strongly about – being able to use financial terms and contract conditions to increase the chance of 'regret' in the previous organization is a very powerful way of increasing ones own positive feelings. Justice literature suggests that individuals will try to redress the balance and make the relationship feel more equitable by withdrawing positive behaviours after ill-treatment. With very few exceptions, views on performance and relationships were poor at both first and second interviews:

> The actual performance of the people here has gone down a lot. The level of service is definitely much worse.
>
> (p. 25-2, UK/private/mgr/male)

Furthermore, there was evidence that this bad feeling impacted upon others who join the group later. Although this was discussed by some participants with respect to new colleagues, perhaps the best quotation is from an electronic interview with a Belgian participant, who had joined a team just as the transfer was happening:

> I believe my negative perception is more related to the team I am working with than to Newco at such. Although I can understand people in my team are a bit anxious because they know for more than one and a half years they will probably be outsourced, in my opinion this is not a valid reason to have such a negative attitude. Maybe Newco management

> should avoid this kind of situation. Or avoid to put new people in such a group? From the management I know they were hoping I could bring some different thinking within this group. Kind of a hard job to deal with.
>
> (p. 40, Belgium/private/staff/female)

Although she does not feel a need to blame the companies directly, it is clear that she feels the situation is problematic. These issues were raised by participants at all levels, and all locations, even two years or more after the transition:

> I think er, they still suffer a somehow disturbed relationship to our, as it is now our customer.
>
> (p. 42, Germany/private/mgr/male)

These disturbed relationships may have been eased if there had been more care taken during the initial transfer, and more socialization of staff into the new organization. What was particularly noticeable was the lack of any clear HR support from the original employing organization, and discussions of poor HR support from the outsourcing company. Although one or two mentioned initial presentations where they were told they had been 'chosen', not many seemed to believe this, and at times it seemed to be linked to the way HR implemented their transfer, to which we now turn.

The role of HR departments

The role of HR management from the original organization was hardly ever mentioned by the participants, and, when asked, it was suggested that they were hardly involved. HR departments in the new organization were often seen to be a disappointment, with their function being 'only' administration rather than caring for their human resources. This indicates that many staff believe the role of HR should be more orientated towards the *human* rather than the *resources* aspects. Indeed some suggested that, in an outsourcing company, where people really should be the key asset, this might be more important. Possibly they had hoped for a human orientation due to the emphasis that many systems houses place on this. Perhaps this view is linked to their feelings of rejection or the anxiety they had experienced during the transfer; often people said they had wanted someone to listen to them. Not being given the opportunity to talk things through can reduce understanding; often, only as we talk do we begin to come to terms with the meaning of a change.

For some, the HR support was a great help during the initial process, but a gaping hole was left once this support was withdrawn:

> We went from the comfort of the Newco HR people being there and then they completely walk away.
>
> (p. 25-1, private/mgr/male)

An important aspect in the socialization literature is the type of socialization organized by the company (individual versus institutional) and the way this impacts directly on staff in their dealings with the HR department, as well as the impact it has on line management, who are often expected to adopt an HR role. According to the official transition documentation, at least some of the responsibility for interventions aimed at increasing 'transfer' in outsourcing is given to the HR department. Yet for nearly all of the participants these interventions seemed to work more to disassociate staff rather than integrate them.

Many of the participants seemed to have an understanding of HR that differed from their actual experience. There was concern that Personnel departments tended to focus only on contracts and not on the human side of the transfer – they were referred to as 'over-rated admin'. For example, after expressing how 'all' HR did was talk him through the contract, one participant said:

> yeah, I mean my perception is that they should be the interested people, but there isn't a Personnel any more is there.
>
> (p. 10-1, public/staff/male)

To put this into the individual context, this participant had taken three months off work with a stress-related illness and was rather surprised that no one seemed interested in how he was feeling. However, many of the other participants who had been, shall we say, less obviously affected still expressed the same sentiments: 'no one has even asked how I feel about all this' (p. 19-1, public/staff/male). The lack of 'soft HR' was often discussed around events also; for example, one participant told of the major presentation they attended:

> No, I think it's all a bit, sharp suited and American, that's what you, when you first meet them, and they rolled out the big guns, y'know once they knew we were going over they rolled out the big bosses, I can't really remember, the big manager, the training manager, human resources, and you really thought, wow they've rolled out some really important people, y'know, and they stress how important they are, and human resources person stood up and she said, Newco's policy on drinking is that you will not drink at lunch-time, and that wasn't quite what I was expecting I suppose from Personnel.
>
> (p. 08-1, public/staff/female)

It seems that many people still have a model of HR as 'Personnel' and anticipate that HR professionals will care for their psychological welfare as well as their contractual situation. This seems to be particularly pertinent because they were moving over to a systems house where personnel are supposedly the main asset, and this was sometimes explicitly discussed.

Few seemed to be happy with the idea that, in the 'new era' of work, the only person who cares about you is yourself[55] – although some tried to acknowledge it:

> Perhaps I should have said devil take the hindmost and looked after myself. But here we have always worked in a sort of community, with a family spirit, and I felt it was the right thing to do, to help. Maybe the world of outsourcing is such that you can't do that anymore. I've been left with a kind of sadness. The process has meant I have clearly taken a dip. None of the existing staff have been helped really, perhaps I find it harder. But I see it a bit like bringing up kids, let's protect them during that transition from childhood to adulthood, but here it seems more like you should put them on the street at 18. My personal view is you can smooth people into transitions. A few swimming lessons don't go amiss!
>
> (p. 25-1, private/mgr/male)

This issue concerning the role of HR may be partly due to the increasing emphasis in outsourcing companies on the line manager as HR/Personnel. Many of the respondents commented that everything seemed to be down to the line manager, that HR was a 'black hole' and that this meant it was the luck of the draw whether your line manager knew what to do and understood the personnel issues. Sometimes comparisons were made between different departments: 'the IT department don't get perks. I guess their manager isn't so keen on motivating people' (p. 15-1, public/staff/ female), whereas others compared the present with their previous organization:

> Yeah, it was nice to have that small group, probably about having control. Stark difference to Newco where, you don't really know many senior people, you don't know the people, so you know your immediate line manager, they don't have much control over what happens, no one really has control, and there is no Personnel department or anything like that.
>
> (p. 17-1, private/staff/male)

This participant had left by the time of the second interview, and his reasons for leaving at that interview indicated a total lack of identification with Newco. He had joined a small company where, he felt, he could understand the values and meet regularly with senior managers to aid his own sense-making.

A number of participants also discussed the importance of the sense of community, which was often lost during the transfer, especially when groups were split up. Being transferred in a small group seemed better in some ways than being in a larger group, as closer ties were forged and this may have reduced the feeling of being 'just a number'. However, even small groups emphasized the lack of support from HR, where one would imagine that there would be less of an excuse for poor support. In one example, a very large group of people were transferred and many complained about the use of temporary staff to manage the HR side. The organization itself had been unable to cope with the numbers being transferred, but the temporary staff were unable to assist to the same depth as the company's own HR employees.

The following is an example of a participant who was extremely happy with her new situation, and definitely felt she belonged to the new company, but still her view was:

> But what I didn't like was as soon as that very hectic period was over, there was a presence here, but the numbers of HR people dwindled but there was still people left with lots of er, problems, and I remember because, there was an admin. office in the old civil service, and any, personal problems, pay-related matters, all went through the admin. department, erm, now you either, over pay you sort out the problems yourself, but if there's any welfare, it has to be through the line manager, so I have to take on that role for all my staff, and I remember having lots of queries to pass onto HR for people, and I think that could have been done better, I think they should have, a greater presence, it was like, 'Oh we've got what we want, we're going to clear off now'.
>
> (p. 21-1, public/staff/female)

Another aspect discussed a great deal was the continual need to monitor salary increases in the old organization due to remaining on old-style 'mirror' contracts. This seemed to create a number of problems, especially with 'letting go' and over a long timescale. One participant mentioned this immediately when contacted for a follow-up briefing over two years after the transfer.

The key change apparent in the second batch of interviews was that HR was discussed more in the context of presenting the option to change to standard contracts, and to some extent their lack of 'personal' assistance was accepted; for example, having said that HR don't really know what is going on out of head office the following participant said:

> By and large the HR people have got their hearts in the right place, but the follow-through is not there – they make the right noises to win the bids. And actually, no one seems to care much.
>
> (p. 25-2, private/mgr/male)

This participant and many of the others tended to place more focus now on the line manager. This seems logical, given that systems houses are generally large and complex organizations (a point made by many participants). The literature suggests that the team can be particularly useful in socializing newcomers, but in outsourcing the entire team is 'new' and the line manager is likely to be particularly important for socialization. However, many suggested that neither the line manager nor the organization was doing much to socialize them. Having suggested that the organization was complex, and that it was perhaps correct to identify with the project rather than with a rather distant organization, this participant suggested:

> To me Newco at the moment is, sort of, at one level its the (senior exec.) message, at the other level it's the individual I deal with on a particular project, the middle field has not really been filled in, y'know, for example we haven't been away, I suppose, to anything that resembles a manager away session or anything like that, that sort of thing where you are away for half a day with all the senior managers in the (org), and that sort of gives you a feel for what's happening.
>
> (p. 13-2, public/mgr/male)

Many highlighted the poor communication and lack of attempts by the organization to socialize them. The emphasis here is on how a manager who has been placed in charge of the department after a transition can demonstrate to those transitioned what are the 'true' values of the company. The importance to participants of the managers in charge, and particularly those placed over them from Newco, in generating an understanding of the company values, cannot be overemphasized. In many outsourcing organizations the line manager is also responsible for much HR work, but this also created issues:

> There is a huge contrast to inside a structured company like Oldco. One of the roles of HR was management development; we would have had discussions about the future. In Newco, every individual, especially at senior levels, the complete onus is on yourself, there is no one watching for high flyers or that sort of thing. Personally I find it strange and difficult. The transition from being over-cosseted to complete anarchy is a challenge.
>
> (p. 25-2, private/mgr/male)

However, this did vary by outsourcing company. There were cases cited where both HR and the management seemed to enable engagement. Problems still arose though, when the contract was under discussion, sometimes even less than two years after the original deal. This situation seems to leave everyone in a difficult situation. If the transfer is done badly, performance suffers and the staff feel a lack of belonging to either organization. They certainly appear very resistant to being returned to their former employer. If the transfer is managed well, and the staff establish a relationship with the new organization, problems develop when contracts are renegotiated (see Chapter 3 on the lifecycle).

To summarize the results, discussions were focused on the poor treatment participants received during the outsourcing process. They emphasized lack of communication, poor explanations for the need to outsource, and a lack of sensitivity or respect shown during interactions. The emotional aspects of the transfer were highlighted, coupled with the lack of control. Perceptions of poor distributive, procedural and interactional justice were in evidence, although at times it was difficult during the analysis to differentiate between these. Future relationships were considered to be problematic, with some openly discussing a lowering in performance and motivational problems. HR was viewed as problematic by most, with an over-focus on contracts and little consideration for employee engagement or even psychological welfare. The concept of employees being of great importance to a systems house was deemed as empty rhetoric. Instead the cry seemed to be 'where *is* the HR department!'

Discussion

Although there are weaknesses in this study, in particular the emphasis on interview data and the relatively small sample size, we believe there is much to be gained from the depth of the information gained. The longitudinal nature of the research is also a strength. Additional cross-sectional research has taken place on manual workers,[56] including 25 interviews across 11 local authority projects. Few differences were found, and we believe these are mainly differences in management rather than differences between professional and manual workers. A key issue may be that there is likely to be a higher attrition rate early on with professional workers, although further research will be needed to assess this. The theoretical implications of our findings will now be discussed, followed by an outline of practical implications and advice for managing transfers.

Many participants emphasized the lack of control they felt while talking about unfairness. This is an interesting finding given that little research on the links between justice and control has been carried out since the seminal studies by Thibaut and Walker.[57] While raising this issue, Greenberg[58] suggests that this lack of interest in control is problematic as the concept is fundamental to understanding procedural justice. The effectiveness of procedural justice is based on a hope that control will change outcomes or because it promotes acceptance in itself. This qualitative analysis suggests the latter. Furthermore, the one participant in this study who had chosen to be outsourced (and was therefore seemingly in control) seemed to experience a form of 'justice contagion', where he felt resentment for the way his colleagues had been treated. Ideally, future research should include outsourcing interventions where staff have been given a sense of control whilst recognizing that outcomes will remain unchanged, to attempt to disentangle motives.

Blame and resentment were clear, and were mostly aimed at particular senior managers, and to a lesser extent the organization. It is impossible with this type of research to comment on whether managers (and organizations) really did handle the change process badly in all cases. However, there was sufficient evidence to believe that some injustices occurred. Theoretically, it has been proposed that managers handle justice poorly despite evidence of its impact on performance and attitudes, because justice is hard work – emotionally and cognitively. On an emotional front they may feel partly to blame, or fear blame, which can lead to loss of face and personal discomfort. Cognitively, they may exaggerate the perceived cost of talking things through, may wish to avoid thinking about their own potentially difficult situation, and may attribute blame to the people being outsourced.[59] Therefore, they are more likely to distance themselves. The decision to outsource is generally made for 'strategic' reasons related to cost or conceptions of poor performance. Explaining to staff that they have been doing so badly that they must be handed over to someone who can handle them is difficult. Cost justifications are often used, although the evidence of insufficient cost savings in outsourcing also weakens this argument. Furthermore, managers may be able to persuade themselves that, if the staff had worked harder or been more efficient, outsourcing would not have been needed. The fact that none of the managers transferred themselves was blamed by their staff, and that they felt they had done their best, but that more senior managers were responsible for poor justice, fits in with current justice conceptions. In particular they were likely to feel blameless, and an increased empathy with their staff, as they were in the same situation.

In the long term (noticeable in both first and second interviews) many participants emphasized that their whole view of work and their relationship with organizations had changed. Rebuilding trust and a new psychological contract seemed to be particularly difficult after these transfers. This seemed to be further complicated by the dual relationships, and is an area that should be studied in future research. There was no evidence that staff accepted the idea of outsourcing more easily because it is now predominant in their area, therefore generating a shift in psychological contract standards.[60] The role of justice perceptions during communication, and the link to employee engagement (or in many cases disengagement) is clear. HR and line management need to develop clear strategies for engaging employees during and after transfers.

Practical implications

Although these have been touched on in Chapter 1, a summary of the practical implications specific to employee transfer is given here. For companies who have outsourced, the staff will still be required to carry out work for them, albeit under the management of the vendor. It is also possible that at some stage the organization will wish to backsource. This study indicates that organizations will experience problems if they do not attend to the needs of their staff during the transfer process. The outsourcing organizations need to ensure that the transfer is managed fairly, with consideration for the emotional aspects as well as the contract, and staff should be socialized in a professional manner to enable them to remain effective.

This research has many practical implications for managers involved in outsourcing transitions, on both sides. I will briefly discuss these, first for the original employer and second for the outsourcing company taking on the staff.

Original employer

The HR aspects of the transition management should be considered well before the formal announcement, and the potential repercussions explicitly discussed. Resistance should not be automatically assumed, but plans should be put in place to help staff feel more in control. In particular, long timescales should be avoided. In the public sector in particular, endless market testing for five or six years would appear to be unhealthy for the staff, in some cases literally.

For most companies, the staff will still be required to carry out work for them, albeit under the management of the systems house. It is also possible that at some stage the organization will wish to backsource. This study indicates that organizations will experience problems if they do not attend to the needs of their staff during the transfer process. Some of the practical considerations for the transfer itself include effective and ongoing communication of the business rationale; a focus on procedural and distributive justice; training of managers to ensure that open two-way communication is enabled; and accepting and working with the emotional aspects of the transfer rather than pretending it does not exist.

An aspect not often considered at all by organizations is the *aftermath* of the transfer. It will be important to ensure remaining staff receive clear communications regarding the changing roles (their own and their ex-colleagues'). A balance will need to be made between letting go, so that transferred staff do not feel they cannot move on, and creating barriers to communication. Most importantly, if the TUPE (transfer of undertaking, protection of employment) agreement includes a mapping-on of salary increases or other awards, it is vital that a process is put in place to ensure that this happens, rather than forcing the transferred staff to continually monitor the situation.

Outsourcing companies

Care should be taken to ensure that, whilst initial presentations are made in a positive way to help staff see the potential benefits of transfer, they do not oversell or mislead those about to join. In the study, what few expectations participants had of the new organization were primarily developed during these presentations. It is also important to ensure that procedures are fully adhered to – staff who had been promised a one-to-one interview were particularly put out if they did not then receive these. Most noticeably, it is possible that additional procedures will need to be put in place to socialize transferred staff into the new organization. Even if there are questions regarding the long-term viability of the main contract, meaning that full socialization into the organization may not be beneficial to either party, action should be taken to maintain motivation and reduce uncertainty. Although a performance link cannot be proven, there were clear indications that performance had been affected by both the poor transfer and the weak socialization. Some staff showed low identification and role conflict, which could lead to burnout.[61] Organizations should take action, particularly to train management responsible for newly transferred staff in developing clear roles and identification with organizational goals. It is possible that increased performance would then improve the likelihood of contract success.

Although there is some evidence in this sample that employees may be more willing to embrace the new organization if they believe the transfer has been badly handled, in general a bad transfer appears likely to damage both relationships. It is therefore recommended that systems houses work more closely with the original organization to manage a smooth transfer, as this is likely to benefit both parties.

Furthermore, it might be important to include existing systems house staff as role models on a long-term basis, rather than relying on a few HR staff during the first weeks. It will be helpful to train these staff and sensitize them to their own behaviour and how this may impact upon transferred staff.

There is a specific issue with developing a relationship with transferred staff, as they are indeed potentially short-term employees. One of the systems house HR directors suggested that there was an 'interesting psychological question of whether an individual should get too attached to any employer!' (HRDirectorNewco2, email correspondence). It is possibly this factor that influences the level of socialization employees (appear to) receive. However, based on the findings of this study, I would suggest that the systems houses would benefit from generating a feeling of identification by more systematic socialization tactics.

A survey carried out by a market research company on behalf of a systems house,[62] indicates that staff uncertainty was a key factor contributing to stress, which in turn affected performance. The study also showed that staff were unhappy with the management of the transfer process and felt that communication was generally poor. The company argued that their focus on 'soft' employee-related expenditures and improving staff communication reduced the stress levels of staff transferred to them. Whilst this was a small study and the method details are not available, it does indicate that systems houses are becoming concerned about the performance of transferred staff, and that some systems houses at least believe that their ability to motivate such staff may be viewed as a selling point. Whether they are actually successful in engaging staff is a matter for further research, although the current study indicates that insufficient attention is still paid to the psychological needs of those transferred.

Conclusion

This study demonstrates that outsourcing transfers are indeed a change process in which justice concerns are paramount and poor management of transfer, coupled with poor socialization into the new organization, can reduce performance. Employee engagement is almost impossible in many cases, due to bad feeling generated by poor transfers. Participants openly discussed issues of fairness, reactions to the breaking of the psychological contract, feelings of lack of control, resentment, a sense of loss, issues of poor socialization into the new organization, and the limitations of HR during the change process. These perceptions have implications for the future relationship of outsourced staff with both the companies involved, as resentment and low trust will impact upon commitment, turnover and performance and may even lead to forms of retaliation. HR and line management need to take the concept of engagement during and after transfer seriously. To this end they should take steps to ensure that the transfer is actively managed, that justice perceptions are considered, and that communication is clear and ongoing.

Notes

1 There is some debate regarding what constitutes a profession. Some distinguish between blue-collar, manual or clerical workers and highly trained and educated staff such as engineers and faculty members.
2 See M. C. Lacity and R. Hirschheim, *Information Systems Outsourcing: Myths, Metaphors & Realities* (Chichester: Wiley, 1993).
3 S. L. Robinson, 'Trust and breach of the psychological contract', *Administrative Science Quarterly*, 41 (December 1996): 574–99; J. McLean Parks and D. L. Kidder, 'Till death us do part – changing work relationships in the 1990s', in C. L. Cooper and D. M. Rousseau (eds) *Trends in Organizational Behavior* (New York: John Wiley & Sons, 1994), pp. 111–36.
4 D. M. Blancero and S. A. Johnson, 'A process model of discretionary service behavior: integrating psychological contracts, organizational justice, and customer feedback to manage service agents', *Journal of Quality Management*, 6 (2001): 307–29; R. Cropanzano and C. A. Prehar, 'Emerging justice concerns in an era of changing psychological contracts', in R. Cropanzano (ed.) *Justice in the Workplace: From Theory to Practice* (Hillsdale, NJ: Lawrence Erlbaum, 2001).
5 O. Gustafsson and P. O. Saksvik, 'Outsourcing in the public refuse collection sector: exploiting old certainties or exploring new possibilities?', *Work*, 25 (2005): 91–7.
6 For examples, see T. R. Mylott, *Computer Outsourcing: Managing the Transition of Information Sytems* (Englewood Cliffs, NJ: Prentice Hall, 1995); and M. Useem and J. Harder, 'Leading laterally in company outsourcing', *Sloan Management Review* (Winter, 2000): 25–36.
7 L, Willcocks, G. Fitzgerald and D. Feeny, 'Outsourcing IT: the strategic implications', *Long Range Planning*, 28(5) (1995): 59–70.
8 M. C. Lacity and L. P. Willcocks, 'Relationships in IT outsourcing: a stakeholder perspective', in R. W. Zmud (ed.) *Framing the Domains of I.T. Management: Projecting the Future, Through the Past* (Cincinnati, OH: Pinnaflex Educational Resources, 2000), pp. 355–463.

9 M. G. Martinsons and C. Cheung, 'The impact of emerging practices on IS specialists: perceptions, attitudes and role changes in Hong Kong', *Information and Management*, 38 (2001): 167–83.

10 R. L. Glass, 'The end of the "Outsourcing Era"', *The Journal of Systems and Software*, 53 (2000): 95–7.

11 Y. Cohen-Carash and P. E. Spector, 'The role of justice in organizations: a meta-analysis', *Organizational Behavior and Human Decision Processes*, 86 (2001): 278–324.

12 For a recent review see J. A. Colquitt, D. E. Conlon, M. J. Wesson, C. O. L. H. Porter and K. Y. Ng, 'Justice at the millennium: a meta-analytic review of 25 years of organizational justice research', *Journal of Applied Psychology*, 86 (2001): 425–45.

13 For a discussion, see J. Brockner, 'Making sense of procedural fairness: how high procedural fairness can reduce or heighten the influence of outcome favorability', *The Academy of Management Review*, 27(1) (2002): 58–76.

14 For example, M. A. Konovsky and J. Brockner, 'Managing victim and survivor layoff reactions: a procedural justice perspective'in Cropanzano (ed.) *Justice in the Workplace*, pp. 133–53.

15 See A. F. Buono and J. L. Bowditch, *The Human Side of Mergers and Acquisitions* (San Francisco, CA: Jossey Bass, 1989); and S. Cartwright and C. L. Cooper, *Managing Mergers, Acquisitions, and Strategic Alliances: Integrating People and Cultures* (Oxford: Butterworth-Heinemann, 1996).

16 J. A. M. Coyle-Shapiro and I. Kessler, 'Exploring reciprocity through the lens of the psychological contract: employee and employer perspectives', *European Journal of Work and Organizational Psychology*, 11(1) (2002): 69–86; S. L. Robinson and D. M. Rousseau, 'Violating the psychological contract: not the exception but the norm', *Journal of Organizational Behavior*, 15 (1994): 245–59; S. L. Robinson and E. Wolfe Morrison, 'The development of psychological contract breach and violation: a longitudinal study', *Journal of Organizational Behavior*, 21 (2000): 525–46.

17 C. Koh, S. Ang and D. T. Straub, 'IT outsourcing success: a psychological contract perspective', *Information Systems Research*, 15(4) (2004): 356–73.

18 D. M. *Rousseau, Psychological Contracts in Organizations: Understanding Written and Unwritten Agreements*, (Thousand Oaks, CA: Sage, 1995).

19 N. Nicholson, 'The transition cycle: causes, outcomes, processes and forms', in S. Fisher and C. L. Cooper (eds) *On the Move: The Psychology of Change and Transition* (Chichester: John Wiley, 1990), pp. 83–108.

20 R. S. Weiss, 'Losses associated with mobility', in Fisher and Cooper (eds) *On the Move*, pp. 1–10.

21 E. Kubler-Ross, *On Death and Dying* (New York: Macmillan, 1969).

22 See S. Cartwright and C. L. Cooper, 'The human effects of mergers and acquisitions', in Cooper and Rousseau (eds) *Trends in Organizational Behavior*, pp. 47–61.

23 C. Bullis and B. Wackernagel Bach, 'Socialization turning points: an examination of change in organizational identification', *Western Journal of Speech Communication*, 53 (Summer, 1989): 273–93.

24 I. Kessler, J. Coyle-Shapiro and J. Purcell, 'Outsourcing and the employee perspective', *Human Resource Management Journal*, 9(2) (1999): 5–19.

25 J. Charara, *The Impact of Outsourcing on Employees: A Guide to Organizations* (Lulu, 2004), available in paperback via website or download at: www.lulu.com/content/66236; M. S. Logan, T. K. Faugh and D. C. Ganster, 'Outsourcing a satisfied and committed workforce: a trucking industry case study', *International Journal of Human Resource Management*, 15 (2004): 147–62; S. Morgan,

'Organisational attachments in IT outsourcing', unpublished Ph.D. thesis, Birkbeck College, University of London, 2003.
26 C. Mayhew, M. Quinlan and R. Ferris, 'The effects of subcontracting/outsourcing on occupational health and safety: survey evidence from four Australian industries', *Safety Science*, 25 (1997),163–78; J. E. Ferrie, M. J. Shipley, M. G. Marmot, S. Stansfeld and G. D. Smith, 'An uncertain future: the health effects of threats to employment security in white-collar men and women', *American Journal of Public Health*, 88 (1998): 1030–49; J. E. Ferrie, M. J. Shipley, M. G. Marmot, S. Stansfeld and G. D. Smith, 'The health effects of major organizational change and job insecurity', *Social Science & Medicine*, 46 (1998): 243–54.
27 A. M. Saks and B. E. Ashforth, 'Organizational socialization: making sense of the past and present as a prologue for the future', *Journal of Vocational Behavior*, 51 (1997): 234–79.
28 B. E. Ashforth, *Role Transitions in Organizational Life: An Identity-based Perspective* (Hillsdale, NJ: Lawrence Erlbaum, 2001).
29 M. R. Louis, 'Surprise and sense making: what newcomers experience in entering unfamiliar organizational settings', *Administrative Science Quarterly*, 25 (June 1980): 226–51; D. A. Major, S. W. J. Kozlowski, G. T. Chao and P. D. Gardner, 'A longitudinal investigation of newcomer expectations, early socialization outcomes, and the moderating effects of role development factors', *Journal of Applied Psychology*, 80(3) (1995): 418–31.
30 T. N. Bauer, E. Wolfe Morrison and R. Roberts Callister, 'Organizational socialization: a review and directions for future research', *Research in Personnel and Human Resources Management*, 16 (1998): 149–214.
31 Louis, 'Surprise and sense making'.
32 S. L. Robinson and E. Wolfe Morrison, 'The development of psychological contract breach and violation: a longitudinal study', *Journal of Organizational Behavior*, 21 (2000): 525–46.
33 For example, B. M. Wiesenfeld, S. Raghuram and R. Garud, 'Communication patterns as determinants of organizational identification in a virtual organization', *Organization Science*, 10 (1999): 777–90.
34 Saks and Ashforth, 'Organizational socialization'.
35 Ibid.
36 D. M. Rousseau, 'The "problem" of the psychological contract considered', *Journal of Organizational Behavior*, 19 (1998): 665–71.
37 See Ashforth, *Role Transitions in Organizational Life.*
38 R. E. Gorman, 'Why managers are crucial to increasing engagement', an interview with Ray Baumruk, *Strategic HR Review*, 5(2) (2006): 199–208; see also R. Thornham and T. Chamorro-Premuzic, 'Time to review engagement surveys', *Strategic Communication Management*, 10(3) (2006): 9.
39 A. M. Konrad, 'Engaging employees through high involvement work practices', *Ivey Business Journal* (March–April 2006): 1–6.
40 M. Stairs, 'Work happy: developing employee engagement to deliver competitive advantage', *Selection & Development Review*, 21(5) (2005): 5.
41 K. Yates, 'Internal communication effectiveness enhances bottom-line results', *Journal of Organizational Excellence* (Summer, 2006): 71–9.
42 *Computer Weekly*, 14 March 2006, p. 55.
43 D. Brown and S. Wilson, *The Black Book of Outsourcing* (Hoboken, NJ: Wiley, 2005).
44 M. F. Corbett, *The Outsourcing Revolution: Why It Makes Sense and How To Do It Right* (Chicago, IL: Dearborn, 2004).
45 S. Khanna and J. Randolph, 'An HR planning model for outsourcing', *Human Resource Planning*, 28(4) (2005): 37–43.

46 A. Arkin, 'Arise, Serco', *People Management*, 4 May 2006, pp. 33–4.
47 Special thanks to Dr Gillian Symon at Birkbeck College, University of London, for her insightful supervision during the main study, and to the ESRC for funding (Grant No. R42200024292).
48 S. J. Morgan and G. Symon, 'The experience of outsourcing transfers: implications for guidance and counselling', *British Journal of Guidance and Counselling*, 34(2) (2006): 191–208.
49 M. Schminke, R. Cropanzano and D. E. Rupp, 'Organization structure and fairness perceptions: the moderating effects of organizational level', *Organizational Behaviour and Human Decision Processes*, 89 (2002): 881–995.
50 Weiss, 'Losses associated with mobility'.
51 See J. McAuley, 'Hermeneutic understanding', in C. Cassell and G. Symon (eds) *Essential Guide to Qualitative Methods in Organizational Research* (London: Sage, 2004), pp. 192–202.
52 K. D. Markman and P. E. Tetlock, '"I couldn't have known": accountability, foreseeability and counterfactual denials of responsibility', *British Journal of Social Psychology*, 39 (2000): 313–25.
53 J. Brockner, 'Making sense of procedural fairness: how high procedural fairness can reduce or heighten the influence of outcome favorability', *The Academy of Management Review*, 27(1) (2002): 58–76.
54 See Morgan and Symon, 'The experience of outsourcing transfers', for an overview of these links to health.
55 W. Bridges, *Jobshift: How to Prosper in a Workplace Without Jobs* (Reading, MA: Addison Wesley, 1995).
56 Masters student supervised by the author: R. Kendall, 'Socialization in outsourcing', Birkbeck College, University of London, 2004.
57 J. Thibaut and L. Walker, *A Theory of Justice* (Hillsdale, NJ: Lawrence Erlbaum, 1975).
58 J. Greenberg, 'Setting the justice agenda: seven unanswered questions about "what, why, and how"', *Journal of Vocational Behavior*, 58 (2001): 210–19.
59 R. Folger and C. P. Skarlicki, 'Fairness as a dependent variable: why tough times can lead to bad management', in Cropanzano (ed.) *Justice in the Workplace*, pp. 86–96.
60 M. L. Ambrose and M. Schminke, 'Are flexible organizations the death knell for the future of procedural justice?', in Cropanzano (ed.) *Justice in the Workplace*, vol. 2, pp. 229–44.
61 R. C. King and V. Sethi, 'The moderating effect of organizational commitment on burnout in information systems professionals', *European Journal of Information Systems*, 6 (1997): 86–96.
62 Benchmark Research Ltd: Steria Press Release (September 2002).

3 The outsourcing lifecycle

Royston Morgan and
Stephanie J. Morgan

Introduction

Outsourcing is now moving into a more mature stage, with not only a large increase in the number of contracts signed, but also an increase in recontracting and bringing outsourced work back in-house. This backsourcing may be increasing because outsourcing is perceived as not bringing the expected benefits; surveys are beginning to uncover high levels of dissatisfaction.[1] This may be partly due to a lack of understanding of the full process – it is important to bear in mind the full lifecycle of events when considering outsourcing, as not allowing for future change from the beginning can lead to issues at a later date. In this chapter we will first clarify different types of outsourcing, and then discuss the lifecycle from a contractual point of view. During these discussions we will consider the related lifecycle experienced by staff involved, and the issues raised, for each lifecycle stage. We will then assess important points to consider for drawing up service-level agreements. Finally, we discuss the importance of understanding employee transfer contract legislation such as the UK TUPE (transfer of undertaking, protection of employment) legislation, and the impact on different stages of the contract.

As discussed in Chapter 1, the term outsourcing is used very broadly, often to refer to processes that would previously have been termed subcontracting. For some, a crucial point is whether the work would have been done internally before outsourcing. Outsourcing is a particular form of externalisation of employment that involves an outside contractor taking over an in-house function.[2] A key criterion for a definition of outsourcing, and a particular area of interest in this chapter, is that the process includes a transfer of staff to the third party while still requiring them to carry out work for their previous employer. This can be compared with more general forms of subcontracting; for example, where outside companies carry out work that is not done in-house. In our view this should not be called outsourcing, as it can lead to confusion.

Outsourcing should also be clearly distinguished from insourcing, when you bring in contractors to assist with work; for example, supplementing internal capacity in setting up an external division – with the expectation that additional business will be found. Offshoring is also becoming in vogue, as business processes are handed over to organisations operating from parts of the world that enjoy a labour cost advantage. However, as no staff are transferred, we will not specifically discuss this aspect (see the case studies relating to Korea in Chapter 10 and to India in Chapter 9). Increasingly, as the market is maturing, the concept of backsourcing (or re-sourcing) must be considered, as more organisations feel the need to bring people and processes back under their control. These differing forms of outsourcing have been introduced in Chapter 1; here we focus on the main outsourcing lifecycle. We begin with a discussion of types of outsourcing and their implications for the overall process, and then discuss each stage of the lifecycle in turn. Figure 3.1 emphasises the importance of stages of scoping, preparation and evaluation, negotiation and selection, transition, maturity and re-scoping.

Our preference is to distinguish outsourcing from other types of external use, by using a definition that emphasises 'the delegation or handing over to a third party (external supplier) mediated via a contractual agreement, all or part of the technical, process and human resources, including management responsibility for transferred staff, for a required result'.[3]

There is a variety of types of outsourcing, relating to the type of service and the form of the relationship with the supplier. Cullen *et al.*[4] outline seven

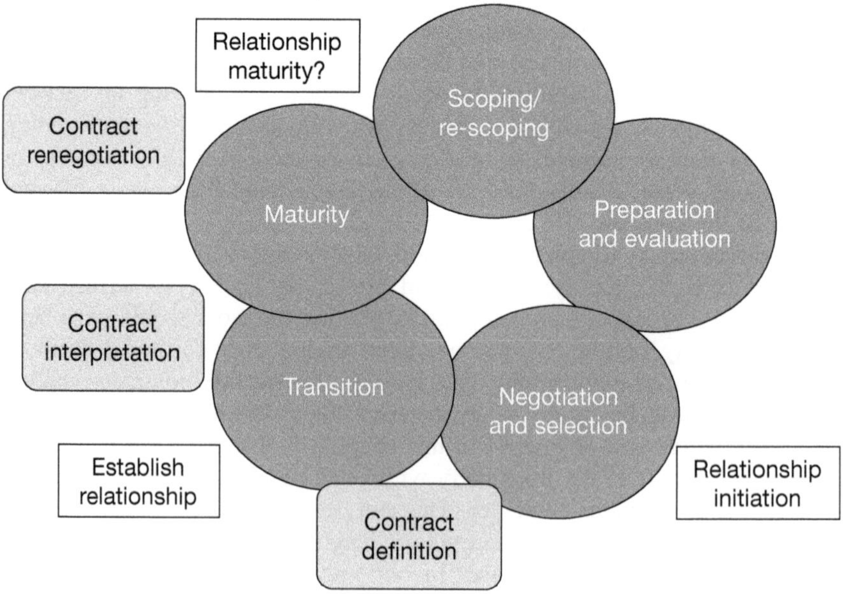

Figure 3.1 The outsourcing lifecycle.

Source: Authors' own.

key attributes: scope, supplier grouping, financial scale, pricing framework, duration, resource ownership and commercial relationship. To simplify here we emphasise differences between full and selective, and single, dual and multi-vendor outsourcing, as well as variations in the process to be outsourced and the scale and duration of the contract.

Full outsourcing occurs when a complete function or department is outsourced, and handed over to one vendor or multiple suppliers. Selective outsourcing is when a specific aspect is outsourced, such as only the desktop management within IT, or the payroll function in HR. There are also differences between single, dual and multi-vendor outsourcing, with obvious contractual issues to be considered as the number of vendors involved increases. The area you are considering for outsourcing will also impact on the process. There are differences in risk between outsourcing cleaning services and outsourcing functions with high specificity and complexity such as IT or HR management. In general, simpler, easy-to-define services carry lower risk – although this will vary by organisation. The scale of the project is also key, not just in terms of value and the number of people involved, but also in terms of whether multinational operations are covered. Differences in cultural values and behaviours do need to be considered when negotiating and managing an international contract. Extra management effort and time will be needed to construct a workable contract and hidden long-term costs in monitoring supplier performance for international suppliers need to be accounted for explicitly. Finally, outsourcing varies by timescale, with some contracts being signed for relatively short periods, two years for example, and others extending for ten or even twenty years. Clearly, the longer the timescale, the higher the possibility that there will be a need for flexibility and consideration of contractual changes. However, short contracts have their own problems, particularly in gaining stability, building trust and stabilising human factors.

The key at the start of an outsourcing discussion is to determine why you are doing this and to question, and to keep questioning, until you have an agreed answer to 'what are our objectives for this?' With a clear consensus up front of the objectives you are far more likely to achieve cost control and other benefits, and strike a good deal with potential suppliers. Just considering the rationale as to whether or not to outsource can be an impetus to improve a function and increase your understanding and control of it. If you can understand then control the costs of the function, and clarify where it fits into your business, you can make an informed decision about whether to outsource. There are some good examples of where access to high-quality management skills, and advanced new technology, can happen, particularly with suppliers who have more experience in your area, but this is not automatic and has to be planned for. Some companies have found an improvement in service quality, especially when the supplier has learnt your business and really understands your specific needs. This can take time and demands a solid relationship between the parties and trust based on delivered performance.

There are also situations where economies of scale can be found, and where outsourcing can increase the future flexibility of your enterprise. However, an increasing number of contracts are being brought back in-house,[5] or departments being rebuilt, and in IT outsourcing over half of the contracts are suggested to have poor or mixed outcomes,[6] which suggests that there are some problems needing further exploration.

Some of the problems surrounding outsourcing are due to the 'hidden' costs that occur at each phase of the lifecycle. It takes time and skill to develop benchmarks, learn how to manage an outsourcer, negotiate with suppliers and develop a solid contract. The transition can also involve a lot of disruption, especially if there is a slowdown in reaction time and flexibility due to prolonged supplier learning. The time and effort spent on building supplier relationships can vary and can be fraught with difficulties – a recent survey showed that some senior managers felt the relationship was adversarial, with continual fighting over objectives and the interpretation of the contract. It is not surprising that this conflict should arise as the objectives are different; suppliers will provide service within the framework of a service level agreement (SLA) that will be commercially coherent for them. The cosy relationship with a former internal supplier is broken, there are no more 'freebies', and each extra service will demand an additional service fee that will engender heated commercial discussions.

Trust has also been shown to be a key element in outsourcing; the development of trust takes time and can be difficult if overarching goals are not shared or defined. On the one hand, these 'hidden' costs increase the more suppliers or vendors you have to deal with, particularly if you manage vendors individually rather than through a prime supplier. On the other hand, experience in outsourcing can reduce these management cost pressures, and they will form a smaller percentage of larger contracts. There are also issues regarding the level of control you have over the performance of the activity. In practice, using the market as a control mechanism when outsourcing can never give as much control as using 'hierarchy', when you keep things in-house. The contract of employment is always stronger (and quicker) in governance terms than resorting to contract law to resolve disputes. Sometimes this is not a problem, but with critical business functions it can be.

The extent to which you will be able to balance the strengths or weaknesses of outsourcing depends in large part on having a clear understanding of what you want to achieve, a good contract, and an awareness of the circumstances that will influence success. These will vary by stage in the lifecycle, which should be considered carefully from the start.

Lifecycle stages

Many managers will be aware of the concept of the product lifecycle. Although vendors may view outsourcing as a form of service-based product, there are some differences in the lifecycle as outsourcing is a continuous and iterative process. Although there may be peaks and troughs in terms of lifetime market value of outsourcing contracts, at the current time a more important aspect for consideration is the different stages of each individual contract or process. Unfortunately, many organisations only consider the initial search for a vendor and handling of the procurement process when considering outsourcing. Research suggests that it is beneficial to take a longer-term view and consider the requirements across the lifecycle of the process. Some models have been developed for specific forms of outsourcing that do allow for different stages. For example, Khanna and New[7] suggest that HR planning during outsourcing should move from analysis/evaluation, contract negotiation and transition, to stabilisation/improvement. They do allow for a return path in their model, but there is little discussion of changes after the stabilisation phase. George[8] suggests stages of selecting the vendor, preparing the contract, outsourcing management, and termination. However, we believe it is vital to ensure you have fully scoped the activity to be outsourced in detail, and made efficiency savings first, before deciding to outsource. We therefore recommend the stages of scoping, preparation and evaluation, negotiation and selection, transition, maturity and re-scoping. These six stages allow for each important aspect of the outsourcing lifecycle to be given full attention. During our discussion we will also highlight the experience of staff during these stages, as their perceptions of the issues can also inform; and, as we argued in Chapter 2, this does need to be taken into account. Figure 3.2 highlights the more emotional stages that staff may experience and that will influence their perceptions. Where we have quoted from our own research interviews, we have used the terms Oldco and Newco to refer to the original employer and the outsourcing company.

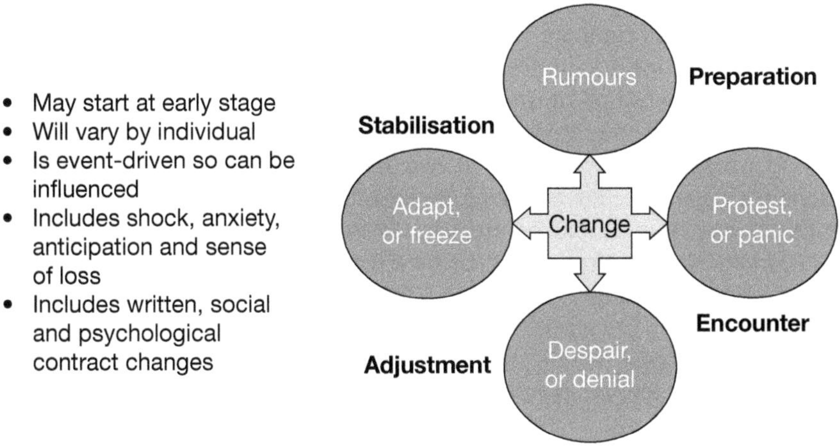
• May start at early stage
• Will vary by individual
• Is event-driven so can be influenced
• Includes shock, anxiety, anticipation and sense of loss
• Includes written, social and psychological contract changes
Rumours
Preparation
Stabilisation
Adapt, or freeze
Change
Protest, or panic
Encounter
Adjustment
Despair, or denial

Figure 3.2 People lifecycle process.

Source: Authors' own.

Scoping

In the scoping stage, you will need to formulate your outsourcing strategy, and identify core activities and the areas you would consider for outsourcing. It will be important to work through the rationale for outsourcing in detail, and assess the risks involved.[9] In many cases, research suggests that a reason for considering outsourcing is the desire to cut costs and/or get a better grip on a process. However, handing over an activity that is not efficient results only in handing excess profit to the vendor. Far better to ensure that you have evaluated all activities, improved processes and reduced costs to the best of your ability before handing over to a third party. Indeed it has been known for vendors to walk away from certain outsourcing tenders once they realise there is no slack – this suggests that a trusting relationship would have been difficult from the start, and therefore is no loss to the client.

The full range of alternatives to outsourcing should be considered. Apart from keeping a function in-house, and setting up an external division or shared services, there are other options available. These include joint ventures and bringing in management changes to enhance knowledge and increase efficiency. The use of flexible working, improved performance management, and regular review of projects can also assist. HR should be involved at this very early stage, as they may be able to assist with these aspects. In some circumstances it may be helpful to encourage the internal department under threat of outsourcing to propose an internal bid. This should be handled sensitively but may encourage further efficiencies and also perceptions of fairness – at the very least it will deliver a grounded baseline of your costs.

Some organisations try to hide the fact from their staff that they are considering outsourcing. This is unlikely to be a good strategy, as the rumour mill is more likely to make things sound worse than the reality. In our own research a number of staff discussed the problems with rumours: 'Well, it all started just as rumours. Which is the worst thing, I think . . . yeah we were uncertain for a long time' (public sector, male). People have a strong need to make sense of situations and will make up information rather than feel they do not know. Reduce the rumours by making clear statements and giving people the opportunity to discuss the impact on their individual situation. Again, if they are being given a chance to demonstrate their own effectiveness, this should be emphasised as a positive thing, giving them some element of control over their own destiny.

An issue with both scoping and the next stage, preparation, can be timescales. Some organisations (especially in the public sector) allow these stages to take years, with a resultant loss in motivation for the staff, as one public sector employee pointed out:

> morale went through the floor, over the last six years, it took six years pretty much, morale started to go down and towards the end, we couldn't get any lower, your pride in working for the (Oldco/industry) had gone,

> and, you were just grateful that you still had a job and you got a payslip at the end of every month, and, you weren't bothered about going into work anymore, nobody gave a damn, including the bosses.
>
> (public sector, male)

However, pushing these things through too quickly can also have its problems, both in terms of the organisation not being ready and contracts not being fully signed-off, etc., and the impact on staff and the work itself. When asked why she referred to the first transfer week as the worst in her life, this participant stated:

> Because everything that I had set up and done, just stopped, and we weren't told it was going to be stopped, now if I had been given warning that it was all going to grind to a halt suddenly, I could have done things to manage people's expectations, to set up various things, to just cope with it, but we were presented with this but we weren't presented with an alternative.
>
> (private sector, female)

Another participant, this time from the public sector, highlighted how too much speed leaves people feeling confused – their department was set up as a separate organisation and then almost immediately outsourced:

> Suddenly we were already with a separate organisation and then we were joining with Newco, that bit I felt was very quick, I mean we didn't I don't think, people didn't really understand what was happening at that time.
>
> (public sector, female)

Whilst this discussion may sound a little like 'Goldilocks and the Three Bears' (not too fast, not too slow), the focus should be on being ready for the change and taking time where possible. Well-thought-out scoping and clear communications will always pay dividends in this area.

Preparation and evaluation

The scoping stage will give you the information to work through a preparation phase, where you will measure baselines, develop evaluation criteria and create a request for proposal. Here you need to consider the remaining stages in far more detail. How do you want to negotiate this contract? Will you need outside help? On what basis will you select the best vendor(s)? Risks here include not fully understanding what you are trying to achieve by outsourcing, not fully scoping the activity, and not employing (or developing) the right skills for managing the future contracts. HR departments should be encouraged to develop clear plans for the transfer of staff, before negotiation has even started. It may be useful to get a feel for which staff are already keen on the idea of outsourcing. Do not assume that all of them are resistant. For example, some IT staff really do feel it could be of benefit to them:

> I think the way that IT in general is going in the civil service that the tendency towards outsourcing, there's not going to be that many IT jobs per se left in the civil service. So I thought if I wanted to stay in that arena then the obvious way to do it was to get out. So I therefore saw the option to be TUPE'd as a gentle way of doing it.
>
> (public sector, male)

Some people will even volunteer to be moved so that they will be transferred, which may give those who are very resistant an opportunity to stay with you. However, do not assume that those resistant to the move are just 'stick in the muds' who you will not need following the transition – often their scepticism comes from a deep understanding of the business process. A concern frequently expressed to us was the potential loss of knowledge, and the weakening connections between the organisation and its former staff that can result from an outsource deal – these 'stick in the muds' may be just the people you need to help you negotiate with the supplier and provide continuity.

In this preparation stage it will be important to reflect upon potential future changes in the organisation. In many organisations reconstruction and refinements are ongoing, but, even in those that appear relatively stable, some attempts at 'future scenario storming' should be made. The objectives for the outsourcing must be clear, consistent and reasonable. Objectives such as cost reduction, refreshing technology, or increasing service may not be internally consistent. Determine the key driver, and include it in the tender documents – the supplier will then be able to pitch the proposal answering the objectives and the chances of a successful deal will be increased. Sign off and agree internally why you are doing this and what is driving the process within the organisation, then use this as the underpinning of the business case for the outsource.

Consideration should be given to all elements of the outsourcing area under consideration and the type of contract that will be required. Cullen *et al.*[10] suggest seven key attributes for consideration: scope, supplier grouping, financial scale, pricing framework, duration, resource ownership and commercial relationship. Although aimed at IT outsourcing, these aspects are likely to be relevant for all types. We would also suggest the inclusion of 'staffing' and 'technology' (not just for IT outsourcing), as these two areas are of vital importance and are prone to rapid change. Do not assume that you will get the best staff from the supplier, or even keep the best of your own.

Negotiation and selection

Then comes the negotiation and selection phase, where due diligence is conducted, SLAs are outlined and selection of supplier(s) is made. The selection should be based on clear criteria, mapped to the business plan – some companies have chosen purely on price, only to regret this later. Linked to these activities are the important areas of relationship and contract development. Research has shown that the type of relationship that you develop with your supplier can be critical to success. Similarly, a poorly negotiated or clumsily defined contract can spell disaster.

Vendor search and selection is one of the hidden costs of outsourcing.[11] However, investment at this stage can reduce other costs and help to avoid problems later in the lifecycle. Trust should begin to develop at this stage, and is built upon reputation, repeated interactions, communication and 'courtship' and, at the highest level, joint goals and shared values.[12] A large-scale outsource can be seen as a strategic alliance where the partners jointly manage the organisations' assets in the form of an alliance delivering best-of-breed solutions for their part of the business. Hidden costs here include the learning curve required for the vendor, and the general disruption caused during the transfer. Expect and plan for a fall-off in service and make contingencies for this eventuality – perhaps by boosting capacity during the changeover. As already highlighted, there are management costs for the customer, and often development or recruitment costs, to ensure that the right skills are in place to manage the transition effectively. Clearly, the more complex and idiosyncratic the area to be outsourced, the higher these costs are likely to be. Paying attention to the entire lifecycle will help to reduce escalation of costs and risks during transition.

Complementarily, strategic and cultural fit become important attributes sought for in a partner. The selection process must also account for the business knowledge brought by the business partner to the table, in process and technology terms, and there must be broad fit in terms of size and distribution. If you are a blue-chip organisation it is of little use outsourcing to a garage operation – and the opposite is also true. Overall potential for benefit comes from the joint leverage of the two partners – doing things that were not possible singly. By such a collaborative integrative model instead of a distributive purchase one increased value can be achieved that can more than cover the increased overhead of the outsource deal.

In order to manage a successful outsource it has to be planned and organised. Remember during the negotiations and initial selection that the vendor does this for a living – often the vendor sales team has been doing this for years (and when this deal is done will move on to the next). The customer side, however, may have never done this before, or the team carrying out the supplier proposal evaluation may be completely new to the outsource process themselves. It is vital to plan the capacities of the customer team that will be creating and then managing the outsource process. In a large bid the job is full-time and often key members of the customer bid team will also have a day job to contend with – do not underestimate this. Time pressure can act in the vendor's favour and allow the skipping of important details. Similarly, do not be put under pressure by either party's optimistic time schedules. Research the vendor carefully – details of outsourcing troubles are rarely reported, and they are likely to give you lists of only their best clients. Contact your industry association to get the inside story and make time for detailed evaluation of vendor client references. Accordingly, interviewing past clients with the vendor not present may be the most reliable method of assessing vendor suitability. A clear set of objectives and a tailor-made contract are also key criteria for this stage. Vendors will often offer a standard contract and ready-made SLA – *never* accept these, but define a specific contract tailored to your needs. We have known proposals that have included standard vendor term sheets returned un-reviewed by experienced outsourcing clients. As is often stated, 'the devil is in the detail' – one of our own participants illustrated this in an outsource that was three years into the contract:

> The project is just, shite, people are ordering things and they are not, things aren't happening and each side is just blaming each other. Newco is blaming the Oldco team and the Oldco team are blaming Newco, and I don't really know who is to blame because as far as I can see, if one doesn't let us down on one issue the other side surely will. Which seems, just stupid things like the need to get a printer (for a site), which should have been the easiest thing in the world, but the printer needed an addition to it because it needed a double-sided copy, and they were arguing about it cos it's not in the contract and the Oldco has got to pay extra. So what, they've got to have the printer, they should have put it in the contract, but every site needs to have this printer, but there is so much politics, I thought you are better off out of this, and people are just pushing bits of paper and trying to score points off each other.
>
> (public sector, male)

If the outsourcing involves multiple nationalities, or you are considering offshoring, do bear in mind the cultural differences in negotiation practices. Hofstede's[13] dimensions have been shown to be useful for understanding these differences, and cross-cultural training may be required to enable those involved in contract discussions to be fully effective. Differences have been found also in negotiating and decision-making style, risk-taking[14] and, for example, in how outsourcing success is achieved – particularly between Western and Eastern cultures.[15] There is evidence[16] that organisations can learn from a limited first exposure to a multicultural contract, and thereby reduce problems for future contracts. This learning should be actively sought and managed. Even within one country, there are differences in organisational culture that need to be considered, and staff (including those staying with you to negotiate and monitor the vendor) may need some priming on how to understand and cope with these differences. The problems can be acute; for example, communication can be reduced. Many of the discussions we held focused around these issues of differences in organisational culture.

This seems to become more apparent over time, although some had become adjusted by the time of the 'maturity' stage of the contract. It is likely that the change in culture and the need to gain an understanding of new ways of progressing one's career within a systems house creates confusion. After discussing the cultural differences between the two organisations this participant in our research suggested:

> I don't think they tend to communicate, because now we have been to like two of their meetings, and when you go in they are all like, robot people, they all dress the same, they are all, like walking round with cups of coffee, they all, they are all sat at their desks and they are not communicating with their colleagues so, the fact that we were hoping they were going to communicate with us is maybe a little bit naive, and they are just working away, munching their sandwiches.
>
> (private sector, female)

The ongoing management of the contract and the process may be at risk if the cultural differences are great. Ensure teams are fully aware of differences in behaviours between cultures, especially in any offshoring or multinational contract.

Do ensure that your decision is final before you announce it to staff. Our own research indicates that staff find it extremely stressful to be told they are moving to one company and then informed they will be transferred elsewhere. They also need some time to prepare for the transfer, and their own preparation stage means that they must be able to gather information about their future employer. Their expectations will be created here, so it may be helpful not only to allow presentations from the vendor, but also to give staff time to check on the Internet, study documentation and discuss any rumours they have heard about the company.

Transition

As you move through the transition stage, the contract will be actually interpreted and the relationships – good or bad – will become established. It is vital here to 'start the way you mean to go on', and set up clear processes for communication and monitoring.

Also of vital importance is the need to retain management and staff who will be needed to manage the vendor. Care must be taken to design the internal organisation correctly, and allow some flexibility. The transition team should work closely with the vendor and ensure that the governance structure and staffing transfers are correctly managed. Extra time should be allowed for facilitating the staff transition, as often concerns are felt a while after the transfer, especially if the contract was completed quickly. HR should not assume that the vendor organisation is communicating fully to staff, as this is often not the case. Furthermore, the client organisation should not assume that HR is not needed after the transfer. Indeed there is some evidence that HR work may become more complex due to the need to assist with managing a dispersed workforce. To support this process it is recommended that the transition team should be composed of peer roles between the client and the vendor and this should explicitly include the HR function.

Staff take this transition period extremely seriously, and, as highlighted in Chapter 2, expect HR to discuss this more than issues concerning their formal contracts. They will wish for their individual situations to be considered. Do not assume, because the supplier says they will have one-to-one interviews, that everything will be handled well. As one of our participants put it when discussing these interviews: 'That was crap, the personnel interviews were to tell us about being TUPE'd, took our bank details and, gave us fuel cards . . .' (public sector, female). What the staff actually want is a discussion about their emotional and personal needs, and about job security and future changes. Another staffing issue to be particularly careful about is the clarity of the roles, for staff being transferred and for those remaining behind. Many of those in our own research indicated that the staff left behind in the organisation did not seem to understand the new relationship, particularly the contractual nature of work with their former colleagues. There were often also misunderstandings and conflicts, with previous managers still contacting staff to give them instructions, or old colleagues asking for favours.

Promises made during a transition cover a wide range, some apparently very minor, others more serious, such as how much downsizing would take place. One manager in an interview we held in Germany discussed how promises became an issue when he had to downsize the organisation, having earlier been assured by Newco that this would not be necessary:

> As soon as I announced that we were going to close, it was a two-step approach, close seven last year, finalised during summertime, and starting September last year I announced the closure of another five locations. So people have been somehow, shocked as well, especially they have said, 'what you had promised us when we joined Newco was not true'.
>
> (private sector, male, manager)

Promises become an issue when they are broken. Downsizing is a particularly serious matter, and promises of this type will assume great importance for staff being outsourced. In the example above, the manager was clearly trying to make sense of his own actions in making promises to his staff that he was unsure about. He went on to explain how he was paid a bonus based on how many staff he brought across, yet was fully aware that redundancies would be needed later. Other transferred managers had suggested that they were unable to make explicit promises to staff, because they were as much in the dark themselves. This suggests that managers have an extra burden of sense-making, in that they are partly responsible for the way staff understand a situation. Promises, or not making promises, may be an important part of this understanding for both parties. Be very clear about what you, and the vendor, can really promise staff.

Management

Not all contracts reach this stage, although ideally you should be aiming for some type of stability, as this is often the most fruitful time. Research suggests a range of factors that can influence the duration of a contract, including knowledge acquisition and relationship-specific investment.[17] An important point to remember is that, as the activities settle down and the mature stage is reached, the contract may need renegotiating, and possibly the relationships as well. This needs careful handling, and is likely to cause upheaval both between you and the vendor, and with staff. The rumours will get out more quickly than you imagine.

Even if the situation appears stable, HR should assess regularly the size, skills and make-up of the outsourced workforce, and assess whether any key staff have been lost to the vendor or elsewhere. The cost of monitoring, bargaining (there are nearly always areas not clearly covered by the contract that suddenly need discussion), and generally managing the vendor should be taken into account right from the start. There is evidence that companies with smaller contracts have to carry a greater percentage of the total outsourcing cost in management.[18] As a result, very small contracts may not be worthwhile once these costs are taken into account.

Staff can find the time between transition and maturity very awkward. They often feel a need to monitor their old employer, even if they have moved to different offices – especially if their own TUPE contracts include salary increases based on their original employer. In one of our studies a participant suggested that Oldco had clearly thought that 'dumping them meant the end of it'; however, participants felt in general that Oldco still had residual responsibilities for their outsourced staff, as one public sector worker put it:

> The commitment [of] the exporting organisation, for want of a better term, doesn't end at the day of transfer . . . we have experienced a number of problems with pay, and things like that.
>
> (public sector, male)

A further aspect of the transfer process is a duality, almost a dissonance, that occurs when newly outsourced managers and staff find themselves 'taking the part' of the old client: siding with the client implicitly against their new employer, attempting to connect with the old organisation by agreeing that Newco are as bad as 'we all' thought. All these behaviours prevent bonding between the staff and Newco, generate confusion and underpin a nostalgia for the old ways of working and, as a result, engender poor engagement and performance. The following excerpt from our work in the public sector is from a participant who has just been promoted within Newco and illustrates that, even when briefing his team on the commercial realities of the new situation, he finds himself drawn back to 'seeing their point of view':

> I have had to say to a couple of people, y'know, you are Newco staff now and you have to actually have to look at it that way, and things are different, the general terms and conditions are basically the same . . . and you might have sort of been feeling that things were this way previously but it is now slightly different, and some of them have a job to get used to that, they're thinking Oldco all the time. (But) it is difficult to actually . . . I came up with something last week in one of the meetings and I thought afterwards I am actually speaking from an Oldco point of view, and not Newco.
>
> (public sector, male, manager)

He begins by explaining how the others in the team find it difficult, then goes on to confess that he himself still thinks from the Oldco viewpoint. During his interview, he suggested that he is finding it easier to integrate into Newco because of his promotion, as he meets more Newco people now, outside the outsourced site, yet still finds his role in meetings difficult as he sometimes drifts into being an advocate of Oldco's position. The confusion in this example, stressing that little has changed, yet a different way of thinking is needed, is typical in an outsourcing process. A few are proud that they have changed their 'mindsets', but others will struggle. As in the above example, some suggested that, whenever they were in meetings, either with the client or about the client, they would have switches in role awareness. They would suddenly realise that they needed to 'change hats' and at times felt guilty whichever position they took and felt caught in the middle between two companies and unclear which side to take.

Finally, the replacing of staff in roles in the areas that had been outsourced provided a rich area of dispute – not surprisingly, this replacing (whether perception or reality) left a 'bitter taste' in the mouth, as expressed by one of our participants from the IT sector:

> They have actually replaced my old group with the twenty-seven people they have lost, and probably doubled it.
>
> (private sector, male, manager)

If you do genuinely feel a need to take on new people during this stage, it will be worth explaining to those who were transferred precisely what role the newcomers will fill, and emphasise the difference between their own work and the work of the newcomers. Issues such as these, and keeping the flexibility that may be required throughout a potentially lengthy maturity stage, can be difficult, but should ideally have been built in during the negotiation stage.

Re-scoping

You may find yourselves back at the stage of scoping, and reassessing strategy, including whether to backsource or change supplier. If you decide to backsource, you will have to assess how many staff will return to your organisation – and how many of them will do so willingly. This is linked to how you managed the transfer process in the initial stages, so it is vital to have thought this through early on. Chapter 2 discussed in more detail the impact of fairness perceptions on staff, and on their willingness (or reticence) to return to their original employer. We give a brief overview below of some of the issues raised.

Changing suppliers necessarily involves risk, and in many cases there are switching costs to consider.[19] These can be multidimensional and must be understood before making the final decision. Changing supplier has not only contractual, but staffing implications. You will have to work with all parties concerned to assess which staff will stay with the original company and which will transfer to the new organisation. Remember the better staff will have the most choice here. Some may have already transferred fully to the vendor (see TUPE discussion above), and may be particularly hard to attract back into the organisation. There have been situations where the best staff were transferred to the vendor and moved onto different client sites, therefore losing any possibility of being re-engaged. This eventuality should be considered and discussed during the early stages, to avoid excessive loss of knowledge. However, staff do have the freedom to work where they wish, so it will be important not only to ensure that the contract protects you, but also that you have treated the staff well enough during the process, and that they still wish to work for you. A crucial thing to consider at this stage is communication with staff. You may need to rely on the current outsourcing company here and that can be somewhat problematic. Certainly staff may feel insecure as yet again their situation begins to appear precarious.

For some of our participants the renegotiations started within two years of the original transfer. For staff to find out that their transfer status is under discussion after such a relatively short time comes as a shock – and may have unforeseen consequences as this public sector manager put it:

> That's the problem Oldco would have, I mean a lot of staff would not want to go back, a lot of senior staff in Newco, who have come in from elsewhere, no way would they go to the Oldco, so, if you took the whole organisation and tried to put it back with the Oldco there would be, a flurry of activity and people disappearing over the horizon.
>
> (public sector, male, manager)

This possibility of people disappearing over the horizon in a 'flurry' was emphasised as being due to the bad feeling generated by the transfer as a result of perceptions of poor treatment and procedural injustice. Furthermore, there were hints that managers had become accustomed to the more flexible 'culture' of a private company, and would not wish to rejoin the 'stultifying' bureaucracy of the civil service. Although this respondent suggested that it would be mainly the managers that would feel this, line staff in similar circumstances also articulated their concerns that another change of employer would not be accepted unreservedly. Furthermore, we found that even participants who were having difficulty integrating with Newco still suggested that they would be happy to further their careers with Newco. Many found the thought of going back to Oldco abhorrent: 'I wouldn't want to go back, not at all'. This has serious implications for any company wishing to 'backsource' and assuming a compliant return to previous roles, with staff putting aside some of the bitter feelings engendered by a poorly managed outsource transition.

For some staff this was their first realisation that their contract of employment was subject to ongoing discussions by senior executives in Oldco. A number of the participants expressed that it made little difference to them, suggesting that staying on the 'mirror' contract provided a safety net, thus making a return transfer easier:

> I am on the image terms, and as long as I can keep those same terms and conditions I don't feel that anything, really changes for me . . . (if) I was standard I would feel very worried . . . if (Newco) pulled out and somebody else comes in, will they want you . . . it's moneymaking and if your job isn't going to make that much money they might decide that they don't want that part . . . at the moment if somebody else came in, there would be a lot of uncertainty for a while, but . . . I feel quite secure with my little package I suppose.
>
> (public sector, female)

The reliance on holding a 'mirror' contract was tempered by a realisation that, should Newco pull out, a transfer back to Oldco was not a certainty. There was a real chance that the contract would be tendered again with new bidders, with all the concomitant uncertainty of where staff would eventually end up:

> I think that would start to be a bit worrying, because, there is talk of that if Newco did pull out maybe it wouldn't be handed straight back into the government, it would be put out to more tenders and then who would we go with then?
>
> (public sector, male)

A way in which some seemed to make sense of this anxiety, and find some sort of stability, was to focus on the job to be done, so that it wouldn't matter for whom they were working. There were indications that some were far from happy with that, but were trying to be positive and make the best of the situation:

> Well, apart from not knowing who I would work for obviously the job would have to carry on . . . they have said they don't want the contract to end and that they would work very carefully to make sure it doesn't.
>
> (public sector, male)

However, there were clear anxieties about what role they might have within Newco, with many saying that they were not impressed with 'being told not to worry, there were always places for people with talent' (private sector, male) and other vague platitudes:

> I would actually look to actually move on within Newco providing something was there . . . I would be happy to carry on with, providing there was a role, with similar sort of things (as) with the Oldco, for the rest of the contract at least. . . .
>
> (public sector, male, manager)

The above participant, and many others, returned to the issue of future roles many times, and worried whether there was a place for them in Newco as well, as there may be no role left with Oldco either. This perception was exacerbated in cases where Oldco started 'backfilling' (taking staff on in their old roles) or rebuilding departments to replicate the outsourced function, sometimes with a new technology base – adding to a feeling that the former employees were to be cut adrift when the contract came to an end. As well as the more obvious consequences of stress caused by a lack of certainty brought about by the transfer, change role theory suggests that, if identification with an organisation is low, the role may become a more important focus.[20] However, the emphasis on role works both ways – the perception that one's future role in an organisation is unclear is likely to reduce organisational identification and loyalty as well as increase anxiety and adversely affect performance. These aspects were discussed in more detail in Chapter 2 on employee engagement.

The service level agreement

We have briefly touched on some of the issues that need to be accounted for while setting up the contract and negotiating the services. Here we discuss some of the key aspects that have to be specifically articulated within the SLA.

As we discussed above, many companies are beginning outsourcing for the first time, sometimes with an inexperienced team who face a growing band of canny outsource vendors who do this every day for a living. As a general rule, particularly for large-scale outsourcing, involving many millions of pounds over the lifecycle – get professional help. This can be in the form of consultants or lawyers well versed in the detail of outsource contracting – at least it will level the playing field. This is particularly important in spotting omissions made during the contracting and negotiation process. As senior managers we all think we know the detail of our business; however, we may be good at checking what is written down before us, but we are not good at spotting significant issues that are *missing*. In terms of the agreements we have reviewed it is not what is in the agreement that is usually the problem but what has been left out. In an IT context the chief information officer (CIO) reviewing the agreement may easily spot errors in a service description, say, for the local area network (LAN) availability targets. However, it is rare to see spelt out how the intellectual property rights (IPR) issues of any software developed during a contract are handled; what is said about the transfer of technology back to the buyer should the agreement be terminated – for example how is the technology upgrade accounted for in the final liquidation of the contract? Will all personnel records be handed over? How will the supplier cooperate fully with a new service provider should the contract need to be terminated? All these types of questions need to be considered and included in the discussions upfront – which makes some of the clauses in the contract look very similar to a prenuptial agreement.

Negotiate all the points, agree them, then write them down in the contract – this is business and it is better to fail in the negotiation than in the execution of the agreement. If it is not in the actual signed agreement it will be difficult to return to unclear or missing points, and many buyers will be confronted with the need to raise a request for change to get any missed points into the agreement at a later stage. At times the negotiation will be difficult – avoid the temptation to fall back on a 'partnership' discourse as a surrogate for a 'handshake' and assume you can 'sort it out later'. Without a process in place to sort out any outstanding issues the agreement will fail before the ink has dried – so clarify, negotiate and specify in the contract.[21]

The success of the SLA is also likely to have an impact on staff. Our research again indicates that staff notice only too well whether their original employer is achieving the aims of the contract – or is being 'ripped off'. This knowledge impacts upon their own motivation and their relationships with both organisations. This excerpt from one of our own studies gives an indication of how staff monitor the situation:

> Newco had people who knew the sites, knew the systems, and so they put a sensible bid in, but there you are, the (clients) have always been screwed over contracts, we don't have a contract team of professionals who know how to handle them. A classic one was, with Newco, they said, part of the system was they wanted, colour printers in certain areas, and Newco could never get this system to work, couldn't get colour

> printing, and in the end there was a lot of banging on the table 'you said in the contract that you would get us colour printing' and Newco turned round and said 'the contract says we will get you colour printers, we did not say they would print in colour (joint laughter) . . . It's absolutely true! So all, the Oldco always got screwed on contracts because they didn't understand what they were reading.
>
> (public sector, male)

A contract is a written statement that sets out the rights and obligations of both parties – it sets down the agreed points of the negotiation. Be careful that any issue covered during the negotiation, and that is intended to be a contractual item, becomes a contractual item. Be aware that claims made during the negotiation that the buyer relies on when making the decision to buy can at a later stage become the subject of a misrepresentation suit – so clarify these issues in the contract. Furthermore, a written contract can help clarify any ambiguities as these will become obvious during drafting, or it can cover aspects that are not necessarily covered in detail during the negotiations, such as IPR and limitations in liability. The contract can also negate terms that are otherwise implied by statute law. This whole area is a legal minefield and this again emphasises the need to seek professional legal advice when setting up a contract – do not rely on internal procurement to provide this expertise.

A comprehensive set of service descriptions, metrics and measures need to be detailed within the SLA. Ensure that the measures monitor key processes such as incident resolution, are measurable (and measured routinely), and are focused on the relevant business areas – these must be the same business areas that will be reviewing the measures. It is also worth considering making the implementation, and auditing of key service processes, a contractual clause. With one of our clients their contract specified that ITIL processes be put in place for the service desk and that ISO accreditation be a stated requirement of the supplier, all of this to be subject to annual audit by the buyer. In terms of a general principle it is not recommended to build into an SLA a so-called 'service credit' process. In such schemes, when the service measure falls below the agreed levels, a form of credit to the buyer is given. As an example, a payment schedule is defined for, say, a 98 per cent service level and, should service be 95 per cent, a lower price band becomes applicable – we have also seen SLAs with performance credits, with increased revenue for a supplier should the 'standard' performance be exceeded. There are several reasons why this is old-fashioned and bad practice. First, the point of a service level is to define the required levels needed to support the business and no more. Improvement levels over time can be defined but the service needed is what the business should pay for – if it is exceeded you may have to increase your targets, but certainly not pay more for just doing the job. Second, with a service credit clause you have no leverage over the supplier to fix the problem. The focus should be to restore the service to the agreed levels as soon as possible. Rather than a service credit clause, it is far better to put in place governance that forces the supplier to act to fix the issue, perhaps to the extent of the customer being able to call in independent consulting advice at the supplier's expense to support service resolution. This use of an 'independent' adviser can be useful in monitoring the overall value of the outsource deal as it matures through its stages. It is important to include this in the SLA and agree the principles and ground rules for such an 'independent' with the outsource partner. Again, staff can often see the problems much later down the line, as one of our research participants described in some detail:

> Because, Newco do have these people, they've got professionals who only write contracts, and they know how to work them, and the Oldco haven't got a clue, eventually they tried using some outside firm of solicitors, to read through the contract, but it's too late then, and even they might not have been professional contract people. And they still got screwed in the end, and they still don't understand, nobody, I haven't met anybody who understands what the hell outsourcing is all about, has it saved them a lot of money, no it's cost them more, have they got an improved service, no it's much worse, why? Why have they done it? They say 'oh well we are saving money on pensions', you are not, you've transferred the pension money over, 'we're saving money on accommodation' well you're not really, 'we're saving money on pay' well you might be saving money on some aspects of pay but look at how much money you are paying the outsourced companies to run these things, and of course the classic mistake they made is, they're paying for a fixed sum of money, millions of pounds a year, for maintenance of the existing system, nobody mentioned, changes to the system, like, I don't want the machine here any more I want it in the room next door or in the new building, ah that's a change to the contract, it will cost you an extra x hundred of pounds, and I think the contract in the first six months was something like thirty million over the estimate, cos, they are moving things all the time, closing buildings, building new ones, every time you get a change of hierarchy, it's new broom, right we will change all this we'll have the (Dept.) over here and that group over there, we'll swap those two over, and they do it regularly . . . and it all gets charged.
>
> (public sector, male)

The governance structure must receive special attention with all the relevant review and management processes, including escalation procedures should things go wrong. Furthermore, built-in mechanisms for changeover time must be included to account for continuous improvement. Obviously, targeted reduction in price is to be expected from normal improvements in technology or process, but buyers should also expect a share of innovation brought by the outsourcing in both cost and performance terms. For example, if your outsourcer moves significant elements of the service offshore, a new model has been introduced that changes the original assumptions underpinning the outsource deal. In such circumstances the buyer is entitled to a reasonable share of the improvement. There must also be room to include extra reward (increased margin, say) for suppliers investing in more risky approaches – but a full partnership needs to be in place for this to really work. In IT fields, it is important to include 'technology refresh' provisions in long-term agreements.[22] Things also change in terms of infrastructure, shrinkage in market, or growth from, say, a merger or acquisition. All of these issues find their resolution in an effective governance process to manage the improvement of service using the SLA as the guiding tool for action. In some circumstances the change will be so significant that the original contract becomes out of date – in such circumstances a renegotiation becomes almost inevitable.

We have discussed the practical aspects of outsourcing and the setting up of an agreement that frames the whole process. Awareness right from the beginning of the demands of these phases will help to reduce unwelcome surprises and increase the chances of success. We have also discussed the impact on staff of these stages; however, it is important to consider carefully the legal protection that many staff are given during outsourcing transfers. We have found that the nature of this protection can impact on both the transfer process and the ongoing relationship with staff; therefore, we will give a brief overview of the legal aspects of transfer.

Transfer of undertaking – legal protection

In the European Union employees have some protection during an outsourcing transition through the transfer of undertaking (council directive 2001) legislation.[23] The UK has had legislation in place since 1981, which was updated in 2006. In other parts of the world, worker rights vary. In the US there is less protection for staff, although many outsourcing contracts will lead to mandatory decision-bargaining requirements under the National Labor Relations Act. There have been examples, though, of all staff being fired and then being asked to reapply for jobs with the vendor. Not surprisingly, this can lead to bad feeling, and strikes have been reported. Even in the UK, where staff are quite well protected, news of outsourcing has led to strikes. It is clear that consultation needs to start early and that relying purely on the concept of legal protection is insufficient. Legislation is continually changing and it will be vital for any organisation to consider the legal situation as well as their moral obligations to employee rights in these situations. Those transferring in a number of different countries will need to assess rights and legal issues for each country separately, in detail.

Many organisations focus only on the legal aspects of the *initial* transfer, forgetting that they may need to reconsider transfer issues when the contract is renegotiated or the process brought back in-house. In the UK, vendors are not allowed to force staff to move onto a different contract, especially if it does not offer the same terms. Staff who have remained on the TUPE or 'mirror' contract often feel they have to monitor the situation at their old organisation, and this can make 'letting go' difficult. This does not mean that staff should be persuaded to take on the vendor contract, as this can lead to problems later when the contract is due for renegotiation, especially if you wish to take them back in-house. However, it does mean that client organisations should be sensitive to the needs of transferred staff and continue to communicate with them (possibly via the vendor) regarding contractual and financial issues.

Recent changes in the UK have further increased the protection given to employees;[24] however, there are some disadvantages to staff as there is still little clarity regarding retaining specific people or maintaining 'mirror' contracts. It is still not possible for outsourcing vendors to harmonise the contracts of transferred staff with their own contracts if the terms would be less favourable than their current contracts – indeed the new TUPE rules make this even more difficult. However, there is a change to the rules when staff object to a transfer – they are now deemed as having resigned. There is a view that this could mean that personnel who object will be forced to take on new terms and conditions – that it may even be possible for organisations to manage the transfer badly on purpose to ensure that staff object and lose their rights. However, as we discussed here and in Chapter 2, this is a very shortsighted view and could lead to more problems than advantages.

The new TUPE rules also ensure that specific details about staff to be transferred are given to the new employer. This improves the situation when re-tendering, as previously these details could have been withheld by the original vendor, as they were often not contractually obliged to give such information about staff working for them on the client contract. Transferors can no longer hide behind the Data Protection Act or imply that this is commercially sensitive information. However, we still recommend that the initial contract stipulates that, when the contract is renegotiated, full staffing details are given. Both parties are now jointly and severally liable for staff consultation in the UK, so this aspect must be discussed in detail. Increasingly, these staffing issues are being cited as reasons for performance problems, and therefore we recommend that the people lifecycle is analysed in detail.

The analysis of the transition process, in conjunction with TUPE considerations, highlights the importance of understanding differences in staff motivation across the outsource lifecycle, maintaining communications with staff who have been transferred, and keeping to the contract, ensuring that any salary increases are managed automatically. This will reduce the need for transferred staff to continually monitor the situation (most likely to impact on their work), and also retains perceptions of fairness, which may be important if the original employer needs to backsource staff. If new employees are brought in to help manage contracts or handle unexpected work following on from the transfer, it is essential to communicate the rationale behind this to the outsourced staff. This should reduce ill-feeling and the risk of retaliation, and maintain a good relationship should the original employer need to bring staff back in-house.

Conclusion

Outsourcing should be considered as a long-term process that will develop through a number of stages: scoping, preparation and evaluation, negotiation and selection, transition, maturity and re-scoping. These stages need to be considered in depth before the initial scoping starts and especially during the preparation stage and development of the contract. Staff will also proceed through different stages, with many experiencing anxiety initially and again as contracts are renegotiated. The special nature of outsourcing, where staff are required to continue working for their old employer, means that their reactions should be taken into account when preparing and moving on through the lifecycle.

To conclude, we present brief summaries of the practical considerations and the transition process, which can be used as quick reference guides.

Practical considerations

- Consider carefully what you want to achieve and why you are thinking of outsourcing – ask and keep asking until you all agree.
- Get your own operations in order first; do not outsource a problem or something you don't understand.
- Assess the whole lifecycle and consider the implications of different stages for your organisation.
- Invest in a good contract that can minimise risk yet maximise flexibility – never accept supplier standard terms; write a specific contract.
- Invest in developing your internal management to ensure that they have the skills to manage contracts and supplier relationships.
- Set clear benchmarks and realistic expectations.
- Do not focus on price alone; there have to be other benefits or the chances are you could reduce the price yourself.
- Consider the potential advantages and disadvantages of shorter contracts and multiple suppliers.
- Plan to manage, set up clear structures and monitor and evaluate performance – create a good SLA.
- Consider also how you can retain and develop knowledge in-house and ensure the supplier does not plunder your intellectual assets.

The transition process

- Communicate fully with all staff and ensure that the transition is managed with tact and consideration.
- Continue to communicate with staff after the outsource if they remain on your TUPE contract, if necessary through the vendor. This will reduce the need for staff to continually monitor your activities, and smooth the path should you need to transfer them back in-house.
- When assessing TUPE issues, remember to consider the whole lifecycle – ensure that you have taken into account the impact of your transfer conditions on any future need to transfer staff elsewhere or back in-house.
- If different nationalities are involved, ensure that you take into account differences in communication and behaviours.
- Make realistic claims and promises based on the realities of the deal.
- Brief managers fully and train them how to handle their staff during the transition.

Notes

1 See, for example, the survey by Deloitte Consulting, discussed in *Computing*, 28 April 2005, p. 40.
2 K. Purcell and J. Purcell, 'In-sourcing, outsourcing, and the growth of contingent labour as evidence of flexible employment strategies', *European Journal of Work and Organizational Psychology*, 7(1) (1998): 39–59.
3 S. Morgan, 'Is outsourcing the answer for IT and HR functions?' Paper presented at the National Housing Federation Conference, London (2002).
4 S. Cullen, P. B. Seddon and L. P. Willcocks, 'IT outsourcing configuration: research into defining and designing outsourcing arrangements', *Journal of Strategic Information Systems*, 14 (2005): 357–87.
5 Deloitte, 2005; see also Cullen *et al.*, 'IT outsourcing configuration'.
6 See Cullen *et al.*, 'IT outsourcing configuration'.
7 S. Khanna and J. R. New, 'An HR planning model for outsourcing', *Human Resource Planning*, 28(4) (2006): 37–43.
8 B. George, 'Innovation in information systems education – III Sourcing Management – a course in the information systems curriculum', *Communications of the AIS*, 15(19) (February 2005): 331–42.
9 Specific risks will vary depending on the nature of the outsourcing – for IT see K. M. Osei-Bryson and O. K. Ngwenyama, 'Managing risks in information systems outsourcing: an approach to analyzing outsourcing risks and structuring incentive contracts', *European Journal of Operational Research*, 174 (2006): 245–64.
10 Cullen *et al.*, 'IT outsourcing configuration'.
11 J. Barthelemy, 'The hidden costs of IT outsourcing', *MIT Sloan Management Review* (Spring, 2001): 60–9.
12 D. L. Shapiro, B. H. Sheppard and L. Cheraskin, 'Business on a handshake', *Negotiation Journal*, 8(4) (1992): 365–77; see also C. M. Lander, R. L. Purvis, G. E. McCray and W. Leight, 'Trust-building mechanisms utilized in outsourced IS development projects: a case study', *Information & Management*, 41 (2004): 509–28.

13 See www.geert.hofstede.com.
14 R. Taplin (ed.) *Risk Management and Innovation in Japan, Britain and the United States* (Abingdon: Routledge, 2005).
15 S. Samaddar and S. Kadiyala, 'Information systems outsourcing: replicating an existing framework in a different cultural context', *Journal of Operations Management*, 24 (2006): 910–31.
16 F. Niederman, 'International business and MIS approaches to multinational organizational research: the cases of knowledge transfer and IT workforce outsourcing', *Journal of International Management*, 11 (2005): 187–200.
17 J. Goo, R. Kishore, K. Nam, H. R. Rao and Y. Song, 'An investigation of factors that influence the duration of IT outsourcing relationships', *Decision Support Systems*, 42 (2005): 2107–25.
18 Barthelemey, 'The hidden costs of IT outsourcing'.
19 D. Whitten and R. L. Wakefield, 'Measuring switching costs in IT outsourcing services', *Journal of Strategic Information Systems*, 15 (2006): 219–48.
20 B. E. Ashforth, *Role Transitions in Organizational Life: An Identity-based Perspective* (Hillsdale, NJ: Lawrence Erlbaum, 2001).
21 See N. Beaumont, 'Service level agreements: an essential aspect of outsourcing', *Service Industries Journal*, 26(4) (2006): 381–95.
22 M. Turner and A. Smith, 'The challenge of changing technology in IT outsourcing agreements', *Computer Law & Security Report*, 18(3) (2002).
23 See http://europa.eu.int.
24 See www.dti.gov.uk/er/individual/tupeguide2006regs.pdf.

4 Making outsourcing work

From service level agreement to partnership

Ivan Schouker

Introduction

Today's increasing pervasiveness of outsourcing and its emergence as a common business management tool in particular in the services sector feed a wealth of debates in corporate strategy and public policy. What is driving concerns and perceptions of threat is the rapid evolution of outsourcing, from farming out non-strategic activities (such as facilities or payroll) for pure cost-reduction reasons to offshoring functions valued in multimillion-dollar deals, and of real or potential strategic impact on the future of the outsourcing company and its local communities.

While the nature of outsourcing deals has fundamentally changed, the thinking, mindset and approaches, even at the senior management and board levels of global corporations, have not evolved. Standard procurement management techniques and processes based on detailed service level agreements (SLAs) and pure cost-driven financial models remain the rule. The most potent challenge for outsourcing today is that, to genuinely mature as an effective tool in the management arsenal of sophisticated businesses, it has to be understood, planned, and managed as a *partnership.*

Outsourcing is a fundamental component of today's large corporate fabric; like any relationship that has to withstand changing circumstances over time, it is hard work and has to operate under guiding principles rather than detailed rules. Often-used performance statistics parallel quite eloquently marriage relationship records in the Western world! One can for instance quote the 2000 Dun & Bradstreet Barometer of Global Outsourcing: '20 to 25% of all outsourcing relationships fail within two years and 50% fail within five.' This does not leave much room for long-term successful partnerships. In the same vein, a 2005 McKinsey study of 30 outsourcing deals signed in the past four years and worth more than $20 billion in total contract value concluded that 'up to 50 percent of outsourcing arrangements fail to deliver the expected value'; the report attributed these failures in large part to continued reliance on 'a standard procurement approach . . . and use of price as the primary decision-making factor.'[1]

This chapter highlights the common pitfalls of outsourcing decisions designed around tactical cost-saving objectives and managed through a detailed document, the SLA, also too commonly seen as the sole guarantor of a successful outsourcing relationship. Most examples here come from the technology and financial services industries, where cost savings, supplier price considerations, and SLA usage are particularly noticeable within large European and American organizations. In a traditionally low risk-seeking and conservative environment, this is where the move to outsourcing core functions is accelerating and is highly sensitive, let alone for regulatory reasons and increasing supervision – including over offshore locations.[2]

In most relationships, what is often overlooked is that the design itself of an outsourcing agreement, from the initial negotiation stage to the ongoing monitoring and management of the deal, can make or break the rationale for entrusting to a third party key production and/or servicing delivery components. Best-practice trends and experience in making outsourcing work point at five operating guidelines (Figure 4.1), reviewed in turn in this chapter:

- Ensure clarity in value creation and coherence with corporate direction.
- Strike a balance between business and legal risk assessment.
- Elevate the SLA into a charter and establish a culture of transparency and trust.
- Manage governance and relationships through cross-organizational teams.
- Plan evolution and scope restructuring upfront.

Failure in laying out the proper foundations of an outsourcing deal, and especially relying on a 'mechanical' or strictly contractual relationship, will exacerbate the negative perceptions both internally within an organization

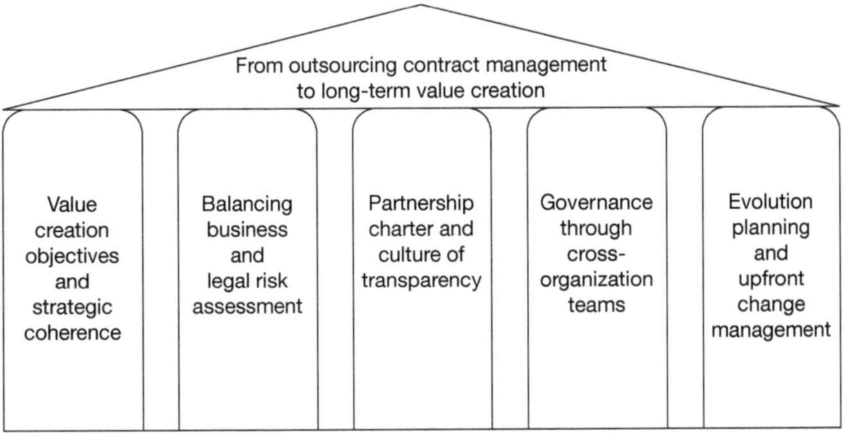

Figure 4.1 Foundations for outsourcing partnerships.

Source: Astwood Partners LLP.

and outside in popular (mis-)understanding, especially in an offshore context.[3] Some analysts will go as far as to argue that ignoring these best (new) practices in the age of globalization is turning one's corporation's back to unavoidable transformations in enterprise management.[4]

Outsourcing through different binoculars

How did we get to have SLAs as a source of controversy in the outsourcing debate? What's wrong with them? How is this changing?

When Dr Michael Hammer and James Champy's book, *Re-engineering the Corporation*,[5] took the business books' best-sellers world by storm in the early 1990s, and by the same token created a whole new specialized consulting industry as well as providing new impetus to the established firms, outsourcing did not make headlines. It was not even mentioned as such in the now classic business book. It was quietly practiced mainly in the manufacturing sector and essentially as part of a more progressive evolution of supplier–producer relationships.

Business process re-engineering (BPR) rapidly became part of day-to-day business vocabulary and of the inevitable and rather tedious basic training ground for graduates fresh out of top business schools and hired by the fast-growing operations of leading management consulting firms. Outsourcing was part of the toolkit, with extensive materials prepared for the analytical commandos swarming across industries and functions.[6] Outsourcing recommendations had to fulfill a number of conditions: the assessment of a process or function as non-core, a recognized internal inability to manage an expected upscaling of the process or function, a propensity for ever-expanding internal justifications and therefore building overhead costs (classically the training function in HR, and even the HR department as a whole), or, again, proven third-party capabilities with compelling cost-value benefits, such as facilities management or security services. Such outsourcing initiatives became 'commodity' offerings and often outsourced themselves to third-party consultants for selection and negotiation, thus becoming standard procurement efforts with set techniques and in some cases limited contact between customer and vendor. As a result, functions such as HR administration are now very commonly contracted out to large specialized groups and form in their own right a significant services sector. HR business process outsourcing (BPO) now represents the highest spending of all large BPO services, and a third of total BPO spend in Europe, running toward 3.7 billion euros of enterprise spending in 2006.[7]

In BPR, the mantra has always been to maintain the right balance of efficiency (lowest cost) and effectiveness (highest output quality). However, cost is the quantitative measure that is easiest to measure and track in and around the re-engineering exercise; it is therefore the one that tends to be the ultimate focus and remains the main driver of subsequent decisions. Eventually, as organizations took a pure process redesign logic, mostly measured by cost reductions that in themselves had to justify significant consultancy and/or project costs associated with large BPR programs, outsourcing ended up as a highly visible result of cost-cutting initiatives. This approach remains particularly prevalent in industry sectors, which have been late 'entrants' in the outsourcing game, most notably the broad services world and in particular financial services. Traditionally quite a protected industry, through regulations, cartels, and infrastructure cost barriers, its breadth of cost reengineering potential has been in the late 1990s and early 2000s the focus of BPO initiatives. Financial services now represent, if not the largest, then among the top three industry verticals in terms of revenue contribution for the global BPO vendor leaders.[8]

This is where the SLA comes into play. As BPR evolved into mainstream management, internal departments started to emerge, called usually business re-engineering (BR) departments. Their justification was actually often to 'insource' the external re-engineering advice and implementation costs that had exploded in the 1990s. These BR functions are designed to serve the whole organization and sometimes have mushroomed within functions and businesses (technology, operations, sales, etc.) as some form of 'cost police', bringing some permanence (or semblance of) to cost control beyond annual budgets and leadership changes. Besides BR departments, all powerful procurement divisions also emerge as the prime guardians of supplier screening, selection, and contract negotiation. The SLA is the critical instrument for these controls and is the vital extension of the outsourcing contract. It is designed or inspired by the BR department or an equivalent project-based function (most often the IT department); its elaboration can be supervised, and even contracted out in complex situations, by the procurement division to be then handed out to the function or business for day-to-day management.

These disciplines are not to be downplayed. They have to be a core component of a transparent relationship. However, their mutation into inflexible rulebooks, or 'Cerberuses', for procurement divisions can be catastrophic.

Use and misuse of SLAs

SLAs are an outgrowth of two corporate development phenomena: first, a growing legal recourse environment in most geographies, and not only in a US context; second, high management turnover at all levels of accountabilities. The latter is being driven by faster promotion expectations as well as tighter and shorter time-frames in individual and teams' performance management. Whereas internal or external suppliers in the past could easily manage around agreed specifications and ongoing relationships between individuals with longer tenure in their roles, today's relationship environment focuses on potential liability, as well as short-term individual and group performance measures. Hence the unavoidable SLA in framing and guiding the day-to-day life of a supplier relationship. Long-term relationships based purely on trust struggle to be sustainable within a more fluid, uncertain, and fast-moving corporate world in which ongoing transparency and documented reference points are necessary.

The use of SLAs in the service provider's management toolkit is certainly growing. This is a positive trend in clearly defining and documenting expectations between internal divisions, especially within a large complex organization, and externally between clients and their suppliers. A key benefit was, and still is, for example in the financial services sector, that it ensures the buy-in of business unit leaders and effective transition when, for instance, IT services, data centers, or other previously dedicated services become consolidated to gain economies of scale. In addition, compliance requirements – not least those of the Sarbanes-Oxley Act requiring mandatory personal attestation of financial statements' veracity and therefore of a wealth of supporting operational processes – have driven the need for evidence of key processes' management and reporting. They are, therefore, accelerating the proliferation in documented evidence of the mechanics of interdependent relationships and critical processes within and outside an organization. Structuring an SLA helps map out clear supporting performance standards and consistent, effective measurements of these processes.

A typical SLA will outline the scope of services, for example:

- serviced assets, equipment and infrastructure;
- provision of types of services;
- responsibilities of the outsourcing provider; and
- responsibilities of the client.

In addition, to a breakdown of fees will also be added both penalty and incentive provisions – amounts per period, work volume covered, quality of work provided, and provision for over- and underperformance. Finally, the SLA should include guidelines for selecting outsourcing metrics, which would include metrics aligned with business goals of the service, as well as metrics helping to diagnose problems, escalate attention, and address performance issues. A practical SLA should limit the metrics for each service category to one or two encompassing measurements allowing ease of monitoring.

However, this standard approach has to be reassessed in situations concerning mission-critical activities that are outsourced based on strategic re-evaluations of an organization's core competencies. For example, highly technical and high-risk areas such as part of a technology security infrastructure (firewalls, intrusion-detection systems, virtual private networks) are very often managed by third-party managed security service providers (MSSPs). Here, well-laid-out SLAs and reporting processes are of the utmost importance.[9] Yet, they cannot fully account for relationship aspects such as quality, communications, availability, and responsiveness that may differ between service providers and also depend on the evolving chemistry between client and supplier.

This trend is creating its own challenge in that the number of people involved in supervision increases linearly with the number of SLAs under management. The knowledge of the specific business logic of the SLA resides in a person's head; when this person moves on, that knowledge needs to be relearned at best if well handed over. Moreover, performance reports are often generated after the fact, all but voiding the ability to impact SLA compliance during a typical monthly tracking period. In large IT outsourcing deals, performance measures are most often tracked in different systems, for example frequency of backups, help desk response time, and system availability, making it quite difficult to correlate the data. Most advanced practices have now introduced automated service level management systems that automate the complete lifecycle of service management.[10] This evolution in automating SLAs is an efficiency response, particularly essential in monitoring IT and mission-critical processes. Broadened and with the inflexibility that automation can bring, it could have damaging consequences on the overall relationship if it is not managed strategically and in a partnership manner.

Where the SLA becomes a genuine hindrance and one of the key sources of outsourcing failures is when it can be described by any combination of the following:

- It is relied upon religiously by the accountable executives; 'Deal structures . . . made too rigid for too long a period of time.'[11]
- It is inflexible in dealing with business requirement changes.
- Its rigid customization eliminates advantages in external scale economies; 'Companies . . . unwilling to accept standard ways of doing simple processes, arguing that their needs are special, when, in fact, industry standards should be applied.'[12]
- Cost performance measures are prioritized over skills access and overall business and strategic rationale.
- It includes penalties-based arrangements over mutual trust and goals alignment.

As outsourcing practices mature and the heavy-handedness of procurement teams in managing supplier relationships is being felt, the actual usefulness of SLAs becomes questioned at middle and sometimes senior management levels; one challenges the tool, forgetting too quickly its benefits and overlooking practices in effective relationship management around a reference set of 'rules of the game.' Dramatic headlines easily misconstrued have started to appear: 'CEOs who rely on SLA lose 40% of contract value,' summarized from recent research conducted by Warwick Business School, Melbourne University, and LogicaCMG.[13] Some analysts,[14] in particular of the IT outsourcing world, probably the most sensitive, precise, and detail-prone sector of all, are debating whether SLAs are worth having at all on the grounds that a buyer should not attempt to tell a supplier that is a specialist at providing a service what to do.[15] This logic clearly could easily misfire!

Carefully laid terms are evidently of little value if the outsourcing partnership is misaligned in the first place and executives manage a live relationship with an SLA in hand, using it like a product users' manual. Indeed, today, such a product mindset unfortunately remains pervasive in many outsourcing deals where a 'make sure it works or I'll demand a refund' approach is applied to a delicate supplier–customer business model that requires careful management. Although it may sound quite absurd and obvious in retrospect, one can observe this outlook in multibillion-dollar contracts managed expensively by specialized teams monitoring every aspect of an outsourcing relationship defined in hundreds of pages documents. Productizing what is generally a complex relationship cannot but lead to frustrations on both outsourcer and customer sides. These tend to be exacerbated in large organizations where SLAs are a simplistic substitute for coordinating intricate internal dynamics of separate accountabilities in procurement, supplier management, financial management, and functional and business leadership. A Booz Allen Hamilton consultant, Paul Fielding, is hence quoted as saying 'Oftentimes, what I see in contracts is people trying to abdicate their responsibility with contractual language, and often the vendors are left in charge of checking themselves.'[16] Leaving suppliers to second-guess their clients' expectations is a recipe for disaster.

In all, SLAs are here to stay and prosper, let alone because best practices in risk and liability management will point at the need to have documentation of reference, separate from or additional to a contract, in a third-party relationship. The SLA cannot, however, be the centerpiece of a relationship, but a component among several tangible and intangible levers within a partnership model based on principles and guidelines.

Principles-based management

A fresh look at major outsourcing deal-making and management inspires itself now from the most successful relationship experiences that borrow more from concepts of partnerships, strategic partnering or alliances, made popular or widely accessible by best-seller business academia authors such as Yves Doz *et al.*[17] Not only do these efforts and supporting research continuously bring to bear the role of good multidisciplinary management and people skills, but they also underpin what enterprise risk management is all about. Rigid and detailed rules that can be handed out to implementation teams can contain more risks than adopting less detailed, directional procedures, sharing respective strategic intent between parties, forming the right cross-functional teams, engaging in regular and transparent communications, and adopting the appropriate steps and flexible design that will build effective relationships throughout the lifecycle of a contract. Relevant, due to the increasing regulatory oversight of outsourced operations in financial services, is the model that the Financial Services Authority (FSA) in the UK has adopted since its inception to regulate the financial services industry. It defines its values as 'an approach to rule-making based as far as possible on high-level principles rather than detailed prescription; a focus on senior management responsibilities; and acting in a proportionate and risk-based way.'[18] Interestingly, this practice is at the center of the debate in the US on reforming intense financial regulations, exemplified by the Sarbanes-Oxley Act, that are held responsible for US financial markets' loss of global capital-raising competitiveness.

Principles-based management allows for flexible supervision of complex relationships that are experiencing ongoing innovation and change. It is the approach that can transform outsourcing contracts into successful partnerships that create long-term value; it is about applied common sense – a most uncommon practice! – and methodical steps in strategic planning, controlled legal input, communications, people staffing and governance, and contingency and exit planning. Successful outsourcing relationships do not happen by chance or by diktat. By taking due consideration of these five categories, an organization can avoid falling into an SLA-driven path and engage in a synergistic partnership leveraging respective core competencies. The direct consequence is a collaborative model rather than a relationship that easily falls into an arms-length confrontational interaction.

There is a way out of the fateful statistics on outsourcing deals' success!

Five action guidelines for successful outsourcing

Strategic planning: ensure clarity in value creation and coherence with corporate direction

> Financial services companies have allowed departments to outsource functions on a case by case basis, often driven by cost savings. But without reference to a central strategy, companies may find they are carrying more risk than they realise. As businesses audit their outsourcing, this risk exposure, as much as any reputational pressure, may prompt companies to think again about outsourcing, especially for core business processes.[19]

A pure cost arbitrage logic, locked in a detailed contract and associated rigid SLAs that are tasked to guarantee the cost benefit, can lead to a wrong decision for the following reasons:

- *Few companies understand the true cost of manufacturing and/or servicing internally.* An outsourcing effort, often laborious and expensive in itself, needs to be compared to taking a harder look at extracting costs and making productivity improvements from existing capabilities. Even research highlights that internal improvements can outweigh savings produced by outsourcing, and this equation is made even worse (for the outsourcing case) if administration costs in managing a supply relationship are included – e.g. from 3 percent up to more than 10 percent of the value of a contract.[20]

- *Broader efficiencies and therefore strategic opportunities are overlooked.* McKinsey estimated in a case study that an insurance company would have captured only 16 percent servicing efficiency improvements if it had focused only on labor costs offshoring, e.g. transferring labor to offshore locations to benefit from reduced costs. Taking a strategic stance by combining a number of associated measures, such as consolidating IT, automating, and re-engineering processes, it actually reaped 45 percent total benefits.[21]
- *An effective long-term wholesale or institutional relationship needs corporate cultures that are aligned if not matching.* Global business giants go to great expense to find out simply that the cultural fit was not there. Hewlett-Packard, for instance, hired a major consulting firm to assess a partnership with Microsoft; the report eventually concluded that the two companies 'were culturally mismatched.'[22]

A sharp focus on value creation is all the more important than the scope of outsourcing possibilities and therefore the array of vendors' offerings has expanded radically over the last 15 years. With the advent of megadeals (contract values exceeding $1 billion – over 100 since 1995 and 15 in 2003 alone[23]), outsourcing has evolved from a wages advantage game applied to tactical non-essential activities, to a broad strategic move akin to joint ventures, divestitures, and even mergers and acquisitions (M&A). Drivers of value are multidimensional – accessing specialized competencies (Schlumberger is, for instance, the unavoidable outsourcer in drilling and related oilfield services for oil companies[24]), restructuring balance sheets through asset transfers (plant, equipment, licenses), creating economies of scale by facilitating the creation of large vendor capabilities, and innovatively mitigating business risk in areas such as product/software development.

The automobile industry showed the way more than 15 years ago. It is now among the most disaggregated industries and one that depends for its survival on the efficient management of its outsourcing partnerships. For example, 70–80 percent of the cost of a motor vehicle for Chrysler, Ford, and Honda is outsourced. Canon buys more than 75 percent of its copier components. Adopting a total value approach, away from unit price, in fact transformed the automotive industry at several points in its recent history, notably saving Chrysler in the 1990s. 'Partnerships with suppliers have helped Chrysler improve performance significantly by speeding up product development, lowering development costs, and reducing procurement costs, thereby contributing to increases in Chrysler's market share and profitability,' assessed Jeffrey Dyer, Assistant Professor of Management at the University of Pennsylvania.[25]

The famous SCORE (Supplier Cost Reduction Effort) program emerged out of a new partnership paradigm. It simply captures and tracks ideas for improvement from suppliers and vendors, then implements agreed initiatives of mutual benefit to both customer and supplier. When such strategic alignment is so tight, outsourcing and partnership become pretty much the same word. In fact, if a function or a process outsourced is non-core (and therefore cost-cutting is the primary if not the only goal), an outright divestiture may be a more appropriate solution. In reality, many of such outsourcing arrangements that transfer assets (often called 'lift-outs') – people, systems, buildings – are divestitures in effect even if managers don't look at them this way. Forcing that thinking allows the validation of a strategic decision to retain a function, contract it out, divest it, or partner depending on the required control and flexibility for future product or service development. For instance, in the securities brokerage industry, an outsourcing decision on part or whole of the back office, middle office, call center, and/or technology development and maintenance functions has direct consequences on the ability of an organization to develop new products and related businesses, especially at an expansion or development stage. Setting aside questions of strategic intent and constancy,[26] American Express in the UK in 2004–05 would not have been able to create market-leading wholesale investment services and aggregation (or 'wrap') offerings if it had outsourced its existing technology and operations functions, as it should have from the pure scale-economies logic of its retail brokerage business. Interestingly, McKinsey, in a 2005 survey of IT costs in 37 European banks,[27] found that the most effective spenders (called 'effective business enablers') outsource sparingly (7 percent of their IT spending) as against the 'high IT spenders' with a 25 percent ratio. The difference appears to be that the better-performing banks carefully choose the areas where third-party skills have a clear advantage over internal resources, rather than take the outsourcing route to 'fix' IT-management problems – a 'give up' option to which the less well-performing institutions would not want to admit.

An outsourcing decision needs today to be part of a strategic planning agenda that includes a clear assessment of core competencies and skills, especially in relation to the outsourcing suppliers. It also requires a clear mapping of where value will be created (new products, redesigned processes, new relationship clusters) and, therefore, where the collaborative model will need to demonstrate results over time.

Controlled legal input: strike a balance between business and legal risk assessment

Selecting outsourcing vendors and negotiating a deal can often be more complex than M&A discussions, largely because, in addition to external negotiations, there is a multitude of internal negotiations with many stakeholders. In addition to board and executive management levels, transactions involve managers in procurement, financial analysis and control, accounting, technology, operations, various functional expert areas, and unmistakably

HR as well. Such complexity, quite arduous for a deal team to tactfully orchestrate, leads commonly to a high reliance on the legal team – internal and/or external – playing the role of internal facilitators but also taking quite naturally the most conservative positions, limiting risks, creating future options, and overall ensuring its client, the company that is outsourcing, retains the upper hand in the contract. If negotiations go wrong, lawyers will be blamed for having made terms too restrictive or too onerous to manage. Usually this is unfair reasoning when:

- executives in charge of the vendor selection and negotiation should manage lawyers, not the other way round;
- lawyers' professional input is to focus on issues of liability, tax, regulation, and structures or governance, not organizational or partnership facilitation, even if they may have some positive contribution ad hoc; and
- lawyers are ethically barred from acting as advocates of a partnership (unless specifically hired for it); they are by the nature of their charter taking the perspective of their client, which, if not controlled in a partnership-oriented outsourcing deal, can lead to a win–lose logic – and again, will be translating into overdocumented and inflexible SLAs.

Having experienced these tensions, one is easily tempted to advise the establishment of three deal teams:[28] the two separate negotiating teams from the respective parents, and a third team whose role is to protect the interests of the intended partnership, to design its business plan, and to identify ways of maximizing a deal for both parties' benefit. Specialized external advisors can fulfill such a role if well recognized, experienced, and trusted by both sides, even if hired, as is most often the case, by the outsourcer.

Alternatively, negotiating executives need to be clear about the scope and the spirit of the outsourcing deal so as to align well to the strategy, but also have a better understanding of the vendors' capabilities. Assessing these and, generically, past performance on SLAs within previous and existing contracts is an important screening factor for selecting an outsourcing partner. However, it is like screening an individual; the CV and the references are only a piece of the jigsaw.

An important lawyer's input is about thinking ahead of the exit. Business executives on the other hand are not inclined to do so nor even address this upfront for fear of it being perceived as a proof of bad faith. Although sensitive, transparency and upfront discussions on exit are critical to the health of an agreement-crafting process (see 'Contingency and exit' section, pp. 99–101). Often, a legal and financial team would separately negotiate exit provisions under the direction of business leadership teams. In cases of multi-year large deals where outsourcing or 'lift-outs' are de facto divestitures, this discipline allows circling back to tighten up the deal's strategic rationale as well as to develop a portfolio of alternative options.

Striking the right balance between functional experts, and in particular navigating legal input to the process, should be the role of an outsourcing deal manager. This manager may not continue on as the actual relationship manager but is the focal point, in a similar fashion to internal corporate finance or M&A deal teams, of the design of the outsourcing deal. Even if external advisors are being hired, this role is critical for the organization to align and manage communications channels between the parties at the early selection, negotiation, and structuring stages. Overall, this balance at the selection and negotiation stage and in subsequent agreement discussions is what can be called 'striving towards a true partnership.'[29] It means that:

- at the negotiation stage both parties are seeking commercial fairness – principles set in the early days of the relationship are maintained irrespective of individual staff turnover;
- if one party is disadvantaged or hurting in some manner, then there is no partnership;
- a governance structure is agreed for both parties to identify and work toward solutions that improve the deal and its components, and to share the benefits among parties according to relative contribution; and
- a structure is defined upfront that allows a deal to be reconfigured if it is not creating the appropriate behavior.

Again, to add some research evidence, in its survey of IT costs in 37 European banks,[30] McKinsey found also that, on the one hand, high-performing banks tend to have negotiated flexible vendor contracts, monitored on an ongoing basis and renegotiated when opportune. On the other hand, other banking institutions are constrained by inflexible contract terms and conditions, thus making renegotiations difficult and the overall relationship arduous and expensive to manage.

Communications: elevate the SLA into a charter and establish a culture of transparency and trust

One never communicates too much. Although this maxim may sound like something out of a personal development bestseller, it is especially relevant in complex organizational systems where contracts and SLAs are often surrogates for candid and regular communications. In fact, hands-on experience shows that management consultants and at times lawyers for one or the other party end up playing the role of the protagonists' 'therapists' or facilitators, called in at a late stage when communication has either not happened when it should have or has simply broken down.

Beyond the SLA, and chronologically before its elaboration as a deal requirement, the parties should agree a relationship charter that sets a benchmark for behavior – the standard would include regular health checks, balanced scorecards, and senior executive dashboards as governance mechanisms for monitoring success for both parties. A charter, in a nutshell, is structured simply with a jointly agreed vision and/or mission statement, a list of major objectives or critical success factors, and guiding principles for the relationship (see Figure 4.2). It is not a legally enforceable contractual agreement. Its objective is to focus the parties on the working relationship and intent between customer and supplier. It means in practice too that, as the relationship matures, the charter becomes the point of reference, rather than a reliance on legal rights and obligations.[31] The latter's SLA-based approach is effective if the charter is the prime reference tool and its operating standards are well respected. Without it, the relationship falls rapidly into a contract management by the book with all its travails. Here, we should not underestimate the importance of aligning the respective client–supplier cultures, or at the very least of understanding their compatibility.

To facilitate these early stages of the relationship, starting at the proposal request step, it is important that the process and the engagement with vendors are highly transparent. The vendor should be provided access for his own due diligence prior to deal agreement and/or be supplied with detailed requirements materials. Besides ensuring that the outsourcer has a true grasp of its assets, resources, and services, this sets the stage and the expectation for ongoing transparency from both sides, facilitating deal agreement and potential future issues resolution. It will also reduce the costs of monitoring and the possible recourse to sanctions.

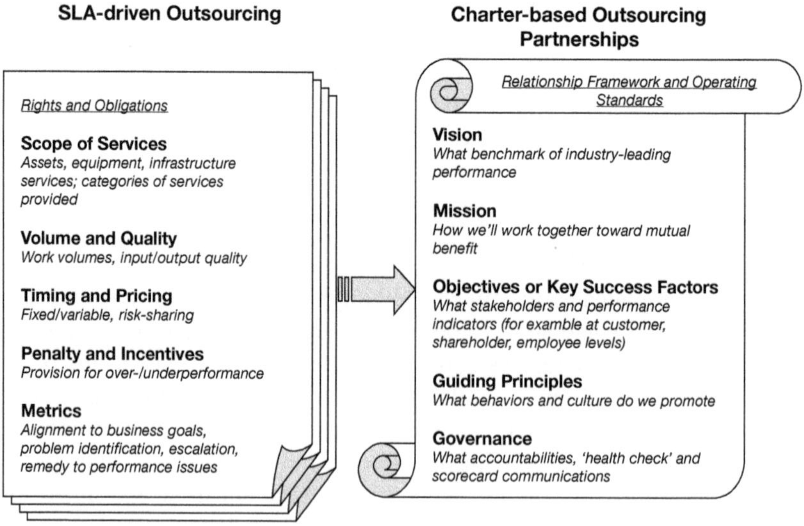

Figure 4.2 From SLA-driven outsourcing to charter-based outsourcing partnerships.

Source: Astwood Partners LLP.

In *Trust*, a study of the interconnectedness of economic life with cultural life, Francis Fukuyama makes the insightful assessment that the creation of trust does not simply come from good information management:

> Trust does not reside in integrated circuits or fiber optic cables . . . trust is not reducible to information. A 'virtual' firm can have abundant information coming through network wires about its suppliers and contractors. But if they are all crooks or frauds, dealing with them will remain a costly process involving complex contracts and time-consuming enforcement. Without trust, there will be a strong incentive to bring these activities in-house and restore old hierarchies.[32]

Communications, rather than information, need to be planned and structured toward building 'social capital'[33] as a foundation for trusted relationships.

A simple best practice is for the parties to address the definition of trust upfront in the relationship – how would you define trust in this initiative? Once trust is discussed and established as critically important for the well-being of the deal, then a process is agreed to proactively build confidence in people's competencies, objectives, intentions, systems, and processes. This means communicating openly levels of empowerment in respective organizations, achievements and successes, ideas, and referrals, and even sharing personal beliefs and values. In a nutshell, the end result is the creation of a strong and shared conviction that individuals or groups will act as they say they will. 'Real trust is not naïve. It comes from planning, is steered by the right people, structures, processes and measurement, and is earned from performance,' says Professor Leslie Willcocks of the Warwick Business School.[34]

Viewed from a traditional 'Western society' perspective, trust is the 'unwritten SLA.' From Fukuyama's thesis on differing social and historical backgrounds to trust, there is an inherent challenge, quite difficult to gauge per se, of large corporations from low-trust, litigious societies, to enter long-term outsourcing partnerships with entrepreneurial organizations based in high-trust societies used to flexible contracts, extended family and family-like relationships, and networked information.[35]

In this perspective, the complexity and literally the extensiveness (and physical size in itself) of the SLA documentation can be – perceived or real, it does not matter – evidence of initial mistrust. Like any relationship, business or personal, the amount of documentation, and the legal time spent on mapping out scenarios of where things could go wrong, never prevent issues from emerging and going awry if mistrust presided at the outset.

A research study spanning 15 years and covering 108 companies in Australia reported that well-managed outsourcing arrangements based on mutual trust could create a 20–40 percent difference in service, quality, cost, and other performance indicators over outdated power-based relationships.[36] Colin

Holgate, chief executive officer (CEO) of LogicaCMG Australia, one of the research sponsors, emphasized that 'none of the organisations in the study cited a good contract as the key factor. Good relationship management techniques, such as flexible working arrangements, willingness to change, and frequent and effective communication, were however regularly highlighted.' Hence, the concept of 'trust dividend' is starting to take some root among outsourcing practitioners and analysts, although this is still in its infancy in terms of performance measures and tracking.

Among the 'transparent intangibles' of contract success is the sense of ownership depth within the vendor's organization. This connection to the client in terms of shared values is a powerful trust-building effort. In one of the leading India-based global BPO organizations in banking and financial services, a visitor can notice a number of staff management approaches that are not SLA-driven but illustrate a strong culture of ownership, accountability, and client service. Characteristics observed are, for example:

- Employees are trained in understanding their clients' stated core values and people approaches. For instance, in sleek Bangalore offices, which look identical in architecture and the comfort of their premises to any of their clients' industrial park buildings in the US or Europe, posters of the client's values and mission statement adorn the walls. Office workers dedicated to this major financial services client speak with passion about their achievements and use the client's language and terminology to talk about how they personally relate to the work undertaken.
- Rotations across a client's organization (even global relocation) and continuous professional development of staff within a contract reinforce this attachment, but also allow the vendor to be 'on the pulse' of the client's organization and have a better day-to-day understanding of the web of relationships and changes in personnel and their significance within their large clients.
- Similarly, the diversity agendas (men/women, ethnic/community backgrounds) of major international groups appear increasingly mirrored within their Indian outsourcing vendors at broader professional and management levels – a significant development noticeable in the traditional Indian context.

This chameleon-like approach to client styles and values facilitates the resolution of stark underpinning cultural differences at individual or group level and ensures better communications in the long term. Whether written and discussed upfront, or driven by the leadership of senior executives as well as of day-to-day managers of both partners, vendor and suppliers, the relationship charter or moral agreement (Figure 4.2) ought to precede the SLA as a reference point to an outsourcing partnership based on trust.

People: manage governance and relationships through cross-organizational teams

Rarely do executives look back at a major outsourcing contract and comment first on how pricing made it or broke it, or how SLAs were not adequate or respected. They are more likely to focus on how people interacted, on the quality of staffing on both sides, and on whether a governance model was in existence, effective, and respected throughout the duration of the relationship. Similarly to marriages, partnerships fail for all sorts of reasons but, in the vast majority of cases, source problems and ultimate breakdown originate from people. When the expenses related to the internal management of the outsourcing relationship are clearly known, the importance of governance, relationship, and team management ought not to be overlooked. Cost estimates range from 5 to 12 percent of total contract value, depending on the complexity involved; this value range can easily double in an offshoring situation, depending on the scope of processes outsourced and expected business results.[37]

A large proportion of these expenses are driven by specialist external and in-house staff resources deployed across several competencies that need to be coordinated with the supplier's own. This model appears quite novel in most major financial services institutions grappling with outsourcing management. It is, in effect, however, nothing more innovative than reproducing standard practices from the manufacturing sector, adopting at the working level 'platform team' structures (engineers, suppliers, specialists) for a vehicle production process for example, or integrated project teams in product development – activities that are in many situations outsourced/partnered with. The more mission-critical the outsourced processes will be, the more 'make-or-break' decisions will relate to the selection of quality teams and of their leadership. Moreover, these cross-organizational teams, rather than individuals, have to receive appropriate commitment, involvement, and leadership from senior corporate management and relevant functional executive teams. We shall see below how this 'ointment' needs to be part of the ongoing governance structure.

Best practices point to three stages to which correspond three types of positions: negotiators and start-up managers for the deal-making and launch phase; deal-responsible executives and operating staff for the operations phase; and relationship managers for the coordination stage handling day-to-day partnership communications and conflict or issue resolution. Successful relationships will depend heavily on defining these positions upfront, selecting and recruiting the right profiles, and developing incentive programs and measurement methods to direct individual and collective performance.

Ideally, best practice would encourage limited changes in the people responsible for the outsourcing relationship. Stability and retention of responsible managers within the organization is at the heart of sustaining the right partnership culture and the spirit of the charter.[38] What happens if you are not yet at the stage where you have a strong, long-term, trusting relationship? Or the key contact departs or changes roles? To a certain extent, it may be like starting all over again. It is, however, unrealistic to expect outsourcing managers and executives to remain in the same position for more than three or five years. The career path or options need to be planned ahead of time, whether the organization has scale of partnership resources or not. The path could include various routes, including a return to a previous functional area or a rotation into business development units and/or initiatives. Critically, this will allow for the retention of the knowledge base and for continuous access to 'relationship memory' and networks built throughout the practice of joint teams.

Team members are not account or contract managers in the traditional sense. The choice of individuals has to be made on a structured understanding of the hard and soft skills required. At the leadership level, core skills in team-building, conflict resolution, and quality management will impact the successful make-up of the group. The soft skill set and character of the selected individuals will determine the culture of the relationship. A dose of 'humanist management,' as defined by Philippe Masson, is neither understood enough nor a well-studied factor of success in outsourcing partnerships:

> Humanist managers instigate trust because they are reliable, honest, courageous, and selfless. They bring about followers by practicing tolerance without negligence and a sense of humor. They know how to combine a healthy anxiety with deep confidence. It is their humility which makes them succeed over time.[39]

People backgrounds and capabilities mirror the requirement distinctions between partnership-led relationships and an SLA-driven outsourcing deal. Some observers would go as far as asserting that 'Partnerships are a place for leaders, not managers.'[40] The skills and behaviors that underpin successful partnership models are already in high-performing organizations, which promote empowerment, accountability, and leadership. Anecdotally, one could observe global corporations known for their strong leadership culture and people development skills as most often being pioneers in outsourcing management (for example, General Electric, American Express, Citibank). For more traditional organizations, these approaches require a complete reshaping of strategy and structure, and people management and involvement, and often from the very top of the leadership hierarchy.

Finally, appropriate team staffing at different stages of the deal needs to be closely defined in relation to the governance that regulates interactions and establishes a 'partnering process.'[41]

Typical governance structures[42] allowing for efficient monitoring and decision-making have a number of design principles, for example:

- Three levels of support: a Board assembling respective corporate executives and monitoring/ defining strategy and performance; an Operations Committee involved in tactical decision-making and resources management; and a Functional Committee executing day-to-day work within the various components of the contract.
- A short document articulating the operations of the joint governance structures – who reports to whom, who does what, what are the milestones, what are the relationship logistics (meeting location, frequency, etc.), and when and how they are modified.
- Membership of the structures is determined by functional responsibility.
- No team limits are set for membership.
- Potentially the right outsider (similar to corporate boards' external non-executive directors) is brought in to ask the unasked questions at critical junctures.
- A definition is laid down as to who will address, and how, the most important decisions to be made by the structures and therefore the escalation process.

Once again, these structures are hollow if they are not driven by a shared sense of purpose, reflecting, and managed through, the charter, but also by a regular reiteration of the mutual benefits of the partnership. They are at the very least instruments for transparent communication and trust-building. Positive developments as well as issues, which may not be directly connected to the relationship (client wins/losses, profitability issues, retrenchments, etc.), need to be aired. These mechanisms go hand in hand with the ability of the partnership to evolve, change, restructure, and even terminate without drama or unnecessary financial and organizational issues. The actual contractual and SLA reviews will simply be consequences rather than focal points of discussions on change.

Contingency and exit: plan evolution and scope restructuring upfront

As mentioned earlier (see 'Controlled legal input' section, pp. 91–3), addressing contingency situations and exit options is what you would expect from your legal staff or external counsel, who would suggest the appropriate clauses. These are, however, fundamentally senior business executive issues that need to be thought through at the outset of any major contract. No relationship is forever, despite what the SLA design effort may want to suggest, and despite all the relevant penalty and exit terms that generally come from non-compliance and service failures. Market and competitive pressures, innovation, technology, and various lifecycles will introduce change as soon as the contract ink dries.

Evolution and potential exit from an outsourcing partnership need to be approached in the same way it was entered into; that is, in a spirit of transparency, trust, cooperation, and following the foundation principles or relationship charter. The first pitfall is to believe one's own press releases that advertise the deal as a marriage that will last forever. . . . Change, redesign, termination, and/or any variations and impacts of these on the relationship are a natural occurrence of the outsourcing lifecycle. Companies must prepare upfront, and this does not mean simply securing a number of contractual provisions around exit or renegotiations.

Such preparation starts with asking a number of questions to structure early on an internal debate and possibly introduce open discussions with the partner. These questions do not need to be answered precisely – they set the stage to plan ahead, for example:

- What is the most likely (as opposed to stated) duration of the outsourcing contract based on what we know from industry trends, competition, and our own business and operational strategies?
- Based on current understanding, what are the top five or ten potential reasons for termination, major change, or redefinition of the deal?
- What is the intensity of the impact of this change on other company processes, products, and services?
- What structures or configurations or asset contributions make the partnership more difficult or easier to disentangle?
- What scenarios exist to address failure early? What are the most challenging tasks?

Working backward from these questions, outsourcing teams can even shape 'change success' well before a contract is signed. At the deal strategy level, a number of considerations needs to be addressed upfront:

- Define objectives for change or, ultimately, exit – these could obviously include seeking better price, but ideally in a compelling way; or regaining control for strategic reasons.
- Map out outsourced functions and processes in the clearest manner to avoid the inordinate cost of separation or change of providers.
- Introduce flexibility in contract duration, especially in uncertain situations.
- Develop staff management policies that encourage career paths so that outsourcing managers avoid being too closely connected with the vendor relationship and the contract itself, and don't lose sight of the company's best interests.
- Entertain potential contingency options, whether they are supported by alternative provider networks and relationships, or driven by potential changes in corporate direction (insource/outsource, offshore/onshore, alliances/acquisitions).

On the contractual side, typically a handful of areas need to be considered: events that trigger a change, ownership of tangible/intangible assets developed, potential transition costs, and post-change/exit demands. At the extreme end, termination triggers would involve performance failure, changes in external conditions, parent status change (ownership change, financial stability issues, key individuals' change of employment), breach of contract, and decision deadlock. Core in contractual terms discussions upfront is the balance in partners' rights even if one is a supplier and the other is the client.

The ownership of potential assets developed uniquely through the relationship will depend on the relative contribution of the parties. One of the parties may straightforwardly be the acquirer, or an independent assessor will set the price and the process if not predetermined upfront. With regard to transition costs, principles should be agreed as to who contributes to what and as to what valuation methods should be adopted. Finally, on post-exit demands and due to close integration or connection to the client organization, future relationships can be defined, especially if there are other areas of value (data management, support). Some future restrictions (such as poaching staff) are commonly placed due to competitive pressure.

Although this contingency approach early on may be counter to the spirit of a partnership, if approached transparently and at the right level, it will make change management a smoother process and reinforce alertness in managing the relationship overall. Fundamentally, it is part of risk-management disciplines, which strengthen the overall quality of the contract and set the tone for a charter-driven outsourcing relationship.

Building long-term outsourcing partnership capabilities

Writing SLAs is more akin to documenting a product's technical specifications than planning for a long-term relationship. Different core skills and capabilities need to be aligned and prioritized to plan for a partnership model, and certainly with better chances of success. With core operations moved to third parties in increasingly global 'digital value chains,'[43] outsourcing and partnering become a mirror of each other. Competencies need to be developed internally to strengthen the chances for highly performing relationships. However, each organization will have its own way to approach institutional capability-building, from ad hoc well-communicated, top-down, competent but informal content leadership, to highly structured, web-based, training-focused dissemination of best practices. In a nutshell, building such critical capabilities should be approached in a similar fashion to any other core management competency, such as acquisitions and post-merger integration management, or quality control and client servicing. These efforts are exercises in knowledge management and dissemination sustained through consistent managerial and leadership development efforts and sponsored at the very top of the organization.

A highly effective approach is to run internal seminars based on case studies, 'post-mortem' reviews, or simply deals 'walk-throughs,' by the company's own senior outsourcing and partnership managers, not by outside consultants or internal training staff. If this commitment is tied to the manager's incentive system, a company can create a virtuous cycle of active transmission of best practices and knowledge-sharing at the core of the corporate value system.

Clearly, in such a growth industry and particularly in the highly mobile and flexible skills retooling US market, new careers, roles, titles, and certifications are emerging to address these competency needs.[44] Especially since 2004, with the setting up of specialized training programs, chief resource officers (CROs) are positioned to be the peers of chief information officers (CIOs) and chief financial officers (CFOs), and to report to CEOs. Support staff can now include certified outsourcing governance professionals (a trademarked title![45]), who oversee outsourcing compliance and contract management.

Besides the essential staff component of this capabilities-building effort, there are three other elements of long-term internal capability infrastructure: tools, organization, and systems. The tools will range from policies to standard contracts and performance scorecards, vendor-screening methodologies, gap analyses, and any other devices prepared and tested to support an outsourcing structure, negotiation, and launch.

On the organization front, a functional unit usually closely associated with corporate business development may be created to be the reference and central assistance point for outsourcing initiatives. Less formal could be an established forum that crosses business units and brings together, on a regular basis and formally, the outsourcing managers and even the heads of the business units and functions concerned, as well as the vendor's relationship contacts. In addition, an organization configuration can help facilitate career paths for these outsourcing managers so that the roles can attract top talent.

Finally, flexible, largely web-based systems are the 'lubricants' that are needed to ensure the existence of these cross-organization networks, which are the lifeblood of these outsourcing relationships. Technology can also help codify, and be the repository for, expertise and training. Even more advanced in the competency maturity spectrum are shared communication systems, such as dedicated websites to support communication, coordination, and various services between partners.

As outsourcing practices become more prevalent in any size of company, these toolkits will be standardized and best practices communities created. Portals and matching services are already emerging and a significant deal track record exists to identify useful benchmarks, from unit pricing to standard process productivity improvement. The more adept at building internal core competencies will be more agile in multiplying successful outsourcing relationships, better at recognizing early warning signals and finding solutions for them, and eventually more creative in extracting long-term value from these partnerships.

Conclusion

As globalization demands ever-accelerating operational improvements and constant re-evaluation of core competencies, the successful organizations will be the ones that transform traditional transaction-based suppliers' contracts into flexible partnerships with their outsourcers. These outsourcing partnerships are to be created to accomplish measurably better business outcomes than could be achieved by the organization alone. They also strengthen the overall buy-in of employees who are part of a coherent transformation of their organization, and not victimized in an ephemeral cost and/or talent arbitrage around the globe. Finally, they are also an integral part of a better-controlled enterprise risk management, where third-party relationships can indeed contribute toward reducing overall business risks and even highlight, on an ongoing basis, potential internal operational risks. Similarly, they can foster innovation in processes, systems, and/or product development based on webs of trusted networks of individuals and teams created over time.

As such, high-performing outsourcing relationships are strategic assets on their own and therefore demand ongoing senior executive investment and dedication proportionate to their importance. They are strategic investments, even if they concern apparent non-strategic or non-core functions; they are not purchasing decisions.

In their predications, industry bodies are increasingly advocating a less contract-focused approach to ensure that the anticipated and inevitable high growth of outsourcing does not backlash. Hence, Martyn Hart, Chairman of the UK's National Outsourcing Association, was quoted as saying: 'vendors that manage to become partners will do better, and practices such as "gain-share," where rewards as the result of outsourcing are split, will increase in popularity.'[46] The early adopters of partnership-driven outsourcing will certainly have a head start in the new paradigm of global services management.

Notes

1 David Craig and Paul Willmott, 'Outsourcing grows up,' *The McKinsey Quarterly*, web exclusive, February 2005. Available online at: www.mckinseyquarterly.com/article_abstract_visitor.aspx?ar=1582&L2=1&L3=106.

2 Datamonitor estimates that as many as 40 percent of North American life insurers were planning to increase outsourcing spending in 2006 – Datamonitor, 'Outsourcing in insurance: perspective 2006,' December 2005. Available online at: www.datamonitor.com/~04035cca884545a298bfbl907b55cd95~/Products/Free/Report/DMTC1144/020DMTC1144.htm.

3 See, however, the various studies 'quietly' highlighting the positive macroeconomic effects of offshoring. For example, research by the management consulting firm McKinsey, quoted in Alpesh Patel and Hemendra Aran, *Outsourcing Success: The Management Imperative* (Basingstoke: Palgrave Macmillan, 2005), p. 6.

4 Thomas M. Koulopoulos and Tom Roloff, *Smartsourcing – Driving Innovation and Growth Through Outsourcing* (Avon, MA: Platinum Press, Adams Media, 2006), Introduction.

5 Michael Hammer and James Champy, *Reengineering The Corporation: A Manifesto For Business Revolution* (New York: HarperCollins, 1993).
6 Most major operations management (OM) consulting firms and the OM groups of general management consulting firms had (and still have) BPR training and guidance documents, not dissimilar to internal auditors' procedures review binders.
7 Sonoko Takahashi, 'European HR BPO Spending Forecast: 2006 to 2011,' Forrester Research, Inc., July 27, 2006. Available online at: www.forrester.com/Research/Document/Excerpt/0,7211,39384,00.html.
8 Firms such as US-based Accenture and EDS, or India-based TCS, Infosys, and Wipro (latest annual reports split earnings by industry sectors).
9 Jian Zhen, 'SLA 101: what to look for in a service-level agreement,' *Computerworld Security*, March 15, 2006. Available online at: www.computerworld.com/securitytopics/security/story/0,10801,109558,00.html.
10 Interview with Yuval Boger, CEO of Oblicore, 'SLAs getting more strategic,' *IT Business Edge*, May 7, 2005. Available online at: www.itbusinessedge.com/item/?ci=3309.
11 Jim Champy, 'Foreword,' in Thomas M. Koulopoulos and Tom Roloff, *Smartsourcing – Driving Innovation and Growth Through Outsourcing* (Avon, MA: Platinum Press, Adams Media, 2006), p. viii.
12 Ibid.
13 Quoted in *IT Wire*, March 29, 2006, reporting on the research report, *The Power of Relationships*. Available online at: www.itwire.com.au/content/view/3770/106/.
14 Notably from the Gartner group. See Linda Cohen and Allie Young, *Multisourcing: Moving Beyond Outsourcing To Achieve Growth And Agility* (Boston, MA: Harvard Business School Press, 2005).
15 James Murray, 'Does outsourcing need SLAs?,' *IT Week*, May 15, 2006. Available online at: www.itweek.co.uk/itweek/comment/2156039/does-outsourcing-slas.
16 *Strategy+Business*, 'Reining in outsourcing risk,' November 30, 2005. Available online at: www.strategy-business.com/press/sbkw2/sbkwarticle/sbkw051130.
17 See Gary Hamel, Yves Doz, and C. K. Prahalad, 'Collaborate with your competitors – and win,' *Harvard Business Review*, Jan.–Feb. 1989; Gary Hamel and C. K. Prahalad, *Competing for the Future* (Boston, MA: Harvard Business School Press, 1994); Yves Doz and Gary Hamel, *Alliance Advantage* (Boston, MA: Harvard Business School Press, 1998).
18 See 'About the FSA,' www.fsa.gov.uk.
19 Stephen Pritchard, 'Financial institutions re-evaluate offshore operations,' *Financial Times*, December 1, 2004 (reviews consequences of JP Morgan-Bank One pulling outsourced services back in-house).
20 Stephen J. Doig, Ronald C. Ritter, Kurt Speckhals, and Daniel Woolson, 'Has outsourcing gone too far?,' *The McKinsey Quarterly*, 4 (2001): 31.
21 Vikash Daga and Noshir F. Kaka, 'Taking offshoring beyond labor cost savings,' *The McKinsey Quarterly* (May 2006), web edition. Available online at: www.mckinseyquarterly.com/article_abstract_visitor.aspx?ar=1784.
22 Sarah Gerdes, *Navigating The Partnership Maze* (New York: McGraw-Hill, 2003), p. 25.
23 Gartner research, quoted in Daga and Kaka, 'Taking offshoring beyond labor cost savings,' footnote 21.
24 Anne Chung, Tim Jackson, and Tim Laseter, 'Why outsourcing is in,' *Strategy+Business*, 3rd quarter (2002).
25 Jeffrey H. Dyer, 'How Chrysler created an American keiretsu,' *Harvard Business Review* (July–August 1996): 42–56.
26 American Express made the global strategic decision, announced early in 2005, to pull out of its investment services business – that is, American Express Financial

Corporation (now called Ameriprise Financial Inc.) and directly related businesses globally.

27 Kanika Bahadur, Driek Desmet, and Edwin van Bommel, 'Smart IT spending: insights from European banks,' *The McKinsey Quarterly*, web exclusive, January 2006. Available online at: www.mckinseyquarterly.com/article_abstract_visitor.aspx?ar=1698.

28 See, in the case of deeper alliances, David Ernst, Stephen I. Glover, and James D. Bamford, 'Crafting the agreement: lawyers and managers,' in James D. Bamford, Benjamin Gomes-Casseres, and Michael Robinson (eds) *Mastering Alliance Strategy* (San Francisco, CA: Jossey-Bass, 2003), p. 103.

29 Interviews with Troika analysts, August 2006.

30 Bahadur *et al.*, 'Smart IT spending.'

31 See example of a partnering charter in Tony Lendrum, *The Strategic Partnering Handbook* (North Ryde, NSW: McGraw-Hill Australia, 2003), p. 216.

32 Francis Fukuyama, *Trust, The Social Virtues and The Creation of Prosperity* (New York: The Free Press, paperback edn, 1996), p. 25.

33 In Fukuyama's terminology, ibid., p. 26.

34 Quoted in *IT Wire*, March 29, 2006, op. cit.

35 Fukuyama, *Trust*, parts II and III.

36 *IT Wire*, March 29, 2006, op. cit.; reported also previously in *Out-Law News*, web edition, November 25, 2005. Available online at: www.out-law.com/page-6386.

37 Douglas Brown and Scott Wilson, *The Black Book of Outsourcing* (Hoboken, NJ: John Wiley & Sons, 2005), p. 134.

38

> There may be a hidden cost when senior managers rotate across jobs every two or three years. What most often prompts a change in strategy in a large company is not a new competitor, new technology, or regulatory upheaval. What most often prompts change is a new executive in the corner office . . . We know of no company that has achieved a ten or fifteen year strategic intent with a succession of two-year executives in key jobs.
>
> (Hamel and Prahalad, *Competing for the Future*, p. 176)

39 Philippe Masson, *Manager Humaniste* (Paris: Editions d'Organisation, 2004), p. 67.

40 Lendrum, *The Strategic Partnering Handbook*, p. 130.

41 Ibid., p. 158.

42 This design does not apply exclusively to large contract situations but to all relationships. At small-size deal level, the structures apply to individual responsibilities, full-time or part-time.

43 Koulopoulos and Roloff, *Smartsourcing*, chapter 9, pp. 161–3.

44 Brown and Wilson, *The Black Book of Outsourcing*, chapter 9: 'New career opportunities in outsourcing management,' p. 150.

45 See www.CROInstitute.com, a UK-based educational foundation, offering coursework sanctioned by the respective American and International Associations of Chief Resource Officers, and the International Society of Outsourcing Business Professionals.

46 Quoted in Lisa Kelly, 'Big changes forecast for UK outsourcing,' *Computing Magazine*, January 9, 2007. Available online at: www.computing.co.uk/computing/news/2172103/bi-changes-forecast-uk.

5 Risk and insurance considerations in outsourcing banking and related financial services

Oliver Prior

Introduction

The Basel Committee on Banking Supervision, in the preliminary papers relating to the New Basel Accord, 'Basel II', has focused on the increased use of outsourcing and cited this as one example of the need to introduce a new capital charge for operational risk event losses. The specifications for risk mapping contained in the paper entitled *International Convergence of Capital Measurement and Capital Standards 'Basel II'* does identify 'outsourcing' as an area that should be mapped as regards risk and insurance, but apart from this little guidance is forthcoming in Basel II on how regulators should view outsourcing risks. In its paper entitled *Risk Management Principles for Electronic Banking*, dated May 2001,[1] the Basel Committee on Banking Supervision is much more forthcoming with regard to their thinking on the subject of outsourcing. The following extract from that paper illustrates this point:

> Banks should conduct appropriate risk analysis and due diligence prior to selecting an e-banking service provider and at appropriate intervals thereafter:
>
> - Banks should consider developing processes for soliciting proposals from several e-banking service providers and criteria for choosing among the various proposals.
> - Once a potential service provider has been identified, the bank should conduct an appropriate due diligence review, including a risk analysis of the service provider's financial strength, reputation, risk management policies and controls, and ability to fulfill its obligations.
> - Thereafter, banks should regularly monitor and, as appropriate, conduct due diligence reviews of the ability of the service provider to fulfill its service and associated risk management obligations throughout the duration of the contract.
> - Banks need to ensure that adequate resources are committed to overseeing outsourcing arrangements supporting e-banking.

- Responsibilities for overseeing e-banking outsourcing arrangements should be clearly assigned.
- An appropriate exit strategy for the bank to manage risks should it need to terminate the outsourcing relationship.

Banks should adopt appropriate procedures for ensuring the adequacy of contracts governing e-banking. Contracts governing outsourced e-banking activities should address, for example, the following:

- The contractual liabilities of the respective parties as well as responsibilities for making decisions, including any sub-contracting of material services, are clearly defined.
- Responsibilities for providing information to and receiving information from the service provider are clearly defined. Information from the service provider should be timely and comprehensive enough to allow the bank to adequately assess service levels and risks. Materiality thresholds and procedures to be used to notify the bank of service disruptions, security breaches and other events that pose a material risk to the bank should be spelled out.
- Provisions that specifically address insurance coverage, the ownership of the data stored on the service provider's servers or databases, and the right of the bank to recover its data upon expiration or termination of the contract should be clearly defined.
- Performance expectations, under both normal and contingency circumstances, are defined.
- Adequate means and guarantees, for instance through audit clauses, are defined to insure that the service provider complies with the bank's policies.
- Provisions are in place for timely and orderly intervention and rectification in the event of substandard performance by the service provider. For cross-border outsourcing arrangements, determining which country laws and regulations, including those relating to privacy and other customer protections, are applicable.
- The right of the bank to conduct independent reviews and/or audits of security, internal controls and business continuity and contingency plans is explicitly defined.

It is clear from this guidance that, where outsourcing is being considered, banks need to carry out extensive due diligence on any potential outsourcing partner and to consider the risks involved and ensure that they are addressed. The process of outsourcing involves the transfer of function and control to a third party and with this risk is automatically transferred. The most important issue is to determine which party will carry the responsibility for risk; many things will then flow from the decision. It would be naive for a major European Union- or US-based 'money centre' bank to assume that an entire process and all of the risks inherent in it can be transferred to a data-processing centre in Asia and that regulators in the bank's principal location will accept this. The bank that is outsourcing a function continues to carry the reputational and legal risk in the view of both its clients and regulators. The distribution of that risk is therefore an internal matter and, apart from the reputational issues, should not impact upon its clients. If, for example, client data is sold by an employee of the bank or by an employee of an outsource firm to a third-party criminal, the bank will be held equally responsible for the loss. Where the data is sold by an employee of an outsource company, however, the bank or its insurers should, in the absence of any contractual waiver, be in a position to exercise rights of recourse against the outsource company in an effort to recover the loss.

It is not the intention of this chapter to provide any specific guidance with regard to the overall conduct of any such due diligence review; rather, it will focus solely upon the insurance implications associated with outsourcing.

The insurance issues fall into three principal categories:

1 Failure to comply with the agreed service level(s)
2 Criminal acts
3 Negligent acts or errors.

Failure to comply with the agreed service level(s)

There is an onus upon the bank not only to conduct due diligence and risk analysis reviews upon the outsource partner, but also, in addition to such comfort, to ensure that the outsource partner is of sufficient substance to support any penalty provisions that may be present in the service level agreement (SLA) or, if they are not, that third-party guarantees can then be established to stand in their stead.

There are specialist law firms that understand the outsourcing process and that have considerable experience in preparing the indemnity agreements that will exist between the parties. The problem often arises, however, not as a result of the language of the indemnity agreements but more over the ability to enforce the indemnities should anything go wrong. However strong the indemnities are worded, they are only as good as the ability to enforce them and obtain redress if anything goes wrong.

Basel stipulates that the various contractual responsibilities of the parties entering into an outsource agreement should be clearly defined, for example:

- What is the service being provided?
- What are the expected volumes?
- What are the expected response times?
- What happens when the service levels are not met?

In the area of private finance initiative/public private partnership – 'PFI/PPP' contracting – where 'risks' are being transferred from government entities to private contractors, the practice of governments seeking to impose SLAs upon private contractors, backed up by liquidated damages penalty provisions for failure to perform in accordance with the service levels agreed, has become standard. Such guarantees of performance are clearly designed as penalties for non-performance and, in order to ensure that they are effective, the private contractors are usually required to provide parental guarantees, cash-collateralised escrow accounts or an 'on demand' guarantee issued by a third party, such as a bank or insurance company.

For example, in the UK, private rail operators are required to provide either cash-collateralised escrow accounts or performance guarantees issued by a third party up to substantial amounts to support their contractual obligations to provide railway services. Should they become insolvent, or fail in their contractual duty and thus have their contract terminated, the government can 'call' the cash or third-party guarantee and the funds can be employed in the continuation of the service by another operator or whatever may be necessary. This process serves two purposes:

1 Should a private rail operator fail, the government has the funds to find another operator to provide continuity of service without additional cost to the public.
2 Since such a performance guarantee is a basic requirement of the tendering process, only companies that can provide such guarantees, either supported by cash or by way of a bank or insurance guarantee, will bid to become service providers.

Banks seeking to outsource services should adopt a similar structure and make it clear from the outset that specific service levels will be required in any outsourcing contract and that failure to meet the service levels will result in a liquidated damages claim and that this in turn will require any bidder to evidence their financial ability to 'cover' any potential claim.

No two cases are alike, but as a general rule evidence of financial ability is normally provided in one of three ways:

1 *parental or corporate guarantee* – a contractual guarantee issued by a company (usually a parent company) that has an 'investment grade'* rating; or
2 *cash collateralised escrow account* – funds held in a separate account that can be called by the bank in the event that its outsource partner incurs penalties by reason of an SLA; or
3 *bond* – a guarantee issued by an insurance company or bank that can be called by the bank in the event that its outsource partner incurs penalties by reason of an SLA.

(Note: * 'investment grade' means an equal or better rating of BBB or equivalent by Standard and Poors, Moodys or similar approved rating agency.)

The amount of the liquidated damages and the size of the 'on demand' guarantee required in support of this provision will clearly vary according to the nature of the services being outsourced and the size of the typical potential liquidated damages claim that might arise. It should be borne in mind, however, that, if an outsource contract has to be terminated as a result of the failure of the outsource partner to meet agreed service levels, the bank outsourcing the work will incur considerable additional cost associated with bringing the work back 'in house' or finding another outsource partner. Each contract may vary, but initially strict provisions can be adjusted slightly for the right potential outsource partner. The absence of any such provision in the initial tender documents could result in extensive wrangling over contract provisions once a preferred service provider has been identified. A potential bidder for an outsource contract needs to know from the outset the types of security that he will be required to provide when bidding for an outsource contract. Pre-qualification of bidders might be a wise move, since this can avoid time-wasting bids by organisations that will not be able to meet any security requirements if they are successful.

Outsourcing does not just involve work being done by an external organisation's employees; it also should seek to transfer the financial responsibility for the risk or a key part of the risk associated with the work. Where risk is reallocated, so the assumption of that risk should change in whole or in part and this will also result in a transfer of costs. To move a function from a secure and well-insured environment to one where controls are less stringent and insurance is absent, or minimal, purely on the grounds of cost savings is a false economy.

It is virtually impossible for the party seeking to outsource services to secure insurance in their own name that will provide an unconditional 'guarantee' of the agreed service levels. It is for this reason that the onus of providing a third-party 'guarantee' should be placed upon the prospective provider of the outsource services during the tendering phase.

Criminal acts

The principal source of criminal losses in any bank is the acts of employees. Bank crime insurers tend to view 'people' as being in one of two categories:

- employees, or
- third parties.

Whereas in practice there are three categories:

- employees,
- trusted third parties, and
- other third parties.

Most standard financial institution crime insurance polices will provide extensive insurance cover in respect of dishonest or fraudulent acts by employees and more limited cover in respect of the criminal acts of third parties, but will probably fail to address the issues of outsource service providers in a satisfactory manner. Employees are usually defined as persons directly employed by the bank under a contract of employment and, whilst in some cases this definition might be extended, it rarely encompasses all outsourcing activity without specific amendment.

Unless a bank's crime insurance programme is analysed carefully and adapted to suit any outsource contracts they may have entered into, there is a danger that full insurance protection may not be in place – or duplicate insurance may be in place (which could complicate the insurance response to any loss).

An outsource partner is, in terms of insurance, usually treated as a third party. In practice, however, an outsource partner's employees are likely to be more akin to employees of the bank, insofar as they have access to confidential information, access codes, etc. and in certain instances the bank's customers.

The difference is that an outsource partner is usually a corporate entity and as such will often have insurance of its own that may be available for the benefit of its clients – for example, the bank. The levels of insurance carried by an outsource partner located in India and a major EU- or US-based bank will be significantly different. For the bank to rely entirely upon the insurances of the outsource partner may be unwise, but, equally, for the bank to assume the entire risk into its own insurance programme could be a mistake (especially since many major banks self-insure significant parts of their insurance programmes by way of deductibles, utilising of captive insurance companies and the like).

The solution is to require the outsource partner to carry a reasonable level of insurance cover for the benefit of its clients and then for the bank to ensure that its own insurance programme takes any contingent risk (i.e. failure of the outsource partner's insurance programme to respond) and/or surplus risk up to higher levels. This issue needs to be addressed in the initial outsource bid documentation so that any prospective bidder knows what type and levels of insurance they will be required to carry if they are successful in their bid for the services in question.

It is important that outsource bid documentation makes it quite clear what type of insurance is required and that the sums insured, retentions and insurer quality are all addressed:

- *Type of insurance.* Insurance contracts tend to be client specific and the use of generic terms such as professional indemnity or crime insurance is not sufficient. The contract should make it quite clear what the outsource partner's insurance should cover (specimen insurance forms can be included in the appendix to avoid misunderstandings).

• *Sum insured.* The amount of the sum insured needs to be sufficient to cover both an expected and an unexpected loss event. It should be borne in mind that the amount of loss may be considerable despite the fact that the gain made by a dishonest individual may not. In a data-processing function an employee of an outsource partner may be 'selling' details about a bank's customer accounts for £5 per set of customer information. The information may then be sold on by a criminal purchaser for a higher amount and ultimately used by yet another criminal to remove all of the funds held in the customer's account. The loss suffered in such cases can be hundreds or thousand of times the gain made by the original criminal. The bank and their insurers will want to recover the full amount of the loss suffered by them irrespective of the modest improper personal gain made by the outsource company's employee who triggered the event that led to the final loss. This issue can often lead to arguments between contracting parties since the outsource partners are often resident in countries where criminal aspirations are low, while in contrast the bank's main customer base may reside in a country where average bank deposits can exceed the lifetime earnings of an employee of the outsource partner.

• *Retention.* The self-insured retention contained in any insurance policy purchased by an outsource partner should not be so large that it cannot be funded out of cash flow. Since insurance premiums tend to decrease as the size of the self-insured retention increases, some insurance buyers may be tempted to assume unrealistic self-insured retentions in order to reduce costs. It is advisable to set a maximum amount of any self-insured retention that can be acceptable to avoid such problems.

• *Insurer quality.* In determining a standard for insurer quality in relation to operational risks, Basel II determined that an insurer should be 'A' rated or better by Standard and Poors, Moodys or any equivalent rating agency. Many banks will apply a similar standard to organisations to which they transfer their own risk via an insurance contract. The requirement for 'A'-rated insurers to provide the cover for the outsource partner can cause problems. For example, in India the insurance industry is closely regulated and insurance must be underwritten by locally established insurers – many of whom will not be rated 'A' or better. In such instances the bank that is outsourcing the function will need to determine whether it is willing to relax its requirements for insurer security. When doing so such issues as quality of reinsurance, etc. will need to be taken into account.

Specific vs. non-specific insurance

For many years banks have been outsourcing cash-transportation services to organisations such as Brinks, etc. These service providers have put in place specific insurances for the benefit of their banking clients, and the banks that take advantage of this insurance as a part of the service then arrange contingent insurance for their own account to protect them if an actual loss exceeds the amount of insurance arranged by the transporting company or if the insurance arranged by the transporting company does not pay for some reason. Cash transportation is an easier area to address, since the amount of potential loss can be estimated in advance. This will not be the case for, say, IT outsourcing, where one employee of an outsource service provider could cause a significant loss far in excess of the contract value or worth. Despite this latter point, the insurance structure that has been developed, tried and tested for use with outsourced cash transportation can be adapted to work in the case of outsourcing of other services.

In any event, a formal review of the policy language of any outsource partner's proposed insurance coverage should be carried out and consideration given to how such coverage 'meshes' with the bank's own policies, since there are various ways in which the two could conflict. Many insurance policies will contain a 'Condition' that states:

> It is agreed that, in the event of loss, this Policy, insofar as it covers loss also covered by other insurance or indemnity, shall only pay claims for the excess of the amount of such other insurance or indemnity. As excess insurance this Policy shall not apply or contribute to the payment of any loss until the amount of such other insurance or indemnity shall have been exhausted.

If the outsource partner's insurances and the bank's own insurances both contain this clause and they both insure the same loss event, then a question will arise over which insurance policy should pay and it is possible that neither one will until a court rules on which, if any, policy should pay.

It needs to be made quite clear in the bid documentation as to whether the outsource provider's insurance should be treated as more specific than the insurances of the bank when it comes to losses caused by the outsource partner's employees or activities.

Meaning of 'loss'

The definition of 'loss' as it appears in the bank's own crime insurance and that of the outsource partner is very important. As has already been stated, it is a normal condition of most crime insurance policies that the insured shall bear a self-insured excess that is applied to 'each and every loss'. The current main area of concern as far as outsourcing is concerned is the sale by an outsource partner's employees of data relating to a bank's customers accounts. As stated above under 'Sum insured', the outsource employee might only be paid £5 per data set, but the misuse of the data by the end-user criminal could result in the bank having to reimburse its customer for a loss that may be £1,000 or more. Whatever the loss may ultimately be, the loss suffered by an individual bank's customer is unlikely to be more than the amount of the self-insured retention applicable to the bank's own insurance. Most financial institution crime insurance policies define a loss that involves the acts of an employee or another party as one 'loss', even though the employee or other party may have committed many separate acts and caused many separate losses up until the date that the 'loss' is discovered. Thus, if a single bank employee sells 100 data sets, all relating to different bank customers, the bank's crime insurers should treat all of the sales and subsequent loss as 'one loss' for the purposes of insurance. The definition of 'loss' is very important, since without a definition that seeks to cumulate the dishonest acts of one employee or third party all single losses could be self-insured irrespective of the overall total amount. If, as stated above, an employee of the bank sells 100 separate sets of customer details on separate occasions and each set of data is then misused by criminals to cause loss to each customer of £1,000, the bank will be responsible for £100,000 of loss suffered by their customers. If the whole £100,000 is treated as one 'loss', as far as insurance is concerned, then it is likely that a significant part of the loss will be recoverable from insurers. If, however, each customer loss is treated separately, it is unlikely that any recovery will be made from insurers. It is important to make sure that an outsource partner's insurance allows for such loss events to be cumulative in the same manner and that the bank's own insurance treats all losses caused by the acts of one outsource partner as being one 'loss'.

In June 2006 various newspapers and radio news broadcasts reported that an employee of HSBC's electronic data-processing centre in Bangalore, India and his external associates were alleged to have removed £233,000 from 20 customers of the bank. The employee allegedly accessed personal and debit card information on the customers in question and passed this through to associates in the UK who conducted fraudulent transactions through ATMs, debit cards and telephone-banking services. In October 2006 an investigative journalist, while making the television programme, *Dispatches*, shown on Channel 4 in the UK, posed as a potential financial services call-centre entrepreneur exploring the market in India and seeking to purchase details about UK bank customers. The television programme in question illustrated that there is a market for such data and that it can be obtained for quite modest payments per data set. This is not just an outsource issue, since it is possible to purchase similar information in the UK that has been acquired by persons working in banks' data centres. Where the complications arise is in determining how a loss will be apportioned where outsourcing is involved. Where banks are concerned, criminals will consider them to be prime targets, since their 'stock in trade' is money. For this reason bank regulators are now focusing upon operational risks as much as they do on credit and market risks.

The major operational risk associated with any bank outsourcing involves employee dishonesty in either the bank's or an outsource partner's operation.

There are other risks, however, that can occur that do not involve any dishonest acts of employees of either party. Most outsource contracts do involve the exchange of data between the bank and the outsource partner. The degree of communication will vary in sophistication, but in many cases the outsource partner will need 'online' access to the bank's systems in order to carry out their role effectively. Most banks purchase specialist insurance policies covering electronic and computer crime risk exposures. Such insurance policies cover the risks associated with third parties penetrating the bank's computer systems or a third party inserting fraudulent messages, viruses, etc. into the bank's computer communications system. When a third party, such as an outsource partner, gains access to the bank's network, it is necessary to look at such insurance carefully to ensure that the cover is specifically adjusted to allow for these changes.

Negligent acts or errors

As in the case of criminal acts, it is highly likely that a bank will be held vicariously liable for the negligent acts or errors of any party acting or purporting to act on their behalf under the terms of an outsource agreement.

Most professional indemnity insurance policies (which address the legal liability of a bank resulting from the negligent acts of its employees) will limit the scope of the cover they provide to the acts of the bank's own employees. Any other party, for whose acts the bank may be held vicariously liable, may not be covered unless the insurance contract has been specifically amended. This is particularly likely in the current insurance market, where insurers have significantly narrowed coverage scope under such insurances.

Where insurers are asked by banks to amend their professional indemnity insurance to include the negligent acts or errors of an outsource company's employees, the insurers will be particularly interested in who the outsource partners are and the extent of any insurance that they may have in place that can be claimed against should a claim be made against the bank. It is as well for the bank to consult with its insurers prior to finalising any outsource agreements, since specialist financial institution insurers usually have a wide knowledge of organisations engaged in financial services all over the world and their input may be valuable.

It is normal for outsource contracts to specify that the outsource service provider must indemnify the bank for any legal liability that the bank incurs as a consequence of the acts of the outsource service provider's employees. As has already been observed, however, there is usually a financial imbalance between banks and their outsource service providers. As a general rule banks will have a professional indemnity insurance programme providing limits of indemnity in the hundreds of millions of pounds, whereas an overseas outsource service provider is more likely to have insurance that provides limits of indemnity in the hundreds of thousands or low millions of pounds. Equally, the service provider is likely to have limited assets to claim against in the event the insurance is for any reason inadequate. It should also be borne in mind that an outsource company's professional indemnity insurance will be in place primarily to defend the outsource company against any claims that may be made against it by a third party, including the bank that has entered into the outsource agreement with them. The fact that an outsource company has a significant professional indemnity insurance policy in place may not necessarily insure to the benefit of the bank engaging them, indeed it might work against them since the outsource company may be in a position to mount a vigorous defence of any allegation made against them.

Another problem that often arises with professional indemnity insurance concerns the 'contractual liability exclusion'. This excludes any liability assumed by way of contract that would not have existed in the absence of the contract. Thus, if a bank or its outsource partner reaches an agreement to apportion liability between them in a manner that would not otherwise exist in the absence of the contract provisions, it may create problems with either party's professional indemnity insurance if the contractual liability exclusion is not amended to take account of the specific contract provisions.

In the area of liability, the exposure created by each outsource contract will vary according to the nature of the service being outsourced. Where customer information is concerned, there is likely to be a considerable imbalance between, say, the liability of an EU-based bank for a breach of confidentiality towards its customer base and the view of the potential liability of an overseas outsource partner. It is unlikely that outsource service providers domiciled in other continents, for example, will have sufficient assets and/or appropriate insurance protection to be able adequately to indemnify a major EU-based bank for a significant breach of confidentiality involving the bank's clients. The issues of liability and how insurance responds to this need to be carefully addressed at the outset.

Conclusion

The process of outsourcing, particularly to overseas service providers, is becoming an accepted practice in the service industries. In a true outsource situation between equal partners, the transfer of services normally involves the contractual transfer of most of the risks associated with providing the services. Where the outsource service provider is not the equal of the party seeking to outsource the service, then the simple transfer of risk via the use of contractual indemnities alone will not sufficiently address the risk issues. In the latter case, insurance becomes vitally important, since a few hours spent during the pre-contract due diligence phase can save hundreds of legal hours (and possibly millions of pounds of uninsured and irrecoverable loss) at a later stage if anything goes wrong.

Regulators have been quick to point out the risks associated with outsourcing services and to provide guidance on how such contracts should be addressed. Any bank contemplating entering into an outsource agreement should:

- consider the allocation of risk inherent in such contracts;
- ensure that, at the pre-contract stage, they have a clear strategy, including the role to be played by insurance, which flows into any proposed contract language; and
- carefully assess, and if necessary amend, both their own insurance arrangements and those required or proposed under the outsource agreement.

Where outsource agreements are concerned, it is also important for banks to keep insurers well advised of the process. Insurers are risk partners who have agreed to assume some of the operational risks assumed by the bank. When the nature of those risks is altered in any material way, such as the outsourcing of a particular function to a third party organisation, insurers expect to be consulted, not just informed after the fact. Failure to keep insurers informed could result in the bank's insurance being voidable, or alternatively cover could be restricted.[2]

Notes

1 *International Convergence of Capital Measurement and Capital Standards: Basel II* (June 2004) and *Risk Management Principles for Electronic Banking* (May 2001), Basel Committee on Banking Supervision (Basel: Bank for International Settlements).

2 The draft Solvency II Framework Directive was published by the European Commission on 10 July 2007. The proposed Directive seeks to update EU insurance law and is designed to improve consumer protection, modernise supervision and improve market integration. Solvency II requires insurance and reinsurance undertakings to focus on the active identification, measurement and management of risks and to consider future developments such as new business plans or the possibility of catastrophic events that might affect their financial standing. Insurers will be required to 'know' their own risk exposure in areas such as Credit, Market and Operational risk in the same way that banking operations are expected to under the rules of Basel II. Solvency II specifically refers to Outsourcing and makes it clear that when an insurance or reinsurance undertaking outsources operational functions they remain fully responsible for discharging all of their obligations under the proposed Directive. The proposed Directive goes on to state that an insurance or reinsurance undertaking shall not outsource important operational activities in such a way that it leads to:
(i) any impairment of its governance systems;
(ii) any undue increase in the operational risk;
(iii) an impairment of the ability of the supervisory authority to monitor compliance of the undertaking with its obligations;
(iv) the continuous and satisfactory service to policyholders being undermined.
Insurance undertakings across the EU have been quick to embrace outsourcing, often with mixed success. The European Commission has made it clear in the draft version of Solvency II that it will expect supervisors and regulators across the EU to ensure that outsourcing of an operational function does not result in an abrogation of responsibility for that area of activity on the part of an insurance organisation. Outsourcing a function is clearly not seen as a valid means of transferring risk. Each new Financial Services related Directive or International Supervisory statement seems to make greater specific reference to outsourcing as an area of activity and the approach of all of them is to place an onus upon national supervisory authorities to ensure that when a function is outsourced the risks as well as the cost benefits are analysed and that the outsourcing organisation has a responsibility to ensure that the party to whom a function is outsourced comes within the scope of their corporate governance. This implies that simply relying upon contractual standards and service level agreements to provide a remedy if something goes wrong is insufficient. The outsourcing party has a duty to ensure, as part of its risk assessment, that the provider of outsource services is capable of providing the same level of governance, service and security that would be in force if they provided the service themselves.

6 The operational background to outsourcing

Graeme Fry

Introduction

This chapter deals with the operational issues surrounding the outsourcing of business processes, often known as business process outsourcing (BPO). BPO is a significant and growing business area. The UK market alone is anticipated to grow by nearly 10 per cent in 2007, representing a market worth in excess of £5 billion.[1] Historically, BPO has proven particularly attractive to organisations that have high-volume, industrialised back-office processing operations. The pioneers in this area have tended to be the banks, insurance companies and other financial services organisations; though it is true to say that in recent years activity has increased rapidly in the public sector and in industries such as telecommunications, utilities and health. The outsourcing industry is now maturing and managers responsible for operations are beginning to understand the pitfalls inherent in moving non-core – but often business-critical – activities outside the organisation. Please see Chapter 1 (pp. 4–5: 'Definitions of outsourcing') for a full definition of what is meant by the terms 'outsourcing' and 'offshoring', as they are not interchangeable.

In most organisations outsourcing non-core activities is treated as a strategic decision based on the business priorities in force at the time. However, experience shows that the success or failure of an outsourcing exercise crucially depends on the preparedness of the operation and its processes before outsourcing takes place. This means understanding what happens at the front line at a detailed level and, for example, knowing that an operation is not dependent on the unwritten knowledge of front-line operators to be workable. Generally, senior management is very rarely close enough to a business unit or its operations to make that judgement, as numerous examples of unsatisfactory attempts at outsourcing bear witness. It is not uncommon for the cost savings and improvement in service quality outlined in the original business case to remain elusive.

Initially, management tends to review the operations considered for outsourcing against data recording overall process performance and costs. The actual day-to-day working of the process to be outsourced is not understood and not taken into consideration. In most operations front-line staff face problems, often on a daily basis, which are overcome with minor process improvements that are not formally recorded. The relationships built with advisers, customers and suppliers and the associated informal support systems are almost certainly overlooked in the outsourcing decision process. Failure to recognise and replicate these successful operational activities can result in an apparently well-planned outsourcing project not meeting its objectives.

The decision to outsource is often to provide additional capacity or to take advantage of lower labour costs in a different location (offshoring). However, there are almost always major cost savings to be had by implementing good operations management within functional areas as they stand. This can usually be done without major investment or IT system developments. If full benefits are to be achieved through outsourcing, the processes transferred should first be made as effective and efficient as possible. This will pay dividends in immediate cost savings and service improvement, allow operations to be transferred to an outsource partner smoothly and allow the partner to deliver business case benefits without first trying to fix broken processes.

There are huge reputational risks for an organisation if an outsourced operation fails to meet customer requirements. In an increasingly dynamic and uncertain business environment, in-depth evaluation of these issues can be a key determinant of project success or failure. Experience gained from rescuing problem projects indicates that, if not approached in the right way, there is a high risk that outsourcing projects can fail to deliver expected returns. The key issue is the importance of proving the robustness of existing business processes before they are outsourced.

Compared to the potential benefits in terms of immediate cost savings and continued reliability of processing after outsourcing, the time and resources required to improve existing operations management are small. The techniques companies have used tend to be simple and address the day-to-day activities carried out by the operators involved in the process. Towards the end of this chapter we introduce a Decision Matrix', which will assist in evaluating the robustness and suitability of an operation for outsourcing and help identify which areas need to be addressed in order to proceed.

Processes – the building blocks

Specialists in operations management who work on optimising back-office activities think in terms of processes. They see an operation as a collection of often interlinked processes working to deliver the outcome desired by the customer. This might be the opening of a new account or the payment of an insurance claim or delivering a new mortgage offer. How well these processes work determines the experience that the customer will have and the processing costs incurred by the organisation. Operations management may be the unglamorous aspect of an organisation, but we will show that getting it right is crucial to successful BPO.

The competitive strategy of delivering cost efficiencies and standardised quality was introduced through the mass-production techniques of Henry Ford, first adopted and optimised in the manufacturing sector. Many years later, a more sophisticated version of volume production has been embraced across most service sectors. An organisation's value-adding activities are broken down into their constituent parts, functionally laid out and linked to facilitate the flow of a product or service. In manufacturing units this is often implemented through a production line, and now this is replicated in service organisations. Instead of a conveyor belt as might be found in a factory, the 'product' is transferred through IT systems or as paper from tray to tray.

In its simplest terms a process consists of a number of repetitive activities that will transform a product or service from one state to another. It starts upon receipt of information or a part-completed item and finishes after value has been added and the item is passed on to the next process or to the end customer. A process can be manned by an individual or a team and ideally it should be standardised through a documented procedure.

The chain of activities or processes that link a customer request to delivery of the final product or service can be seen as a 'value chain': each step or process adds value until the customer's requirements are met. The customer's perceptions of the value-adding activity are often determined by the last step in the value chain. This step may consist of answering a query, delivering a product or providing a quotation and often this is where the blame is laid when things go wrong. These parts of customer interaction more than any other can damage a business's reputation if not delivered in a reliable and sensitive manner. A business determined to reduce costs may select these areas for early outsourcing. If the process has not been optimised, the potential for damage to the business's reputation is high.

An understanding of the processes and the value chain that they deliver is the first step in any improvement activity. The value chain may include processes that are manned by low-skilled workers in some parts with high-skilled professionals being employed in other parts. Regardless of the level of professional skill required, these front-line operators should be considered the true 'process experts'. They hold the key to any pre-outsource improvement activity.

Another issue is that, over time, processes can unfortunately degrade. This may be due to activities changing within the process and standards slowly drifting away from earlier design standards, but more frequently it is due to changes outside the boundaries of the process. It is not unusual to find processes that have been modified several times to meet external demands and consequently the once streamlined process has become a Heath Robinson fix loaded with inefficiencies, unnecessary practices and duplication. Waste becomes institutionalised into everyday business practices. As this breakdown occurs, the discipline of the process team is often lost. The old way of processing no longer works, so individuals each find their own best way, thus causing further inefficiencies and inconsistent output.

The waste is frequently not obvious to those outside the process and those working within the process may come to accept the inefficiencies as normal or may be too busy to address them. This can result in the inefficiencies and costs built into the process being exported through outsourcing, thereby reducing the potential benefits. It will also make life very difficult for those trying to take the process over.

Case study: Offshoring an underwriting operation to India

The following case study concerns a large financial services organisation. It highlights how a logical strategic development led to the outsourcing of an apparently well-established, simple process to an experienced Indian partner. The problems encountered at first appeared to be minor, but eventually they absorbed a high level of management time resulting in failure to deliver expected benefits.

Introduction

This case study describes some of the issues a major UK life and pensions business (the Company) encountered in the outsourcing of an operation to India. Although the Company was initially convinced it had made a sensible strategic business decision, it quickly became apparent that it had overlooked many operational considerations that undermined the business case. Unanticipated costs were incurred and there was a serious risk of damaging customer confidence.

The underlying causes of many of the problems encountered and the options to overcome them are discussed.

The business problem

The Company identified the opportunity to aggressively grow its market share in the life insurance market. An analysis of the operation indicated that it was the underwriting process that required most time to complete and was also the most complex process. It requires highly skilled and qualified underwriters to make complex underwriting decisions and correspond with doctors and other health professionals.

Qualified underwriters are in demand, take several years to train and are therefore difficult to recruit. The business calculated that, with its current structure, it would have to increase its underwriting capacity by 30 per cent to meet planned growth targets. An industry-recognised system for training and qualifying underwriters also tends to limit supply. Applications from customers are underwritten by an underwriter in line with his or her accreditation level. Over time an underwriter can reach higher levels of certification up to the ultimate level of 'unlimited underwriter'. This progression takes several years even for the most able individuals.

An automated decision tool for the simplest underwriting decisions was purchased by the Company and became increasingly effective at dealing with simple cases. As many as possible of the simple contracts were processed by the decision-making tool, thus avoiding the need for highly qualified underwriters. It was also recognised that further advantages in cost and capacity were available if some of the remaining manual underwriting process could be outsourced to an offshore partner with low labour costs.

The decision to outsource was further encouraged by the fact that the Company had already successfully outsourced some basic administration tasks to an Indian partner. This comprised the scanning of handwritten proposals from customers, which were then sent electronically to India. These were then read on screen and loaded onto the Company's customer information system by agents at the outsource partner. The transfer of this basic process replaced the same activity in the UK and had been achieved in line with target cost savings.

Signs of breakdown

Initially, the transfer of the process was considered to have been very successful. Software was installed at the partner's site and seemed to work well. Process maps documenting the flow of activities already existed and were handed over to the new operations team. Training of local staff was completed. A process performance measurement system similar to the one used in the UK was implemented and production was started up.

When operations went live, however, the throughput was lower than expected. At first this was thought to be due to the steep learning curve being experienced. After some time it became apparent that the new team would never be able to deliver the expected output. An investigation was launched to discover the cause of the underperformance.

The investigation revealed that the process was not as robust as initially thought. The process maps that were transferred with the outsourcing project and used as the basis of the training were revealed to be no more than the initial process design documents. The experienced UK staff had over time introduced a number of work-arounds to fix or improve elements of the process. These improvements had been developed by individual operators for their own use, and therefore the amendments were not recorded. As management did not consult with the operations team before transferring the process, they had incorrectly assumed that the process documents fully reflected operational practice.

The automated decision tool was also found to be limited and inflexible. The UK team had consisted of experienced operational staff supported by highly qualified colleagues who were consulted when difficulties were encountered. Software short cuts and system overrides had been gradually introduced, and when these failed the team resorted to consulting the underwriters to solve problems. The process transfer removed this support mechanism, so when problems were encountered by the outsource partner the solution was several thousand miles away in the UK.

It also became apparent that staff retention in India was not as good as expected. The Company's outsourcing partner was located close to a series of outsourced operations used by other UK insurers. The industry standard for underwriting training means it is possible to transfer between employers part way through training, in much the same way as 'part-qualified' accountants transfer between firms in the UK. Unfortunately, the Company's partner was not the most attractive firm to work for locally and it proved difficult to retain the required numbers of staff beyond the most basic qualification level. This was the very level of work that the automated underwriting system was increasingly taking away from the manual process.

Finally, the new process still required some communication with medical staff based in the UK. The distances involved obviously incurred delay, but the major problem was caused by relatively inexperienced staff communicating with professional UK staff who were used to a specific and technical language shared by fellow professionals. The correspondence became confused and extended as each side requested further clarification of what had been provided or requested.

These problems started to absorb UK management time, thereby eroding the expected cost benefits and adversely impacting the customer experience.

Pressure increases

The contract agreed between the Company and its outsourcing partner was on a fixed-fee basis. Fundamentally, a number of people had been employed to deliver a capacity that would meet an expected increase in demand. As UK management had not appreciated the extent to which the documented process had been amended to overcome systems shortcomings, the capability and capacity of the documented process was overestimated.

Due to natural seasonal variations, demand varied throughout the year and the outsource partner's team found on some occasions that they had spare capacity. One of the largest wins of this process transfer was expected to be cost reduction. The identification of spare capacity at certain times of the year was seen to be yet another factor eroding the business case benefits. UK management therefore took the decision to keep the Indian team fully occupied to maximise the cost savings. This was achieved by transferring work that had initially been classified as too complex in the hope of maintaining the efficiency levels. As a result, underwriters in India were asked to underwrite work for which they were not properly qualified. This necessitated moving properly qualified UK underwriters out to India on secondment. These underwriters then checked the work of the less-experienced local underwriters. The volume of work that could be processed did increase but only at the cost of double handling.

Although the Indian team remained fully employed, the final cost of supporting the offshore outsourcing partner increased well beyond expected levels.

Impact on performance

Ultimately, the desired processing times and cost benefits were never achieved. The process was continually amended to handle certain types of work and the UK arm of the business frequently provided assistance to help overcome problems that the partner's staff could not resolve.

Backlogs and waiting times extended to levels greater than those experienced in the UK. It became apparent that UK management had not appreciated the value of the informal relationships built over many years between their operational staff and the professionals they dealt with. The new team was not as adept at developing a working relationship with distant professionals and therefore could not efficiently manage the flow of information as well as the UK operation once had.

To summarise, the process transfer had not delivered the expected increase in capacity or cost reduction. A new support team in the UK had to be created to assist the outsource team and the time to turn around a piece of work increased with potential knock-on damage to customer relations.

How could it have been improved?

Could anything have been done to make the outsourcing project successful?

Most significantly, the experience of the front-line operators was overlooked in the transfer of the process. It was assumed that the process was being worked as designed, and the enhancements contrived and implemented by the operational staff were overlooked.

The success of the process transfer could have been greatly increased if the 'as is' process had been thoroughly understood and documented at operator level. Whilst this may have required training for the operators and perhaps the extra cost of facilitators, the resulting process maps would have established the process as it was being worked by front-line staff. With this as a starting point the true capacity, staff skills required and level of training needed could have been worked out.

The efficiency of the process could have been reviewed before outsourcing to remove in-built waste (see 'Productivity' section, p. 126) and inefficiencies. It is not unusual for this exercise alone to deliver a 20 per cent or greater increase in process capacity. These efficiencies can be crystallised through standardising the process, making it robust and easier to transfer. It is even possible that such significant increases in capacity may undermine the case for outsourcing altogether.

An operational risk analysis should have been completed. In this case, most of the experience and skills were with the operators; unfortunately, they were not consulted. A team of operators cannot be expected to complete a risk analysis on their own, but a focused workshop to draw out the key issues would have extracted the critical information very easily. There is often a temptation to skip risk analysis; however, it was later shown that such an exercise could have identified many of the problems in advance and contributed significantly to the decision to outsource or not.

Finally, the capability of the IT system was overestimated. The business had assumed that there would be limited variability in the type of work being processed. Unfortunately, this was not the case and the system was too inflexible to handle a high percentage of the workload. This resulted in hand-offs back to the UK where highly qualified underwriters could manually process this work. A better analysis of the type of work suitable for the outsourced operation would have identified 'rarities' and diverted them to another work stream, thus avoiding the cost of transfer, failed processing and the inevitable return to the UK.

Key learning points

The case study highlights that what at first appeared to be a logical and profitable decision to outsource to an offshore partner can quickly turn into a management problem that may never be fully resolved and that may undermine the expected benefits and jeopardise the business's reputation.

Unfortunately, the problems identified in this case study are neither unique nor comprehensive. Outsourcing can lead to unintended operational consequences. In another example, an organisation outsourced a process to a specialist organisation within the UK, the intended purpose of which was to increase capacity and allow the business to focus on more critical work. To manage output the amount of work completed daily was measured with agreed targets. Penalties and rewards were written into the contract.

It was not until some time after the transfer that the process was analysed systematically. This revealed that throughput times had increased dramatically due to the amount of work in progress (WIP), which led to complaints about customer service. When this was checked with the outsource partner it became apparent that, in order to achieve the contracted targets and rewards, they were cherry-picking the easier work out of the WIP and fast-tracking it through the process. This resulted in some customers receiving an extremely poor service.

Another organisation thought it had a successful outsource project. However, when it analysed the time required to prepare documents for transfer, make copies and duplicate files, progress chase, quality check returned work and file the original documents, it was found that the benefits were trivial.

The Outsourcing Decision Matrix

Developed from the experience of working on many outsourcing projects and the resulting problems, an Outsourcing Decision Matrix has been developed to enable organisations to fully evaluate the factors that will impact on an outsourcing project. The decision tool comprises a matrix of ten key business issues that an organisation needs to address when considering a potential project for outsourcing.

The critical areas identified by the Decision Matrix are:

Productivity	Quality
Independence	Stability
Boundaries	Training
Predictability	Financial viability
Inputs	Reliability

These process attributes are described in detail in the next part of this chapter.

Productivity

Is the true productivity level of the process in question known?

Analysis reveals that, in many cases, processes are being operated inefficiently with lots of in-built waste. Process waste is an operations management concept developed by highly efficient Japanese manufacturers and used to identify activities for which customers would be unwilling to pay. The discipline developed by this approach encourages teams to question and then strive to remove activities that do not add value; that is, activities that previously may have been seen to be integral to the process. This is particularly relevant to service organisations. Over a short period of time productivity improvements of the order of 20 per cent are achievable. Customer service improves and the analysis explores and records at a working level how the process operates.

Process inefficiencies that are exported with an outsourced process can prove difficult to remove. The new team are usually instructed to follow existing procedures and tend to focus on how their process integrates with other parts of the business. They are therefore cautious about making changes. The result is that, despite a level of cost saving stemming from lower labour rates, the operation continues to underperform.

Only those areas of the business and associated processes that have already been optimised should be considered for outsourcing, where further cost improvement can only be delivered by lower labour rates. At the same time, analysis of the benefits of outsourcing can fail to take account of hidden costs when it comes to the demands of running an effective outsourced operation.

Independence

Is only limited customer interaction required – that is, are other external inputs required to complete the process?

A process can be located at any part of a value chain with the inputs and outputs perhaps linking into other in-house processes. In these situations lines of communication are short and often immediate, relationships will have been built over many years, and there is also the possibility that process team members have experience of working in the neighbouring processes. Some processes are, however, dependent upon external contacts. These may be with customers, suppliers or professional advisers. The effectiveness and reputation of an organisation can be dependent upon the views of these external bodies.

It is possible to formalise the communications with the outside world and, if offshoring is being considered, to select locations with appropriate time zones to facilitate the communication process. This should all work well providing the inputs needed or the outputs generated are simple and repetitive. If the process, however, requires or delivers a bespoke service or product, then specific information may be required or requested. In these circumstances the formalised systems are not so helpful and communications become more dependent upon the individual. If the skills required to manage communications have not been developed there is the potential for delay and conflict.

Complex processes interacting with the outside world are dependent upon good working practice, but also upon informal relationships and the ability to empathise quickly with others. To assume that a distant outsource partner has these skills in-house may lead to problems that cannot be easily overcome and could eventually cause significant damage to the business's reputation.

Boundaries

Are the start and end points of the process defined and clear, thus enabling confident hand-off?

From a senior management perspective the structure of an organisation may appear to be clear if not obvious. Organisation charts show reporting lines and areas of responsibility, process diagrams may have been prepared and job descriptions will be available. The business will give the impression of being designed, organised and perhaps functioning as a well-oiled machine.

At the front line this model of a well-functioning business often breaks down. Equipment fails, sickness depletes the workforce and unexpected demand or customer complaints require the business to adjust constantly. The model organisation described by the charts and process maps may be no more than a rarely achieved ideal.

Many operations managers see their role as being the manager of this daily chaos and in most instances they are very good at it. Staff are moved around to fill gaps created by absenteeism or to meet unexpected demand, processes may work at a lower capacity so resources can be diverted elsewhere or specialists may be inserted into teams to help them overcome unexpected problems.

The whole business at the operations level can be very fluid, moving constantly around the official structure with boundaries between processes changing to accommodate the most recent problem. A process can be identified for outsourcing from the formal business charts and maps, but if the boundaries are flexible then problems may be experienced when the process is extracted for outsourcing.

Further confusion can be created when the processing team does not encompass all of the skills required to complete the work. This may be due to the absenteeism mentioned earlier, but also some processes are designed to be dependent upon external specialist help. This requires partially completed work to be transferred out and then returned to the process. The hand-offs and returns have to be monitored and managed carefully. This creates more work and extends throughput times. It is also highly dependent upon the working relationship between the parties involved in the hand-offs. Consequently, this type of process is usually unsuitable for outsourcing.

A consistent process with dependable boundaries that clearly show when a process starts and ends and what the expected inputs and outputs are should be demonstrated to perform well under normal working conditions before being considered suitable for outsourcing. Evidence obtained before outsourcing that the process boundaries are stable and consistent will limit the risk.

Predictability

Is the process predictable – that is, is Step A followed by Step B? In other words, is the same process followed for each and every item going through that process?

A firm of solicitors opened a new arm to its business that focused on simple repetitive work. The new department was managed by an experienced solicitor who had been involved in this type of work for several years and knew the market very well. Within a few years they had four teams, each with several administrators. The manager designed the working practices and ensured that no one deviated from them.

Eventually the manager moved on and the business was considered to be strong enough to continue without her. An analysis of the business approximately 18 months after she had left revealed not only that every team had developed their own way of working but that they were all aware that the others were 'doing it differently'. The consequences were that the customer experience depended upon which team they worked with. Also, success in winning new work and the time taken to complete the process varied with each team. Strong leadership was missing and work was being completed to serve the interests of the team members rather than the business.

The above example demonstrates how quickly a process can degrade and some of the problems this can cause. There can only be one best way of completing a process. This needs to be agreed and recorded so that everyone can follow it.

Processes do, however, develop over time and consequently the documented way of working needs to keep pace with change, thus ensuring a consistent and predictable approach that delivers the one best way of working. The documents themselves can provide further benefits if they are presented in a simple, easy-to-understand format that can be used to guide day-to-day work and assist in the training of new team members. An indication that such a document is successful is when the local team take ownership and start to update the procedures when change or improvements are implemented.

Confidence in the ability and structures of the process to provide predictable and repeatable practices without the need of constant management interventions is required of any process considered for outsourcing.

Inputs

Have rarities been removed from the flow leaving only Runners and Repeaters – that is, is only the mass of standard items to be outsourced?

Anything requiring special treatment or expertise to complete should be kept in-house. An analysis of the work being received by a team will indicate that there are different types of input. The majority will be similar and the process will probably have been designed principally to work with these inputs. There will, however, also be items that occur occasionally, that are often more complex and less familiar to the team members. There is also a third type of input that tends to lie between these two groups.

These three groups may be described as:

- *Runners* – high volume, easy to process and requiring low skills;
- *Repeaters* – medium volume, not too dissimilar to Runners, with low skills still being required; and
- *Rarities* – low volume, more complex, requiring high skills or experience.

The value chain in a service organisation should ideally mimic a production line and attempt to make the items flow rapidly through the process. When a process encounters a Rarity it slows down and a queue develops behind. A small percentage of the incoming volume can therefore slow down the processing of the majority of work.

To improve the efficiency of the process, the Rarities should be filtered out and dealt with by an experienced specialist team. In the very best operations the team addresses the cause of the Rarities and eventually turns them into Repeaters or Runners.

A process that is outsourced with the Rarities included in the work flow will require a more flexible and higher-skilled or more experienced team than one that is dealing only with Runners and Repeaters. This is obviously not desirable. Best practice is to remove the Rarities from the process and have the outsourced process deal only with the simpler Runners and Repeaters.

Quality

Is the process capable – that is, is the defect rate under control?

An operation should consistently deliver high-quality output. Customers should receive the product or service that meets their expectations. Ideally, the operations should eliminate additional costs incurred in rectifying problems, dealing with complaints or investigating the causes of quality failure. The management of quality in the manufacturing sector is now well developed and sophisticated statistical tools are applied. However, most of the service sector has not developed its quality management to this level.

Quality management systems can range from simple 100 per cent checking to sophisticated statistical control. When a process is stable and predictable then the outputs will be consistent within limits. An understanding of this output will allow the process capability to be defined.

The ideal position is to have a process that always delivers the required quality levels. This provides a level of confidence that the quality will always be at an acceptable level. Checks are still required but they are carried out by the operators to ensure that the process is not drifting away from the expected levels of quality.

Process that provides consistent quality outputs with minimum checking will be suitable for outsourcing. High levels of checking or quality failure will prove to be expensive and require skills that an outsource partner may not yet have developed.

Stability

Is the process in a stable condition?

Any process that has just been changed, for example by recent IT introductions, service level agreement (SLA) changes or interface changes, is not suitable for outsourcing, as further adjustments may be needed to make it work properly. This can cause huge problems in outsourced operations.

The benefit analysis that is required before the decision to outsource is made will make assumptions about the cost, quality and delivery times of the process being considered. Recent changes to the process, its systems or its inputs may adversely affect the consistency of its outputs. After the changes have been made it may well take some time for the process to settle down to a new normal operating level.

Changes may also require that modifications are made to procedures and training material or that new controls are implemented. Processes that have recently undergone, or are scheduled to undergo, change should not be considered for outsourcing until the process is stable once more.

Training

Has the receiving outsourced operation been trained and accredited by the in-house team who actually operate and understand the process?

There can be a steep learning curve causing problems and extra cost, if the receiving outsourced operation has not been trained and sufficiently accredited. In many organisations training is seen to be a specialist position perhaps linked to the Personnel/HR department or an external organisation. If the training is to be delivered to an outsourced partner, then professional trainers or even managers may be required to take on the responsibility of knowledge transfer.

However, the best understanding of the process rests with the people who have worked with it and have assisted in the optimisation of the process. An effective route for passing on this knowledge is to capture the skills and experience of the process operators by training some of them to be trainers themselves. They can then build into the training they offer to the outsource team anecdotes that explain how the process has developed and what problems to expect. Their knowledge will allow them to speak with conviction and to answer any questions in detail and with confidence.

The training should encompass the teams' 'user guides' and process maps and include an accreditation system to ensure that the training is effective. The outsourced partner will experience a level of staff turnover and, to minimise future costs, the training programme should assist in the development of local trainers.

The transfer of skills is critical to the success of an outsourced project and these skills will always be found with the current process operators. Failure to take advantage of this is to accept unnecessary risk.

Financial viability

Are finance calculations based on reasonable and accurate assumptions – that is, level of productivity, attrition rates, erosion of salary differentials, management and travel costs, etc.?

The impression gained from many outsourcing projects is that the potential benefits appear so great that a cost-benefit analysis appears almost irrelevant. This is particularly so when a process is considered for offshoring, where the difference in labour costs can be very high. This may result in opportunities for cost reduction being overlooked as the focus remains only on hourly costs.

There are several areas that need to be investigated and included in the cost-benefit analysis. Wage differentials, for example, are being eroded between the West and the favoured locations for outsourcing, such as India. In Bangalore and Mumbai, for example, there is 15–20 per cent annual salary inflation.[2]

Support and management costs are also often either overlooked or underestimated. This is an area where costs can quickly escalate, particularly if the operational management issues have not been fully addressed.

Finally, the outsourced operation may struggle to reach the levels of productivity achieved by the in-house operation. This may be due to the lack of experience or to staff turnover. A sharp focus on cost alone and reducing hourly rates may also drive outsourced staff to take their newly acquired skills elsewhere.

Reliability

Has a full risk assessment been carried out and have contingency plans been created?

Inevitably things will not go exactly to plan. A formal procedure to identify risks and anticipate them should be undertaken. This is known as a failure mode and effect analysis (FMEA).

Even if all the financial analysis has been completed and the operations management issues addressed, there is still the potential for unforeseen problems to occur. Techniques such as an FMEA use a team to brainstorm potential process problems and the effect they can have on the business and then to generate ideas on how to avoid them or minimise their impact. These techniques should feed into the development of contingency plans. If the process is to be offshored, then the breadth of analysis and level of detail needs to be thorough. The impact of problems on the business is very often directly related to the distance from the home office. What may appear to be a small problem when encountered in a home office may turn into a disaster in a distant office, where the problem has not been seen before and where there is no in-house experience or proven local support.

Detailed and systematic preparation will enable the operation to avoid major problems. Only after all of the above potential pitfalls are taken into account should the attractiveness of outsourcing be assessed. If the operations management issues are seen to be under control then the business is in a position to move forward with confidence.

Decision Matrix – the structure

The Decision Matrix (Table 6.1) has been created using the experience gained from assisting businesses to prepare operations for outsourcing, to

Table 6.1 Outsourcing Decision Matrix

	1	2	3	4	5
Productivity	Continually seeking further improvement	Waste analysed and addressed	Process team understand the waste concept	Capacity planning implemented	Productivity not measured
Independence	Process independent from inputs external to the business	Limited reliance on external input	Service Level Agreements in place with consistent supply	Suppliers and communication channels are reliable	Processing is dependent upon external information
Boundaries	Boundaries of process defined and adhered too	Consistent handovers in and out of the process	Process Maps regularly reviewed	Process mapped	Process has not been documented
Predictability	Team continually improve process and update User Guides	New team members trained in the one best way of working	Process team designed User Guides	Documented procedures in place	Process teams decide on best way to work
Inputs	Volumes of rarities investigated and reduced	Process organised to isolate rarities	Concept of runners, repeaters and rarities understood	Team recognise some types of work take longer	Process team handle all work they encounter
Quality	Statistical tools used to drive quality	Capability of process is known and remains consistent	Quality assurance implemented	Process outputs inspected before release	Complaints and process quality not measured
Stability	Change process has been applied successfully	Change process in place	Process has had no recent changes or plans for major change	Plans in place for new technology, products or systems	Process requirements, inputs or systems have changed recently
Training	Trainers experienced in training novices	Trainers identified within the process team	Training plans in place with post training assessments	Standard training available for new team members	Process team have not recently undergone training
Financial Viability	Changes in salaries and exchange rates estimated	Potential drops in productivity estimated	Costs of support processes and management time is known	Potential gains in productivity have been considered	All current process costs are not recorded
Reliability	Contingency plans prepared	Risks and anticipated problems assessed	Process team involved in risk analysis	Risk analysis prepared	Plans for potential problems not prepared

rescue outsourced processes or to return processes back in-house. It has been designed to be as flexible as possible, avoiding jargon so that it can be applied to all processes being considered for outsourcing. Each process attribute included in the matrix should be considered before making a decision on an outsourcing project. None of the ten attributes should be overlooked even if the performance in all other areas is high. Ensuring that all of the operational issues are examined in detail is important as the costs and potential reputational impacts of getting it wrong are significant. The descriptors provided in the matrix against each attribute should provide an indication of where weaknesses may lie, and how much work may be required to prepare the process for outsourcing.

The columns of the matrix describe how the attributes of the process may develop from being immature and inappropriate for outsourcing (column 5) into the high-performing attributes found in column 1. Process-improvement work should not be considered as pure additional cost as it will deliver benefits prior to outsourcing. It is worth noting that the process Independence attribute, unlike other parts of the matrix, very often cannot be changed without redesigning the process.

The scoring approach is fundamentally one of self-assessment and care should be taken as to who should be involved. An outside assessor could be used but this is not the best solution. Ideally, a team should be enlisted to complete the assessment and recommend the actions that need to be taken. This should include in-house specialists and representatives from the current operations team. The team leader must be willing to challenge and pursue answers to uncomfortable questions, obtaining supporting evidence wherever possible. This work, if completed correctly, will provide benefits in terms of eventual process reliability, the cost of outsourcing and performance improvement.

Interpretation of results

How might the Decision Matrix have been used with the previous case study?

THE TEAM

The business described in the case study (see pp. 121–5) is a large and well-known financial services organisation based in the UK. The first step in assessing the business against the matrix would be to select the team leader. He or she should ideally have a good understanding of operations management and of process and risk analysis but would not be directly involved in the division that owned the process being considered for outsourcing. This person would be respected, capable of directing the team and able to take a dispassionate view of the outcome.

A small team of approximately six individuals would then be assembled. The team should include an operator who works in the process being considered for outsourcing. This person may be difficult to select; he or she must be willing to contribute to the discussion without feeling constrained by more senior people and, more importantly, to assist in achieving the correct business solution rather than trying to defend the existing situation. The team leader's skills in managing the team will be crucial in ensuring that the operator is not alienated and that their knowledge is fully utilised. In some instances it may be necessary to involve more than one operator to ensure that all the relevant knowledge is drawn out. In some businesses a pre-meeting with the team leader, a facilitator and several operators has provided a valuable list of issues that one volunteer can present from and explain to the outsourcing evaluation team.

Other members of the team will probably have specialist skills, possibly including quality, IT, finance or HR. To ensure that a good balance is achieved the team leader would be involved in the selection of the specialists. A good team leader will ensure that the team is well balanced, selecting experience that complements his or her background and skills.

It is also important to have a 'naive' team member who can ask the simple questions. This is someone who is bright and articulate but who has absolutely no connection to the process being considered. These people are very good at challenging and identifying the obvious problems that can be overlooked by the specialists and those close to the project.

The first role of the team is to examine the matrix. They may find that some of the attributes need to be explained or the descriptions of progress in the horizontal panels may need amending to fit their business's culture and language. External expertise may be of help in ensuring that the team fully understands the application of the matrix.

ANALYSIS

The team leader decides in which order the attributes are considered. An area where plenty of information is available is often where most people prefer to start. It helps if a non-controversial decision can be made first, giving the team confidence and demonstrating how the process works.

When the team consider the 'Boundaries' attribute, one of the specialists will most probably have cited the documented process maps as evidence that the process was clearly defined. After consulting the matrix the team will, however, find that this evidence alone leaves them in the 'Not suitable for outsourcing' zone. To move to the 'Some development required before outsourcing' zone the matrix will show that the process maps need to be regularly reviewed and updated. This information is sufficient to guide the team leader and allow him or her to ask specific questions about the documentation and the robustness of the process. The representative from operators on the team would be able to explain quickly why the process maps are no longer appropriate and give an indication of the amount of work required to improve the position in terms of the matrix.

The matrix has now led the team to explore in more detail an area that was initially overlooked. An improvement plan can quickly be prepared and the costs and potential damage caused by working with inappropriate documents avoided.

Similarly, the analysis would have revealed that the existing 'Productivity' of the process had not been examined and concepts of waste were not understood; the risk analysis was not robust, operational contingency plans were not in place and the team did not understand the importance and costs associated with exporting Rarities. The team could then use the matrix to direct their analysis and quickly identify areas requiring improvement prior to outsourcing, thus greatly improving the chances of success and removing some existing costs and reducing the risk of additional costs.

The analysis of the 'Independence' process attribute would, however, be more complex. An experienced team leader familiar with the matrix may have wished to address this part quite early in the analysis. It is a critical area that is very difficult to improve if problems are found.

The matrix would have shown that the process is dependent upon external information and consequently fits into the 'Not suitable for outsourcing' zone. This alone should have flagged up concerns. To move along the improvement axis, suppliers of information and the communication channels would have to be reliable. This analysis has a number of dimensions that a good team leader would ensure were explored. Time zones, technology, technical language and the cooperation of suppliers would all have to be considered. The cooperation of suppliers who were highly skilled professionals depended principally on the existing good relationship with the business's UK staff. Could this be exported or, if not, built afresh by their outsourced partner?

The team could have proposed improvement projects to address the other areas identified, but for the 'Independence' attribute their conclusion would be: 'do not proceed until evidence of the ability to manage external information providers is available'. This would have resulted in a review of the outsource project, which, with the benefit of hindsight, would have been the correct business decision. This might not have meant aborting the project. The conclusion of the analysis would have been that the identified partner was possibly not suitable. This should have led to the search for a new partner, but this time with a specific requirement in mind.

Conclusion

The successful outsourcing of an operation can bring significant business benefits by reducing costs, improving capacity and freeing up management time to focus on more critical issues. In some instances the potential benefits can seem so large that the decision to outsource appears to be self-evident, requiring little or no cost-benefit analysis.

Sufficient experience of outsourcing is now available to demonstrate that many projects develop operations management problems that erode or completely destroy the planned benefits. The viability of the outsourced operation, even though it has been transferred to a lower-wage economy, can be undermined by these operational problems, many of which could have been identified and resolved prior to transfer.

The causes of many of these problems are often apparently minor and would in the normal cause of events be resolved quickly. However, once a process is outsourced and separated from the experience and the expert support it had previously received, then the minor problems can become large and expensive management issues.

Techniques and tools similar to the matrix described above are now available to ensure that operational issues are identified prior to outsourcing. The successful application of such tools depends upon the participation in the analysis of front-line operational staff. They are the people who have the experience of operating the processes being considered for outsourcing and overcoming the normal day-to-day problems encountered by the operation. The matrix and other such tools can identify problems prior to outsourcing and allow realistic and informed decisions to be made with regard to the suitability of a process for outsourcing. If they indicate that the operation is currently unsuitable, there is little point in proceeding.

In some organisations a mindset exists that an operation can be passed to an outsource partner and at that point all the problems and risk are also transferred. This is clearly not the case, as the analysis in this chapter shows. There is no substitute for a clear understanding of the operational issues surrounding a decision to outsource. If they are not taken into account very early in the process then subsequent problems can come back to haunt the organisation as it tries to achieve its business goals.

Notes

1 Samad Masood, 'Market trends: business process outsourcing', published online by Ovum, www.ovum.com, 17 January 2007.

2 Michael Imeson, 'BPO providers must make sure the price is right', from an interview with the Managing Director of LogicaCMG, Guy Warren, *The Banker* (July 2004).

7 Insourcing in the finance industry

Cint Kortmann

What business are we in?

The choices companies have to make are complex. The financial services sector is going through a period of change, much like that of the manufacturing sector some time ago. Whilst organic growth, acquisitions and mergers are very positive and exciting, there comes a time and a need within the period of growth to consolidate and optimise structures and procedures. During this period the business will need to be focused, and in becoming focused it needs to define what the core business is. This process is complicated – the management of a company will have to decide what constitutes core activities, whether that be client-relationship management, database management, administration or product design, to name but a few. On the flip side, the management will also have to decide what the non-core activities of the company are, and what potential there is for streamlining: are these activities best handled internally or externally and if so by whom? Obviously, if an activity is core to the business, management will want to keep full control; however, there may still be a desire to optimise utilisation of resources and, if so, insourcing may play a part.

What is insourcing?

Insourcing can be defined as a way of resourcing personnel. The benefits are clear: by having personnel working within your business alongside employed staff, without having to actually employ them, you have a flexible workforce that can be increased or decreased as the workflow requires. It allows the business management team to focus the overheads and responsibilities of the employed, full-time staff members on the core company activities, leaving the peripheral work to be dealt with on a more streamlined basis. It also frees up management time – there isn't the same need for day-to-day management involvement with those individuals who are insourced as they will generally take their direction from the management of the insourcing company.

Insourcing is already a common feature in certain business departments such as IT, HR and Finance. Project managers are also often used on an interim basis to add an additional skill set or manage a shorter term aim. In certain business areas, particularly technology, it is often useful to be able to 'parachute in' the requisite skill set and know that the business can extract what is required on a short-term basis, rather than having to make a longer-term appointment.

In the financial services sector there has been a great deal of change in the regulatory burden of businesses. At times of change and additional workload it may be advantageous to flex the volume of the workforce to manage certain administrative, non-core operational areas, or where certain skill sets are required for projects that lie outside the normal core operational skill sets of an organisation. Businesses have long understood the insourcing advantages for certain activities, such as in managing the security of buildings, the cleaning and hygiene services or the staff canteen, and individuals also recognise instances of personal insourcing, whether that be a personal fitness trainer, a business mentor or even a driver. More and more temp agencies and interim management and consultancy firms ensure that business organisations have access to the right resources at the right moment – this is a form of insourcing.

In his book *The World is Flat*,[1] Thomas Friedman identifies that even the largest companies in the world are trying to make their structural, traditional core activities flexible, by moving the structural cost to a variable one. The example used within Friedman's text is Toshiba, which has outsourced UPS (United Parcel Service) not only to deliver laptops and computers that need repairing, but also to do the repairs. It should be noted that the difference between insourcing and outsourcing is the devolution of responsibility for delivery. In an outsourced facility the management devolve responsibility for delivery to the supplying party. In Friedman's example the responsibility for what might be considered a traditional core activity is being outsourced. An alternative would have been to 'insource' sufficient resources to continue delivering the repair of laptops in house, utilising additional personnel provided by a third-party supplier. However, it should be noted that, if the management team at Toshiba see their core activity as manufacturers of equipment, then all ancillary activities become non-core and can therefore be delivered by an appropriate third party.

Why insourcing?

Fast-moving and volatile markets, new legislation, challenging local conditions, new players entering markets, global economics, new information and consistent challenges from a competitive environment make it tough to take the right business decisions at the right time. Such decisions are taken among the mêlée of delivering the business on a daily basis and therefore critical decisions with regard to growth, success and failure are taken under pressure.

The ability to be able to see beyond that daily mêlée is of paramount importance. Insourcing assists in a number of ways, mainly by reducing the management time required in managing day-to-day activities, as the personnel delivering the project or 'back-office administration' are doing so under their own volition and are controlled by an external supplier, who will undoubtedly have stringent quality standards. As it is the suppliers who control the work flow, the quantity and quality of personnel needed to deliver the aims and objectives of the work is also their responsibility. Insourcing therefore delivers the right number of people, at the right skill level for each phase of a project, ensuring that an optimum work rate is maintained at all times. Thus, there is no more worry for the business management about seasonal or workflow fluctuations, people on holiday or sick leave, or leavers and joiners. Together with the business management, the insourcing company identifies the work to be done and the strategy to deliver and then reports back to management, thus ensuring that the company project aims and objectives are delivered, on time and within budget.

Insourcing fits perfectly within the insurance and banking sectors, by making it easy to adapt to changing markets, seasonal fluctuations, new business regulations, employment legislative changes or the specific demands of a new contract or opportunity, for example when a business needs an immediate increase in workforce numbers or specific skill sets to win and implement a deal. In addition, there has been much in the financial services press over the last few years regarding how difficult it is to attract new bright young talented individuals to the industry; insourcing may be a way of plugging some of the gaps.

Talent&Pro – an insourcing company

Talent&Pro has focused the delivery of their insourcing model within the financial services industry, thus allowing the companies within the sector to focus on the optimisation of their own core activities.

Talent&Pro was established in 1999, and their insourcing concept has been continually developed into the refined, innovative concept it is now. Fundamental to the concept of Talent&Pro was the need to create a shared win-win mechanism for clients. Encouraging companies to move their traditional overhead structural costs to a variable cost model, Talent&Pro ensured that companies could rely on a high-quality, flexible personnel pool, which has the right skill sets and can provide the right personnel at the right time. The company aim is to deliver, by using fresh, dedicated, young, enthusiastic personnel, a higher level of return through customer satisfaction than was traditionally delivered by a normal workforce.From the personnel side, Talent&Pro provides young, bright graduates who have just completed their Bachelors or Masters degrees with their first few years of structured work experience. In combining this with professional training, coaching and mentoring, the 'package' Talent&Pro offer becomes an attractive proposition to the graduate individual, attracting the brightest and the best. The time the young 'Talents' spend in the first phase of their professional development is finite (a maximum of five years). Ensuring a turnover of Talent&Pro employees provides the creation of a talent pool for the insurance and banking sectors; these are individuals who have gained a professional qualification, and who have had both concentrated and wide experience across many aspects of the industry. Working in harmony with the aspirations of business organisations and the needs of young bright Talents, giving them a career development path and investing in their future, has allowed Talent&Pro to become a successful company with a per annum growth of around 30 per cent and a healthy profit margin.

The philosophical concept of the Talent&Pro business model and corporate approach provides an intelligent solution to the various changes and challenges occurring in resourcing personnel to cope with the new information society.

From vertical to horizontal orientation

The introduction of horizontal process organisational models in the financial services sector, instead of the old centralist business organisation in which only a few senior management personnel had the right to make decisions or organise daily activities, means that there are new challenges to overcome in the integration of the workforce. Today's business models make for a totally different way of relating to peers, management and other work colleagues. Personnel need to be more aware of an organisation's goals and the entire business process in this information-sharing age. There is a need to take an opposite approach to the old traditional silo mentality of getting one's individual tasks done (still necessary!) and to ensure that a more holistic view and responsibility is taken, so that the business is stronger as a whole. The business management in conjunction with the workforce has the job of defining the processes, utilising information and systems to optimise the efficient and effective use of scarce skills. All this demands a different level of commitment and application from employees, but management and leaders also have to adapt.

With the change in organisations from the vertical structure to horizontal working patterns, it becomes a colleague or a peer who defines what you do on a daily basis, and another colleague who judges that your input is of the requisite quality and quantity – you will also need to judge the work of your colleagues. In this flattened management structure, the managers need to be concerned with the strategic aims and objectives of the business and the results. Management can no longer become involved in the detail. Having good personnel resources at the basic level is therefore crucial to the success of an organisation, while the flattened structure has the benefit of reducing management costs and delivering more transparency.

Real bright young Talents have the ability to oversee the horizontal process – they are full of energy and enthusiasm. However, they still need training to deal with the horizontal new world; our traditional schools, colleges and universities do not equip them beyond the silo, vertical mentality. In school or university we are all trained in specific subjects, and to answer a set of specific questions; the value is on producing the right specific answer, not discussing the range of answers that may add value.

From cost to investment orientation

Life is about a series of stories, whether they are told to your best friend in confidence over a bottle of wine, over the dinner table with a group of friends or at a family gathering. Talents – bright young things – want to develop and have good stories to tell their friends and families. They look for organisations that can provide them with the requisite development, so that they can have good stories to tell. Talents understand that development costs money and generally understand that a period of 'apprenticeship' will need to be worked through. If organisations do not offer the right level of investment in a Talent's future, then the Talent will generally look for a higher salary to fund the investment themselves. A structured investment programme will ensure that a Talent stays within the company that is investing in his or her future. A company that provides investment and still gives a Talent a good story to tell regarding the interest of daily activity will be high on the list of any bright young individual.

Many companies look at the cost of training as a negative, benchmarked against the direct costs and the need to gain short-term shareholder value. These are generally not the companies that will attract bright young things looking to invest in their future; they will generally have to pay higher salaries to attract individuals. Money is everywhere, so there has to be a reason for an individual to stay with a company – there is less reason to stay with an organisation that doesn't invest in the individual. Organisations that are looking at increasing shareholder value over the longer term will look to both create the investment opportunity in the right talented individuals and ensure that they have a career opportunity and stories to take home. An investment-orientated company sets an example for the employee, providing a two-way loyalty and ensuring that the company will attract and be able to employ the best people who deliver the highest-quality work and will therefore be cost effective in its own way.

The attractive workplace and individual lifecycles

Every individual goes through different phases in life. As Talents leave university they are full of life, energetic and enthusiastic – they are like infants seeing things for the first time as they absorb every impression they see. However, you cannot stay a Talent forever! They soon go into a second phase, where they are more serious and focused about what they want to achieve – they become Professionals. Generally, a phase of stability with friends, family, children and a mortgage ensures that certain responsibilities are taken on. Some individuals will prefer to stay in this phase for the rest of their working life, while others will have the drive to go further and explore their capabilities; they will find mentors – friends, bosses or others – who awaken them to further challenges and possibilities. Every individual will find his or her own way. They will find a company they like and they will leave it when they like. The company they are with at any one time is simply a vehicle that helps them develop – an entity that is willing to pay for their time and ideas. However, a company that doesn't excite the aspirations or give one a good story to take home is less likely to be an attractive proposition to the individual – thus a higher salary will be required to compensate for the lack of interest in the job.

Every Talent desires an attractive work placement as a start to their working life, and every Professional desires a great story to take home to friends and family. The more a Professional does not get a return from the business, the more he or she will seek compensation from elsewhere – bigger house, more expensive car, travel, movies, theatre, sports and fancy clothes; a Professional has a need to tell a story, and where that story comes from depends on the company they keep.

A changing world – HR in the new age

The HR management role is a key factor in success. HR management knows that the financial services industry is in the midst of change. We go to conferences, read books and survive training programmes, so we should know the theory. But are we prepared to act? Are we capable of doing something with the new theory, in the real world?

If we look at manufacturing outsourcing in countries like India, Bangladesh and China, the care of human resources is not the critical factor in the key to success. Ensuring good working conditions and adherence to human rights is cost orientated and certainly not attractive as a proposition with respect to bottom-line profit. However, in the services sector the proposition is a different one. Delivery of a good service is dependent on these individual human resources and therefore there is a need to treat them with care. We are therefore confronted with big challenges and big risks. In service delivery the real product is the interaction between the customer and the employee. It is this that the customer is effectively buying, whether that is the delivery of a loan or the acceptance and completion of an insurance claim. In the delivery of complex services the situation is more acute; more complex services require more complex skill sets and specialisations, and therefore a more intelligent delivery is required, but unfortunately there tends to be less Talent available at this level. Whoever can best facilitate the customers' needs will have the most successful business; however, this means facilitating a range of skill sets across the needs of a customer's service lifecycle, as well as the management of personnel to ensure this, which is undoubtedly a challenge.

The daily reality for the HR professional is changing as the business world transforms itself. Moving from traditionally motivating people to do what was best for the company, to now understanding the needs and aspirations of the individual and utilising that energy and direction for the good of the company is a very different proposition. The challenge for the financial services industry is as startling as the difference in manufacturing, where there has been a movement from traditional 'job enrichment' for production workers to allowing individual specialisation for Professionals as they grow within the company, not least because you cannot get those specialised skills from the wider labour market. Managing the transition from a good local name or network to a global brand, to attract the right personnel at both Talent and Professional levels is another challenge – if there are not the right skill sets locally, can you look, and are you looking, further afield? The shifting geographical power of knowledge means that you cannot look at recruitment and people resourcing in the old way. Traditional HR policies are now outdated in today's world.

Overall, these changes have a big effect on society: there is an increasing need for Talents in the global market, yet a decreasing set of organisations that provide the 'nursery facility' for those Talents to develop and grow. Professor Wee Chow Hou from the Nanyang University in Singapore likens the current movement between cities of different countries to that which previously existed between cities within the same country. Talents travel the world, speak English and look for other like-minded young Professionals to interact with, to debate the latest theories and practices with or to just have fun with. Talents are looking for an attractive company, in an attractive city, in an attractive part of the world. Ultimately Talents will look for the most attractive company to work for, but additional consideration is given to setting; interesting cities that are alive are an important consideration – as this makes for a more interesting life story. Business needs to be flexible enough to move or set up new operations if a change in location is what it takes to attract the best.

The HR professional cannot stick to old tried and tested methods of recruitment and procedures any more because that is not how business today operates. To be relevant, the HR professional needs to look at the overall vision and strategy of the company and then be able to think out of the box to deliver the right resources for the business to enable delivery of the strategy. Business organisations want the right people, with the right skill sets, at the right time, in place and operational. They also want operational flexibility, so that their people resource is hard-working in times of high required activity or workflow and not hanging around with nothing to do in the low season when operational workflow requirements are fewer. Yet increasing employment law makes adjusting the workforce numbers as required by workflow more difficult than ever. Business management, however, focuses on the need to get the job done, so HR needs to deliver the resources to get that job done by guaranteeing the right Talent at the right time with the right skill sets. If HR professionals can overcome their need for 'ownership' of employees, insourcing may be just the answer they are looking for.

Case study 1: Insourcing Avéro Achmea Zorg & Inkomen (Health Care & Income)

Period

The period covered in this case study is March 2006 to the present.

The customer

Avéro Achmea Zorg & Inkomen (Health Care & Income) is an insurance company established over two hundred years ago. It focuses on both the personal lines and commercial business sectors, utilising independent brokers as a primary distribution channel. The company is part of the Achmea Group, one of the largest players in the Benelux financial services industry. Achmea is a market leader in health care, and has significant market share in the life, pensions, material damages and social security sectors.

Why insourcing?

On 1 January 2006, a new social security scheme was introduced, with the aim of increasing competition among insurance companies and health care institutions. The objective was to lead to shorter waiting lists and thus a greater utilisation of the available capacity in the health care sector. Following a successful marketing campaign, Avéro Achmea Zorg & Inkomen has seen its collective health care contract grow from 1,300 to approximately 9,000 contracts (500,000 individual clients). The resource required to service this additional business growth would mean at least doubling the workforce of Avéro Achmea. In addition to the increase in new business and resulting administration, it was anticipated that there would be a 100 per cent increase in the number of incoming claims. To ensure that company service standards were maintained throughout this growth period and that there was no adverse impact on retention levels, Avéro Achmea identified the urgent need to expand capacity in the claims department with skilled employees. The extra capacity required needed to be highly qualified, given the complexity of the health care claims they had to handle. Talent&Pro was called in to provide a strategic solution to the resourcing problem.

Key requirements

Key requirements were identified as:

- An immediately available insourcing resource (up to 40 personnel).
- Personnel who were fully operational within a month, and capable of achieving the required productivity and quality standards.

- Minimal effort on behalf of the customer.
- Transparency for the customer in respect of the costs and performance measurement for the duration of the project.
- A trust-based relationship built with the customer's own employee teams.

Operational orientation

A strategic solution was outlined by Talent&Pro, working in partnership with Avéro Achmea Zorg & Inkomen, clearly defining objectives, goals, project scope and control mechanisms such as time, quality, money, communication, planning and risk management.

Programme training

Talent&Pro instigated an intensive training programme for the insourcing team to ensure that all necessary skills were there to support the project, and to provide a highly motivated and dedicated pool of Talents. By 4 April 2006, all these dedicated personnel were operational at Avéro Achmea.

Organisational integration and management

To ensure total integration between the Talent&Pro insourced team and the customer, a Project Board was set up to ensure that all key performance indicators were met. The Project Board meets at least once a month to assess the performance of the project, and is comprised of five members: two Avéro Achmea Zorg & Inkomen managers, two managers from Talent&Pro and a project manager also from Talent&Pro. The Talent&Pro project manager is responsible for the management, the motivation of the insourcing team and the overall success of the project.

Talent&Pro are convinced that strong people management and individual focus is of paramount importance in focusing each individual project employee and thus every individual that is within the insourced project team has one-to-one meetings with their People Manager to ensure optimum personal reward and maximum professional delivery. The objective of the one-to-one meetings is the development and individual motivation of personnel; it also identifies their commitment levels, eagerness to learn, delivery enthusiasm and mental flexibility.

Project lifecycle performance benchmarking

Talent&Pro chose to implement a strict performance management protocol in order to monitor all facets of the project, ensuring that realistic reporting forecasts could be provided to Avéro Achmea. Department objectives were defined, and then the most relevant key performance indicators were identified, making it possible to monitor progress and to pinpoint when success had been achieved and also, just as importantly, when to intervene. This strategy puts the team manager in the position where he can support his project co-ordinators and project team members on the basis of objective figures. If there are difficulties to deal with, they are flagged early and therefore can be proactively dealt with when they arise, followed back to their root cause and resolved.

Project objectives

Project objectives are identified as:

- the improvement of quality and productivity;
- clearly defined objectives and procedures;
- transparent reporting for both progress and costs; and
- realistic forecasts.

Project planning and protocols

Avéro Achmea was impressed with the results achieved by Talent&Pro's methods and supporting process templates, and have now implemented similar protocols within their own business departments for performance bench-marking and planning. Key items adopted by Avéro Achmea for use in their own benchmarking are:

- personnel time sheets and resource-planners; and
- performance management tools.

Changing environments

There are now some 44 flexible, insourced personnel working within the Avéro Achmea team, processing a significant proportion of both complex and straightforward tasks. The daily management of the Talent&Pro team and integration into Avéro Achmea departments is handled entirely by Talent&Pro, including all the traditional HR management processes, such as placement of new project team members, replacements, extensions and absenteeism.

The environment at Avéro Achmea has changed significantly (as is normal in a period of growth) and, through the capability to immediately implement the right resources at the required time, the pressure that could have been placed upon the existing infrastructure employees and management has been alleviated. This has ensured that Avéro Achmea management can focus upon the company's core activities and the continuance of service at a high level. In addition, because the insourcing team members have been trained to cope with the changing nature of activities within Avéro Achmea, they are able to be assigned to other departments if the workload in those areas of the company becomes too great.

The inclusion of the Talent&Pro insourcing solution within the Avéro Achmea business strategy has provided significant increases in efficiency and adoption of new management and measurement techniques within Avéro Achmea departments. The Talent&Pro ethos has made a positive contribution towards the environmental conditions under which Avéro Achmea work is performed, encouraging a hardworking mentality in a pleasant atmosphere, which has also encouraged and motivated Avéro Achmea staff.

An outstanding relationship with Avéro Achmea Zorg & Inkomen has been established, ensuring a firm foundation for the future; and, following a recent benchmarking of Talent&Pro comparable competitors, Talent&Pro has been reappointed as preferred supplier – gratifyingly, it scored better than the competition on all levels. The Avéro Achmea Claims department manager has been delighted with the commitment and delivery of the Talent&Pro insourcing team: 'This project carried out by Talent&Pro should be an example for all future projects at Avéro Achmea.'

Case study 2: ABN Amro Hypotheken Groep (formerly Bouwfonds Hypotheken)

Both ABN Amro and Bouwfonds will be used as the name of the company in this case study as it helps to denote time-frames.

Period

The period covered in this case study is 2003 to 2006.

The customer

ABN Amro Hypotheken Groep is an organisation that sets a high strategic relevance on operational excellence. Since 2003, Talent&Pro has been actively involved in insourcing quality personnel into the operational MidOffice and insurance departments at Bouwfonds Hypotheken, part of the ABN Amro Hypotheken Groep.

Over the past few years Bouwfonds Hypotheken has built up a prominent position in the mortgage sector. With a current market share of 7 per cent, Bouwfonds Hypotheken is one of the largest specialised providers of mortgages in the Netherlands. The mortgages are sold largely through a network of independent brokers; the quotation and acceptance of the mortgage and the comprehensive range of home insurance products are managed through the operational team in the MidOffice.

Why insourcing?

Based on the operational excellence strategy, Bouwfonds Hypotheken has been working over a period of years to successfully optimise working processes, including the deployment of personnel within the MidOffice operational set-up. Talent&Pro developed a strategy in 2003, in conjunction with Bouwfonds Hypotheken, to deliver a flexible insourcing pool.

It should be noted that the Netherlands mortgage market is characterised by a high degree of volatility. The operational workflow therefore shows major peaks and troughs in the need for resources to cope with the swings of the market, predominantly caused by fluctuating interest rates. Brokers and customers alike allow themselves to be led by the various interest levels offered by providers; this means that, when interest rates change, there is a sharp increase in demand for mortgages to be processed and quoted within a matter of days. The mortgage process takes some three weeks to complete after quotations have been issued.

Estimating the resource requirements with the swings in interest rates and changes in product offerings, and aligning resource requirements to those needs was a major challenge for Bouwfonds Hypotheken. A strategic solution was therefore developed in conjunction with Talent&Pro to optimise service delivery and effectively manage resource overheads in line with workflow needs, as well as delivering the operational excellence quality standards.

Key requirements

Key requirements were identified as:

- Creation of an insight into the true service delivery workload.
- Assessment of the required complement of permanent staffing levels.
- Creation and implementation of a flexible insourcing pool consisting of 50 Talent&Pro employees capable of immediate operational deployment in the event of an increase in required service.

Operational orientation

The flexible insourcing pool acts as an extension of Bouwfonds Hypotheken's own staff resource to ensure the right number of personnel to maintain an optimum workflow. As soon as there is a major increase needed in productivity the customer contacts Talent&Pro, and within an agreed time-frame, from a few days to a period of three weeks, the requisite numbers of personnel are insourced into the Bouwfonds Hypotheken process – this could be only a few employees or alternatively a whole team dependent on requirements. This enables Bouwfonds Hypotheken to cope with an influx of mortgage applications or administration and continue to meet its service levels. It also means that Bouwfonds Hypotheken is able to limit full-time permanent staffing to a level that does not have to cope with the peaks in activity, making it a leaner organisation than some of its competitors. To determine the key features of the flexible insourcing pool, a number of operational qualitative and quantitative aspects were addressed, as follows.

Size of the flexible pool

It is essential that the number of personnel is sufficient to be able to impact on the workload and deliver the right solution immediately. Due to the lack of empirical data and the number of permanent staff in 2003, Talent&Pro started with a group of 15 people. Within 2005 the group on standby within Talent&Pro's flexible insourcing pool had grown to 50.

Quality and skill sets

Delivering the right skill sets within the pool is essential. Talent&Pro were required to implement specific training programmes to ensure the right level of knowledge within their employee pool. The mortgage quotation process requires detailed knowledge and precise application, both to protect the person taking out the mortgage from errors that could have significant financial consequences and also to protect Bouwfonds Hypotheken from potential fraud. Talent&Pro is aware that it has continually to attract the right Talent to fit the customer company ethos – bright enough to adapt to different needs within short timescales, eager to learn, enthusiastic to deliver and mentally flexible enough to dovetail with the needs of different customers and mindsets.

Deployment period

At Bouwfonds Hypotheken workflow requirements can increase dramatically in a very short period of time. The time-frames for deployment of employees from the flexible insourcing pool can be no more than a maximum of two to three weeks. Bouwfonds Hypotheken do not have the capacity to train new employees at peak times and it should be noted that it takes at least one month for an employee to become competent with the mortgage process.

In ensuring that Talent&Pro is able to maximise delivery for Bouwfonds Hypotheken, a specific development programme has been set up for the flexible insourcing pool employees. Prior to any period of insourcing, personnel will have passed their professional qualification and have been familiarised with the Bouwfonds Hypotheken processes and systems. Bouwfonds Hypotheken ensures that trainers are made available for the Talent&Pro insourcing team, the result being that all employees in the insourcing pool have the right knowledge and competences prior to being insourced, thereby being fully operational immediately.

Management of the flexible insourcing pool

At peak workflow times, 30 insourcing personnel can be deployed into Bouwfonds Hypotheken, which becomes a significant proportion of the workforce when you consider that the permanent staffing level within the company numbers 70. Clearly, to increase the personnel resource by nearly

50 per cent would place a significant burden on the customer management team, therefore Talent&Pro also provides the ongoing management of the insourced team.

Project lifecycles

Talent&Pro's aim is to have an open partnership with Bouwfonds Hypotheken, this being essential in delivering an integrated solution to a customer who has insourced personnel delivering core activities. It is important to be able to share ideas and implement requirements quickly and efficiently.

Throughout the project lifecycle, Talent&Pro has been able to offer its employees individual development. Of those employees who reach a required level, they can in turn become coaches assisting in the training of less-developed staff. So, whilst there is a project lifecycle, there is also a cycle of learning within the project, and the ongoing personnel development signifies the continual development of the Talent&Pro ethos.

Talent&Pro personnel work across the entire quotation and acceptance process, under the direction of a Talent&Pro team leader, while other personnel are deployed within Bouwfonds Hypotheken teams under the direction of its own personnel. The Talent&Pro team leader attends both Bouwfonds Hypotheken meetings and also Talent&Pro meetings to ensure that the right level of resourcing is achieved at all times in the project lifecycle. Whenever Bouwfonds Hypotheken require it, a fully operational, externally resourced team can be called upon to cope with the increases in workload within the company's premises; the team act as fully integrated personnel ensuring achievement of the required operational standards of service excellence.

Changing environments

As a learning company, Talent&Pro has assimilated much during the project process. Complete transparency is of paramount importance in delivering an effective and efficient service, particularly when the insourcing team is deployed within the core areas of a client's business. Various changes in the original implementation plans have been tried out and either maintained or discarded depending on success. Different personnel development initiatives have been set up with varying skill sets, knowledge and experience. The selection criteria for personnel have been refined, with the development of a much more focused profile regarding knowledge, skills and personality.

Whilst the environment within the flexible insourcing pool has changed, refining both the selection criteria and training, so has the external environment. Bouwfonds Hypotheken has been taken over by ABN Amro, which means new changes in internal processes. Quality requirements have been altered to comply with new markets, leading to different responsibilities being placed on the insourcing team personnel.

It is clear that the flexible insourcing pool has become a fundamental part of the operational process at Bouwfonds Hypotheken. Talent&Pro undergoes a continual process of refreshing the insourcing pool, thus providing Bouwfonds Hypotheken with a fresh stream of well-trained talent.

The strategic solution of the flexible insourcing pool has given Bouwfonds Hypotheken the opportunity to adjust its permanent staffing capacity, thereby maximising operational overheads by ensuring that it does not have to employ staff full-time to cope with the peaks within the business. Talent&Pro continues to deliver a fully functional team, with the right skill sets at the right time to meet operational needs.

Note

1 Thomas L. Friedman, *De aarde is plat* (*The World is Flat*) (New York: Farrar, Straus and Giroux, 2005; this translation Nieuw Amsterdam), pp. 147–56.

8 Outsourcing in the automotive sector

Japan, Europe and the US compared

Garel Rhys

Introduction

Outsourcing has always been a feature of the automotive sector. The plain truth was that no vehicle maker had the expertise, the human talents or the financial resources to make all the items that were needed to build a car, van, truck or bus. In the main, the vehicle makers produced major components, such as bodies, floor pans and chassis, engines, cylinders, camshafts, transmissions and gears. Even here some firms always outsourced some of these items, especially some of the heavy commercial vehicle makers. At the same time, some vehicle firms made other components, such as electrical items, radiators and metals. However, for items other than the major components listed above, the vehicle maker depended heavily on component makers.

The degree of outsourcing varied from company to company and from country to country. This depended on corporate ambition and strategy, and also on the degree of manufacturing development of a country at the time of the formative years of the automotive industry, that is before 1920. Therefore, the Ford Motor Company and General Motors took vertical integration to its highest degree. Ford even owned forests to grow the trees whose wood had many uses in the pre-1940 motor industry, particularly in vehicle bodies before 1930. The UK, as the birthplace of the industrial revolution, had a major engineering sector that the budding vehicle makers could use to obtain the parts and components necessary. Indeed, when William Morris established his Morris Cars operation in 1913 in Oxford rather than Birmingham, there were adverse comments questioning the ability of the firm to survive so far from the West Midlands engineering heartland. On the other hand, in order to obtain many of the components required, Fiat, based in Italy, had to make them itself. In a very real sense Fiat was the industrial revolution in Italy.

During the last 20 years outsourcing has grown further in the automotive sector. The very vertically integrated firm has found it necessary for largely the same reasons cited above to replace in-house activities with new arrangements. This has involved either outsourcing or the halfway house of the joint venture, where a number of vehicle firms bring together particular product manufacture or particular functions. All this has been high profile and has led to the popular view that the automotive sector has engaged in a revolutionary change from in-house manufacture to largely outsourcing. Nothing of the sort has happened of course; there has merely been a change in the existing and time-honoured boundaries between outsourcing and in-house activities. Indeed, there may be a trend emerging in which vehicle firms outsource some traditional functions, for example foundries and casting, but develop new in-house activities at the sharp end of development, such as electronics, systems and networks. At the same time, the emergence of the Japanese automotive industry as a world force in the 1970s created an impression by the early 1990s that anything the Japanese did was germane to their success story. Therefore, what was perceived (erroneously as it turned out) to be the Japanese industrial structure, that is that the vehicle makers outsourced most of their activities, became a structure to be emulated.

In short, the automotive sector is a master of outsourcing, but the boundary between outsourced and in-house activities has never been firm and constant. Also the terminology used to express these activities has also changed. For instance, the activity now called outsourcing has in the past been called buying out (i.e. from *outside* the company) and confusingly buying in (i.e. *into* the company from outside). Activities carried out by the vehicle maker have more often than not been called 'in-house' activities, or something similar.

It must be said that outsourcing is not confined to the vehicle firms. The component makers also buy in items to be utilised in the manufacture of the completed part or system. This is especially so with the major items such as transmissions and, more recently, modules. The latter are a result of the attempt to duplicate the Japanese industrial structure: the vehicle makers have to deal with far fewer suppliers as the suppliers themselves perform the role of liaising with other suppliers on their behalf. That is, instead of dealing with up to 2,000 suppliers, as was usual in North America and Western Europe, the Japanese supply sector consisted of tiers of suppliers. The relatively few in the top tier dealt with the vehicle firms, and also with the second tier to build up more extensive modules of components (e.g. a complete front suspension system). In turn, the second tier would deal with the third tier and so on. There would still be a large number of suppliers but, instead of 2,000 or so having trade links with the vehicle firms, only about 300–400 would do so. In addition, they would have trade links with what had become the second tier of suppliers instead of those in the first tier, and so on down the pyramid. Thus, there was a change from a system where a vehicle firm dealt directly with thousands of suppliers to one that involved tiers, including the outsourcing of the administration of the supply function to the top tier. It could also include the transfer of in-house functions.

All this affects the backward linkages of the vehicle makers. At the same time, developments are occurring with forward linkages. This mainly involves vehicle distribution, retail, service and repair, and also links with vehicle finance. The tradition has been for the *de jure* outsourcing of sales, service and repair to independent firms and groups (although there are some examples of vehicle firms owning their own outlets in certain markets; for example, Mercedes Benz has factory-owned dealers in Germany and the UK). The de facto position was that the vehicle firms exercised a great deal of control. It remains to be seen whether various regulatory moves in the EU by the European Commission will loosen these ties sufficiently for the sales and service function to be freed from the vehicle makers' control. Similarly, with vehicle finance, all vehicle firms have in-house schemes that compete with independent finance providers. Again, there is a state of flux at the boundary between the two types of product. The vehicle firms want to retain as large a part of the vehicle financing market as possible as this is a highly profitable part of their activities.

The interest in outsourcing

The incentive to outsource is to improve the efficiency of operation, that is to reduce unit costs and to increase productivity. The purchase of components from outside specialists who also supply other vehicle firms means that relatively few items can be made by vehicle manufacturers at the same volume or unit cost as the component makers. This allows the vehicle firms to reap external economies of scale that are related to the scale of an industry rather than to an individual firm. At the same time, the vehicle firms have had to prioritise their own activities on the basis of what was most cost-effective. In the event, the vehicle makers have not had the resources to do everything and most items have been outsourced. As a result, only about 45 per cent of the unit average cost of a family car are internal, the rest representing outsourcing. Of course, not all this represents parts and components as car firms have a myriad of other suppliers, such as utility providers (e.g. electricity and gas), systems support, food and drink and so on.

The scale of operations in a mass-producing car company is enormous. On a two-shift basis the optimum size of a final assembly plant is 250,000 units a year, but for an engine plant it is 750,000 and for the press lines stamping out body parts the figure is between one and two million depending on the precise part involved. These internal figures demonstrate how large is the volume of component making, especially as the firms involved mainly supply more than one vehicle firm. Of course, the vehicle firms do not always buy from just one supplier, often preferring to spread risks and maintain freedom of action by having more than one supplier per part.

During the last 20 years a further incentive to outsource has been the wish to emulate the work practices and organisation within the Japanese automotive sector, as already touched upon briefly above. The Japanese auto industry's structure appeared to be one where a much higher proportion of a car's costs were outsourced (see Table 8.1), although, as will be shown later, matters were not always as they seemed.

Table 8.1 Proportion of parts made by vehicle makers, 1971

Vehicle maker	*% of parts made by vehicle maker*
Mazda (Japan)	46
Toyota (Japan)	41
Nissan (Japan)	35
Subaru (Japan)	35
GM (US)	54
Chrysler (US)	40
Ford (US)	39

Source: *Japan: Its Motor Industry and Market* (NEDO, Motor Manufacturing EDC, 1971), cited in Parliamentary Select Committee report, *The Motor Vehicle Industry*, Expenditure Committee, Session 1974/5, CMND No. 617 (London: HMSO).

As the Japanese industry was perceived from the 1970s onwards as being super-efficient, then anything the Japanese did was of interest to Western car makers wishing to increase efficiency and meet the Japanese challenge. At the same time competitive pressures generally were increasing.[1] This put further pressure on vehicle makers to obtain cost reductions, which in turn put extra pressure on suppliers of all sorts. The cost reductions emanated both from increased economies of scale and from non-scale improvements. This meant movements along the long-run average cost curve and downward shifts in the curve itself. The latter can come from reduced administration costs, a more focused operation and the removal of operational inefficiencies such as overmanning. So outsourcing and the quest for greater efficiency became complementary activities from the 1980s onwards.

Outsourcing and the changing structure of the supply industry

Intensified competition in the last quarter of the twentieth century forced European and American car firms to seek out cost savings from component suppliers. This applied to in-house component manufacture as well as supplies from outside specialists. Often the pursuit of cost savings meant the transfer of in-house supply to an outsourced one. Part of the cost-down process was the fuller exploitation of economies of scale in parts production. This meant rationalising the vehicle makers' supply structure and reducing the number of suppliers. During the 1980s, a major rationalisation occurred with a reduction in the number of suppliers to the US and European car makers from a range of 2,000 to 2,500 at the beginning of the decade to between 1,000 and 1,500 at the end. At the same time, these car makers were trying to reduce the number of suppliers to each assembly plant to between 350 and 500. This goal was reached by the early 1990s.[2] However, the number of suppliers per Japanese assembly plant was 170.

This development happened concurrently with another, which was that vehicle firms began to increase outsourcing. It was judged that more parts than hitherto could be produced more economically by specialist suppliers than by in-house divisions. Sometimes these divisions were closed and production re-sourced, or they were hived off as legally separate entities, or they were bought by outside specialists, or they underwent some combination of the above. There is a number of ways in which vehicle firms can reduce the number of suppliers.

First, they can tier suppliers by assigning whole components to a first-tier supplier. Seat making has been an example of this. A development of this is the so-called tier 0.5 supplier, which takes on the manufacture of a combination of components assembled into a module. This replaces some of the assembly work in a vehicle plant, hence the name tier 0.5. All this can reduce the number of direct suppliers considerably, thereby also reducing a vehicle firm's administrative and coordination costs.

Second, even without tiering, assemblers can cut the number of suppliers by reducing the parts count in components. This can be due to the ingenuity of a supplier compared with that of in-house production. Hence, the switch to a component or system with fewer parts and therefore fewer suppliers can involve outsourcing as well. This does not always occur, but sometimes it does. Of course, because vehicles are becoming more complicated to satisfy consumer demand and legislative requirements, there can be a growing number of systems. This gives opportunities to extra suppliers and more often than not, because of the specialisms requested, these new systems are outsourced from the beginning.

Third, parts can be sourced with fewer suppliers than previously. Although it was suggested in the 1990s that the aim was to replace multiple sourcing with single sourcing, the latter has not become general as the vehicle firms do not want to become totally dependent on a particular supplier. After all, this would give the supplier increased bargaining power and vehicle firms have become used to 'calling the shots'. So the benefit of maximising economies of scale could be offset by the degree of monopoly power that could be given to a single preferred outsourcer. This is not to say that there is no single sourcing, but this is often on the basis of a single source per vehicle model, or using a supplier that can be substituted by another relatively easily. That is, the market remains 'contestable'. A further problem with single sourcing is that the vehicle firm is vulnerable to supply disruption. This can occur if strikes occur at the suppliers, or there is production disruption due to shortages of supplies into the component supplier.

Vehicle firms have become more willing to outsource where previously there was a reluctance because of quality control concerns. Now, with various quality control monitoring techniques, beginning with statistical process control (SPC), there is much more confidence in suppliers' ability to perform at the highest standard. In addition, the greater willingness to share detailed information on the cost of each production step improves the trust between supplier and vehicle maker. In the lexicon of lean production, this was the way to replace the adversarial power-based relationship. However, this is very much an ongoing process as there is much still to be done before the adversarial system is replaced. Even so, progress in these areas is seeing a greater use of market-based relationships rather than internalised firm-based ones.

The structure in Europe

Historically, the suppliers always had a larger role in the total cost structure of cars in Europe than in the US. This was because the European car companies have always been smaller and more numerous than their US rivals, Ford and General Motors – the US motor industry worked at a North American continental level so the inevitable shake-out of producers as competition took its inevitable toll occurred on a continental scale. In Europe many countries protected their motor industries with tariffs. Hence the shake-out was on a nation-state level not a continental one. It is only after the creation of the European Economic Community, the Economic Community and the European Union that a continental market approach and a second shake-out on a continental level appeared and still continues: at the time of writing, MAN, the German truck maker, is bidding to buy Scania of Sweden.

These historically smaller assemblers did not have the scale or funds beyond their formative years to perform the range of activities themselves that Ford and General Motors did for 50 years. Furthermore, and partly due to this, there has always existed a number of strong European suppliers, such as Bosch, GKN, ZF and SKF, with a clear technical lead in certain component areas. So the tradition in Europe has always been for the large suppliers to be more talented.[3] In practical terms this meant, for instance, that, rather than working to drawings supplied by the vehicle firms, many have engineered complete components for the assemblers. Hence, as vehicles became more complex many suppliers were in pole positions to provide the technical, but also commercial and economic, solutions needed. This meant such advances reinforced, not weakened, outsourcing.

The size of the leading European suppliers reflects the fact that the European components market is the largest in the world. The top 20 component firms in the 1990s accounted for 33.3 per cent of total sales of components to the assemblers, net of the supplies to the after-sales market for service and repair. In the slightly smaller US market, the top 30 companies account for one-third of total component sales to the vehicle firms.[4]

Traditionally, the component makers supplied the home-country assemblers and relatively few of them had a major export business. The export business has grown rapidly in the last 20 years as the single market in Europe began to really develop. At the same time, European producers availing themselves of the wider range of suppliers opening up to them saw the new economies provided by such suppliers as an opportunity to increase the degree of outsourcing. The large component makers are becoming as multinational as the vehicle firms, with plants not just spread throughout Europe but also on a global basis.

As the reduction in the number of suppliers can lead to greater outsourcing, as the vehicle firms have to recalculate the costs and benefits of retaining as many in-house activities as previously, then the huge number of component firms in Europe (11,500) compared with North America (5,000) in 1989[5] meant that the opportunity for rationalisation was immense and new opportunities for rational outsourcing occurred.

A major driver of outsourcing in the American and European industries was the perceived position in Japan, where, it was believed, outsourcing had been taken to an art form. However, in reality, the position was very different and the degree of Japanese outsourcing in the auto industry was a mirage.

Outsourcing in Japan – myth or reality?

One thing must be clarified at the outset: outsourcing in Japan was not done to some carefully thought-out and considered master plan by the Japanese vehicle makers. In fact it arose out of desperation.

Although there are nine Japanese car brands (Toyota, Daihatsu, Nissan, Honda, Subaru (Fuji), Mazda, Isuzu, Suzuki and Mitsubishi), and four heavy commercial brands (Hino, Nissan Diesel, Isuzu and Mitsubishi), traditionally over 65 per cent of production has been accounted for by Toyota and Nissan. Hence, they and latterly Honda form the production core of the Japanese motor industry.

In the spring of 1950, Toyota was in very poor shape. It had to lay off workers because of a lack of demand for vehicles in Japan and its inability to break into export markets. The workers, resenting this, organised a bitter two month-long strike that left the company disheartened and disunited. Earlier in the late 1940s, Toyota had misjudged the market and overproduced. Even worse, customers found that they could not pay their instalments on credit and returned their cars to Toyota. The Bank of Japan eventually saved the company by injecting a large amount of new capital. The bank also demanded a change of company structure into separate sales and manufacturing companies. This is the structure that has served the company so well.

As the company was under-financed and in dire need of new products, this could only be achieved, even with the Bank of Japan's help, by transferring a large amount of the costs of production to suppliers. The suppliers took on the role of the Western car companies in the range and depth of components they made for Toyota.

This included the component firms buying expensive equipment, and providing working capital and the production expertise to make a large proportion of a Toyota car. Nissan went through largely the same experience. Eventually the growth of the car makers was phenomenal and they, in turn, dominated their suppliers. However, initially the degree of outsourcing in Japan was the salvation of the assemblers: a structure born out of necessity.

This close relationship between vehicle firm and component supplier determined the nature of the structure of the Japanese auto industry; that is, the true relationship between the two and the true nature of outsourcing.

The common perception of industrial organisation in Japan is of large companies that belong to a corporate group, or *keiretsu*. So vehicle production sees intermediate goods and services vertically supplied via an extensive network of subcontracting relationships with smaller firms at the base of the pyramid serving successive layers of firms through to the apex. The smaller firms are usually tied in one way or another – contractually, by minority shareholding, by interlocking directors, etc. – to the larger firms right through to the vehicle firm. These vertically linked firms therefore do business with each other.[6] In fact, the Japanese auto industry, especially inasmuch as it applies to Toyota, Nissan, Honda and Mitsubishi, is a classic example of Japanese industrial organisation. The precise link between the links in the chain determines the real scale of outsourcing in the Japanese auto sector.

This industrial organisation has not reduced the total number of suppliers to the vehicle firms in Japan in relation to the numbers in Europe. In Europe in the 1990s, there were 1,500 major suppliers and 10,000 minor suppliers, or 11,500 in total. In the second half of the 1990s in Japan, there were 10,000 smaller producers supplying 1,400 component makers who, in turn, supplied the vehicle firms, or 11,400 in all.[7] These 1,400 component makers supplied nine car firms and four heavy commercial firms compared with 20 large groupings in Europe, including Japanese and US firms.

The tiered vertical structure in Japan is far from straightforward. Some idea of this can be seen in publications such as *Industrial Groupings in Japan*, issued for various years by Dodwell Marketing Consultants, Tokyo. However, even in such a sterling compendium as this the true nature of the relationships is not always clear. This is not surprising as the waters are muddied by not just the equity shareholdings held by vehicle firms in component makers, but also the vehicle firms' involvement with senior managerial appointments, the contracts held, and the influence of the vehicle firms on the sourcing policies of their suppliers. This implies a large degree of vertical control. In addition, both the vehicle firms and the top-tier producers hold ownership stakes in smaller companies further down the pyramid or supply chain. All this is controversial and leads to accusations of there being barriers to entry and competition by European and American suppliers wanting to enter the pyramid of supply. So, does the industrial structure of the Japanese auto sector represent vertical integration, quasi-vertical integration, or genuine outsourcing of massive proportions? The answer lies in what equity ownership level is taken as the benchmark for effective control.

One analyst[8] made comparisons between vertical ownership links in Toyota and Nissan on the one hand and in General Motors, Ford and Chrysler on the other. Cusumano pointed out that the comparative degree of vertical integration was sensitive to the percentage ownership levels held by the vehicle firms in their suppliers' equity. Hence, when a minimum 50 per cent threshold was selected, the US firms were more integrated. If the threshold was lowered then the Japanese firms were the more integrated. As a 20 per cent threshold of ownership has long been regarded as sufficient for effective control by a firm with a stake in other members of an identifiable interest group,[9] then at the 20 per cent level the Japanese car firms are more vertically integrated than US ones and the high degree of outsourcing in Japan is a myth born of a misunderstanding of the Japanese vertical relationship and the obsession with a 50 per cent shareholding as the benchmark for control. Anyone perusing the Dodwell volume for, say, 1980/1, had to come to the same conclusion. This volume has long shaped the present author's analysis of the Japanese effectively vertically integrated industrial structure.

This is a very important point. It explains the seeming willingness of a Japanese car company such as Toyota to entrust their operations, products and future to what appeared to be independent suppliers. The amount of confidence and cooperation involved to produce this state of affairs appeared enormous. However, the Japanese car firms did not really hand over responsibility to *outsiders* – these suppliers were inside the operation. Once the true nature of the links between the vehicle firm and the top tier *and* lower tiers as well is taken into consideration, the Japanese vehicle firms were engaged in huge amounts of in-house activity and the so-called transfer of responsibilities was not so dramatic. Therefore, when a firm such as the Chrysler arm of DaimlerChrysler reduced its in-house activities in the US in order to slim down and survive, and insisted on vetting the lower-tier suppliers to its top tier, it was not really in contrast to the way the Japanese operated their outsourcing. The de facto vertical integration and the close control of the supply chain meant that Japanese car firms were also keeping a close eye on their suppliers to ensure that all was in order and that the future of the vehicle assembler was not put in jeopardy by a malfunctioning supply chain.

Interestingly, due to the traumas faced by all Japanese vehicle makers in the 1990s, apart from Toyota-Hino, the mythical Japanese corporate structure may after all become more of a reality. Following the de facto takeover of Nissan by Renault, the myth of all-round Japanese efficiency in part and component making was demolished by the revelation of sundry problems. As a result, Renault let it be known that it was open to offers by outsiders of whatever nationality to take over companies in the Nissan Japanese supply chain. Hence, far from leading the present trend towards outsourcing, the Japanese industry may be just on the verge of trying to catch up.

Consequently, the success of the Japanese motor industry was not due to its unique level of outsourcing. Indeed, the problems faced by the industry in the 1990s were not prevented by the quasi in-house system. So will genuine outsourcing make a difference? This is probably unlikely. The strength of the Japanese supply chain emanated from elsewhere.

The relationship between Japanese vehicle makers and suppliers is not based upon partnership and trust alone. There is no evidence that Japanese suppliers love their assembler customers any more than suppliers do in the West.[10] This is not inconsistent with the relationship between the vehicle firms and their suppliers in an integrated system. After all, the relationship within an integrated car company between the in-house engine or transmission plants and the assembly lines is not always the smoothest. Some tensions appear even though the overriding relationship is one of partnership and cooperation. The relationship between the Japanese vehicle firms and their suppliers eschews power-based bargaining in favour of an agreed rational structure for jointly analysing costs, determining prices and sharing profits. As a result, an adversarial relationship gives way to one of cooperation. However, this cooperation is also a result of the quasi-vertical relationship. It would be a strange vertically integrated group that did not foster cooperation between its constituent parts.

Outsourcing: consequences and controversies

Within the context of the automotive sector, outsourcing is not without its controversies. This is unsurprising given the implications of the process and the consequences involved in any waxing and waning of the degree of outsourcing.

If outsourcing increases then work can be transferred to either a domestic or non-domestic supplier, each of which eventually has its own consequences. In the former case there is no great job loss to the domestic economy but there is certainly a switch from one enterprise to another. This can have major implications for individuals, localities and trade unions. In the latter case, there is the issue of transferring work abroad to the detriment of the home economy. Clearly, this can lead to a reduction in domestic jobs with all its implications for sector prosperity, individual well-being and economic activity. Often the transfer of sourcing abroad raises issues of domestic content, which is a proxy for factors such as the degree of extra economic activity stimulated by vehicle assembly via the multiplier effect (i.e. a lower domestic content is often seen as lowering the value of the multiplier) or the replacement of domestic jobs by foreign ones. In turn, this can stimulate controversy concerning switching employment to lower-wage countries and factories. Indeed, even outsourcing to another domestic source can involve issues about transferring work to a company that pays lower wages and that has lower-value terms of employment generally. This has always been an issue in Japan. The jobs-for-life philosophy of major manufacturers did not apply to their suppliers. Hence, if a Japanese vehicle firm experienced a surplus of labour, or aged labour had become too expensive, personnel were transferred to subsidiaries. The vehicle firm did not sack them but the 'subsidiary' might. Such issues produce trade union and political responses.

The increase in outsourcing that involves a transfer of sourcing abroad also became embroiled in the general issue of offshoring, a matter of particular concern in North America. Of course, offshoring can occur independently of any change in the degree of outsourcing, but the two issues are interlinked. After all, a change in location of a source of supply for a given component, from a domestic outsource to a foreign one, means that on occasions the two processes are almost synonymous. Furthermore, the trend towards offshoring means that it is the country that is buying in the products and services. Therefore, offshoring is outsourcing on a national level.

At the level of the firm, outsourcing can mean the abandonment of traditional competencies, some of which in a previous age may have been regarded as core. When this involves research and development functions then there is concern about the long-term viability of the vehicle firm as a sustainable long-term player. That is, outsourcing may be a medium-term positive in that it can reduce costs, but in the longer term the vehicle firm loses the ability to compete. In the case of outsourcing abroad, such concerns are raised to a national level and cannot be dismissed out of hand. For instance, BMW is considering insourcing and developing competencies in electrics, electronics and software in order to avoid loss of expertise and power. A particular issue is that the product cycle of an electronics provider may not be the appropriate lifecycle for the vehicle firm. At a national level, outsourcing abroad can mean the hollowing out of activities and expertise so that the remaining critical mass is too small to be sustained.

The growth in outsourcing is of particular interest to trade unions who see a consequent erosion of their membership or a harmful effect on a particular group of their members caused by the transfer of activities from the car companies. During the last decade, outsourcing, in its various guises, has become a major concern of trade unions in Europe and North America. This does not just involve work transferred abroad, but also the switch of activities from vehicle company-owned facilities to outsourcers and whether the outsourced facilities are unionised or not. Hence, they view with alarm any continuation, leave alone acceleration, of the trend towards outsourcing even though it has always been part and parcel of the auto sector. It could well be that they have reason to be concerned.

Figures suggest that the proportion of the value of various automotive activities carried out by the vehicle firms will decrease significantly between 2002 and 2015 (see Table 8.2). Clearly, the precise figures for 2015 are unlikely to be confirmed in the event, but it is the trend that is interesting. Apart from vehicle interiors, electronics and electrical components, there will be a significant increase in outsourcing. This will be so even if only 50 per cent of the predicted increase in outsourced share occurs. These are the major components that hitherto have seen the most involvement by vehicle firms, and some areas have been dominated by them.

We could therefore see strong employment growth in the supplier industry, while that in the vehicle firms falls. At the same time, this will need a large growth in investment by the suppliers and this need will underpin a continuing process of consolidation. A by-product of all this will be the importance attached in the future to value-adding clusters: a form of networked

Table 8.2 Estimated change in vehicle firm–supplier work ratio, 2002–15 (%)

	2002		*2015*	
	Vehicle firm	*Supplier*	*Vehicle firm*	*Supplier*
Chassis	23	77	15	85
Power trains	37	63	20	80
Engines	30	56	36	64
Body structures	96	4	59	41
Body exteriors	56	45	29	71
Interiors	16	84	14	86
Electronics and electrical components	16	84	16	84

Source: S. Roth, paper presented at a closed conference of the Ford European Works Council, Belgium, September 2005.

cooperation among vehicle firms, suppliers, research institutes, universities and so on. Such clusters will offer stronger innovation capabilities and greater efficiency. Where outsourcing is concerned, these clusters will weaken the case for more pure cost-cutting moves, and could reduce the incentive to offshore to low-wage countries. That is, the clusters will anchor firms and create benefits that outweigh any achieved by offshoring.

Outsourcing and the brand

If a vehicle is to consist increasingly of bought-out materials and components, and the vehicle firm outsources an increasing number of contracts to independent service suppliers of all sorts, including independent research houses such as Ricardo, Magna and Tickford, what then will be the status of the vehicle firms? Will the brand switch from Ford or BMW to a group of top-tier or tier 0.5 specialists? Will the vehicle look like a Formula One or Indy car with different companies' logos dotted all over it? Will the reality of the brand be so diluted that a vehicle firm's name becomes one of many?

In answer to these questions, there has certainly been a change in the hierarchy of the auto industry's structure. Traditionally, as discussed above, the vehicle firm dealt with thousands of suppliers and by doing so it exercised a position of dominance in the industrial structure. The system of tiering, which in some ways is still in the process of construction, changes this. At the top of the pyramid is still the vehicle maker, but below them suppliers of modules and integrated systems have positioned themselves at first-tier level in the supply chain. In the second tier are systems specialists (but not integrators) and in the third tier are suppliers of parts and components. Indeed, some 'integrators' are taking on functions associated with final assembly and are thereby described as tier 0.5 actors. So, on the surface it appears as if some suppliers could attain a position where they could establish an image and profile that spreads their 'brand' to the vehicle itself. In truth, however, such an eventuality is unlikely. The lesson of history is against them and, anyway, the vehicle firm especially in the car sector is still of an order of magnitude bigger than the largest supplier. If a supplier does appear to be of threatening size or profile, then the vehicle firm will still find it possible to switch or augment suppliers when new models are developed.

There are already vehicles that are largely made up of bought-in major components. These are mainly to be found in the heavy truck and bus market. A vehicle such as an American Peterbilt truck is made of a bought-in cab, transmission, engine and electronics, etc., yet it is still a 'Peterbilt'. About the only other name that is discernible is the supplier of the diesel engine. This also once happened in the UK, when an assembled ERF or Seddon truck would carry the badge of the Gardner or Perkins engine on the radiator. In other industries, such as consumer electronics, where products are assemblies of bought-in items, only the name of the assembler is on the machine. So, those who suggest that the vehicle firms who outsource more will threaten their own brand are unlikely to be vindicated. The motor industry hierarchy may be changing but the vehicle firm will remain firmly in charge.

Before the suppliers could contemplate moving up to be brands in their own right, they have to get their own houses in order by organising their supply chains. After all, the assemblers did not outsource activities to top-tier suppliers out of philanthropy. The latter are expected to undertake the function previously done by the vehicle assemblers of organising the supply chains. This is something that few suppliers had experience of, certainly at the scale now required. This has been a long process of learning and the results have often been less than perfect. Hence, the recent growth of outsourcing for the suppliers has not come about without its costs. At the same time, many of the top suppliers engaged in a major merger mania and a frenzy of consolidation. Often it was a case of eating one undigested meal after another. The vehicle firms, if they were to outsource more, wanted the large suppliers to become larger, to demonstrate that they had the resources to support the vehicle firm in the long run and to follow them overseas. This resulted in the creation of a super-league of suppliers, but also in some of the corporate disasters of the future waiting to happen. The growth and the consolidation was too rapid and some firms would end up in financial difficulties. This was soon confirmed by the problems at Federal Mogul and the Ford hive-off company, Visteon. Also, as most component firms had set up to supply the local vehicle assembly plants, only a tiny number had any experience of international trade, let alone running a multinational operation. The requirement by the vehicle firms that their suppliers follow them around the world created its own raft of challenges and problems. This illustrates that the motor industry is one that knows how to operate contracts between supplier and buyer, and that the buyer is all-powerful. It was alluded to above that the issue of offshore supply was of growing concern in some countries, especially the US. This controversy has spilt over into the question of outsourcing as they are seen as linked issues: that is, the outsource may be to an offshore location. Hence, the debate concerning offshore supply will have implications for the outsourcing movement.

Offshore controversies

There is alarm in the US that underlying structural costs are slowly eating away at the ability of manufacturers to compete effectively. These costs – corporate tax rates; employee benefits such as pensions and health care; tort litigation; regulatory compliance; and energy – add an estimated 22.4 per cent to the cost of production of US firms, relative to major foreign competitors.[11] It is argued that, once these underlying cost pressures on companies like General Motors, Ford and their US suppliers are understood, it becomes clearer why US production is moving offshore. These added costs in the US are currently nearly as high as the total production costs in China.

Given this backdrop, when a move to outsourcing occurs in the US, this is often seen as an opportunity or excuse for the supplier to move offshore, hence the pressures in the US for car firms to identify the precise locations and companies that supply each facet of a vehicle's costs. Already Nike has succumbed to such pressure and the vehicle makers believe that public opinion will force them to do likewise.

This is not just an issue of moving output to an outsource in a low-wage economy, but also concerns the precise wage and employment conditions involved. Are the cost reductions obtained by the vehicle makers at the expense of worker exploitation elsewhere? If consumers find this unacceptable, then trade unions and others can utilise this to stem the flow offshore and in the process perhaps limit the trend towards outsourcing as well.

Outsourcing in the national sense – that a part is bought from another country rather than being made domestically – does widen the outsourcing debate. What happens at a company level is magnified to occur at a national one. In many ways the issues are the same: attempts to lower internal costs and to reduce the total unit costs of production. The results can be the same in that jobs are often displaced. However, on a national scale the jobs are 'lost' outside the country, whereas on a company level this may or may not be the result depending on where the new supplier is or whether the supplier has taken over the old in-house facility.

Offshore outsourcing is often manifested in the debate about and, often, controversy concerning the local content of vehicles. That is, precisely how much of the value of each car ex-works is generated in the home country? This again is a proxy for arguments over job levels, the de-industrialisation of a country and the hollowing out of manufacturing. The local content is yet another way of looking at the national level of insourcing, and outsourcing in the broader sense.

The precise measures of local content can be important where trade regulation is involved. For instance, it used to be that a car made in the EU had to have a minimum local content before it could have free circulation within the EU. This was a measure really aimed at Japanese cars made in the EU, mainly the UK. The UK measured the local content as the difference between the customs-declared prices of imported components and systems per car made and the ex-works price. The UK argued that this difference was around 80 per cent, more than enough to make the cars EU products. However, the Italian and French car makers who stripped down these cars and components said the figure was much less. They were probably correct. If a component made by a Japanese supplier located in the UK was supplied to a car factory, the part was regarded as 100 per cent British. In fact, the component was made to some degree of imported bits and pieces. In truth, the only way to obtain an accurate picture was by creating detailed input–output models, which no one was inclined to do. Thus, the level of national outsourcing can be higher than realised. This was also the nub of the problem in the US. As the US car makers came under pressure and the cars made by the Japanese in the US and Canada took a larger share of the market, then US trade unions, politicians and component makers argued that US-made Japanese cars were no substitute for the job potential of US cars. This has been an issue since the early 1990s (see, for example, *International Business Week*, 18 November 1991, 'Honda: Is it an American Car?'). In a nutshell, replacing outsources to GM or Ford with outsources to Toyota or Honda meant a net increase in national outsourcing (i.e. imports). This meant that the replacement, with Japanese inward investors, of US vehicle firms relocating factories offshore was not a solution to the de-industrialisation of the US or the loss of jobs. The movement of Japanese car assembly to the US was also outsourcing from Japan's point of view. However, its degree, and therefore the controversy, was minimised by the export of components in one form or another to the US. Interestingly, while one arm of the US government was challenging the American content of Japanese cars, another was trying to convince Europe that Japanese cars made in the US were as American as apple pie and should not come under the European–Japanese 'quota' arrangements for cars. However, the attempt to impose local content rules either officially or unofficially can be protectionism by another name unless the domestic suppliers are as efficient as the offshore ones. If the local suppliers are not as efficient, then any attempt to make an inward investor use that supply chain means that they are as exposed to supplier inefficiency as the traditional domestic makers. Hence, their cost advantage is constrained. So, when national insourcing can be about jobs, investment, research, development and economic dynamism, it can also be about inefficiencies and barriers to trade.

Whereas outsourcing in the narrow and traditional sense means buying a part, component, system or service from another company rather than making it yourself, the substitution of the word 'country' for 'company' legitimately widens the scope of the terms outsourcing and insourcing. This threatens to be much more controversial than the traditional view of outsourcing ever was.

A sense of proportion

Although outsourcing is a growing phenomenon in the automotive sector, it is growing from a high base. By the end of the 1930s, about 50 per cent of the ex-works value of a car was represented by outsourced costs. By 1975, the figure had increased to around 55 per cent. In the case of some heavy commercial vehicles made by companies that bought in almost everything, the in-house content was around 20–25 per cent. Heavy buses and coaches that used bodies made by independent bodybuilders had an in-house content by value of around 25–30 per cent. The industry has always found it advantageous and necessary to buy from an extensive supply chain.

It is clear that these considerations still apply and the vehicle makers are increasing their dependence on the supply chain. However, a sense of perspective is necessary. The vehicle makers are still highly dominant within the automotive industry in general. Also, it is important to put the claims of the efficiency and effectiveness of outsourcing into a proper context.

For instance, when vehicle makers made their own seats for fitting into cars no great comment was made when the seats arrived alongside the assembly lines at the right place and at the right time. Now that seat making has become an outsourced module, often in a factory close to the assembly plant, it is almost regarded as a logistics miracle and a testimony to lean production techniques that the seats do arrive at the right place at the right time. Hence, this synchronised delivery is seen as the highest form of the logistics profession's art, whereas in fact it is merely the continuation of business as usual. The only real change is that the ownership of the seat-manufacturing plant has changed and what was an internal arrangement bounded by the firm has become a market transaction.

It is not surprising, therefore, that outsourcing in itself changes very little. An assembler must still run its operation efficiently and make products the consumer wants. In the same way, lean production may be a necessary condition for sustainability, but the sufficient condition requires the optimum scale of operation for maximum economies of scale, and the manufacture of vehicles the market, that is the consumer, wants. There has always been a major degree of outsourcing in the motor industry, but it has not been a panacea for all ills. Firms have waxed and waned despite the precise, industrial structure. Consequently, outsourcing per se does not equal prosperity – there are other factors at work here.

It is also wrong to believe that outsourcing has been boosted by the more flexible production systems in the vehicle plants, as this does not require a supplier to tool up with dedicated equipment with no other purpose than to supply the needs of a fixed and standardised production run. Such equipment at the suppliers would have no other use and therefore suppliers might baulk at the risks of such a venture; that is, if heavy investment is made in one use, and if that use falters because of a change of policy by the vehicle assembler, the investment is at risk. However, the contrast between the inflexibility of mass production and the flexibility of lean production is a myth. Mass production may have meant large volumes, but there was a large degree of variety in that output – it was not inflexible. Hence, there was no real barrier on this score to outsourcing. To repeat, outsourcing has always been a feature of the automotive sector. In Japan, which was regarded as the home of flexible production in the car plants, the system was one of quasi-vertical integration rather than pure outsourcing.

The Japanese system may have been shown to be something other than supposed in the West, but innovative ways of outsourcing have appeared. For instance, a joint venture between a supplier and a vehicle assembler allows the latter to tap into knowledge without losing access to a particular expertise. The joint venture between Ford and ZF in gearboxes is a good example. Similarly, the joint venture between vehicle firms is a halfway house between full merger and going it alone. If the joint venture is placed into a jointly owned company, then this is a mix of outsourcing and in-house manufacture. Neither part is self-sufficient in its expertise and must buy some from each other. The major joint venture between BMW, Daimler-Chrysler and General Motors in hybrid technology is in response to the fully in-house approach of Toyota. The 'shared' approach means buying in and selling out. The joint ventures may also allow activities to remain on-site without the disruption to workers and locality of full buying-in.

Of course, outsourcing does not solve all administrative problems. The supplier is faced with a logistic challenge to keep the vehicle car plants operating. There is now someone to blame if things go wrong. Clearly, in an in-house operation, a failure to supply major components to the assembly tracks causes controversy, but the problems are kept in the family and the threat to switch sources of supply is hollow.

Outsourcing does not mean that there is a cosy relaxed atmosphere between supplier and vehicle firm. Far from it, as there is constant pressure to improve performance. However, the link between tier-one and tier 0.5 suppliers with the vehicle firms is increasingly based upon cooperation and mutually shared goals, which is in the interest of both parties.

Forward linkage

In some instances, there are forward linkages in the motor industry in which the vehicle firms are part of a supply chain. One example is in the commercial vehicle sector, where outside suppliers supply the body the customer specifies. That is, the bodybuilder is between the vehicle firm and the final customer, hence the forward linkage. The vehicle maker is the main contractor. The body is sometimes supplied in to the vehicle maker, but alternatively the vehicle maker supplies the vehicle in chosen form to the bodybuilder. In the case of trailers, the customer buys direct and marries the truck and trailer.

Another forward linkage concerns the retail and service networks. In the motor industry vehicle dealers are contractually bound to their vehicle suppliers and, in the main, only these dealers can sell a particular brand. Hence, there is a quasi-vertical integration between vehicle firm and dealer. However, in Europe, the control of the vehicle firm over its independent vehicle dealers is being diluted under the auspices of the European Commission. Hence, the vehicle firms are increasing the depth of the outsourcing of sales, service and repair. The European Commission sees this greater freedom of dealers vis-à-vis their vehicle suppliers as a possible contribution to increasing competition to the benefit of the consumer. In Japan, vehicle dealers are more closely linked to the vehicle supplier even if they are separate legal entities.

Conclusion

Outsourcing has always been with us in the motor industry. True, in the early years of the industry in the first decade of the twentieth century, some pioneers tried to make everything themselves, but outsourcing soon became a feature. There is now another surge in the degree of outsourcing that contains some new features: namely, the degree of responsibility given to the top tiers of supply, with them running most of the supply chain instead of the vehicle makers. The vehicle firms will, no doubt, keep a watching brief.

Japan has been regarded as the epitome of the disintegrated motor industrial structure. In fact, if the benchmark of effective control is lowered to 20 per cent of the equity, then the Japanese motor industry becomes the most integrated in the world. If this is so, then many of the features of the Japanese relationship, which were seen as the necessary conditions for a successful outsourced structure, must be reassessed. Instead, they take on the characteristics of an in-house arrangement. However, the conditions needed to allow an in-house relationship to work, where the supplier is given a degree of autonomy, can be those needed where outsourcing is prevalent. The difference is that they will take more effort to install and operate. Nevertheless, the Japanese experience is still informative.

Outsourcing can also apply at the national level. This encompasses the phenomena of companies moving offshore and also the purchase of components abroad for use in domestic production, thereby increasing foreign content. This can apply to subsidiaries of the vehicle firms as well as to independent suppliers. Both these developments lead to controversy inasmuch as they reduce home-country economic activity and employment. However, the improved cost base of the domestic vehicle suppliers can result in greater output because of greater competitiveness. This will increase domestic economic activity.

Clearly, outsourcing is about more than just the pursuit of lower costs and economic efficiency. It has implications for labour and localities, all of which bring in the views of trade unions, politicians and the public. In the main, however, the vehicle buyer has little interest in who makes the parts that are used in the vehicles they buy. They are interested in buying the best-quality vehicle at the lowest possible price. The fate of the vehicle suppliers has been a high degree of anonymity as far as the public is concerned. Even the greater level of responsibility given to the higher-tier supplier is unlikely to change that.

Notes

1 D. G. Rhys, 'Competition in the auto sector: the impact of the interface between supply and demand', *International Journal of Automotive Technology and Management*, 5(3) (2005): 261–83.
2 J. P. Womack, D. T. Jones and D. Roos, *The Machine that Changed the World* (New York: HarperCollins, 1990).
3 Ibid.
4 Ibid.
5 Richard Lamming, *Causes and Effects of Structural Change in the European Components Industry* (International Motor Vehicle Programme, Massachusetts Institute of Technology, USA, 1989).
6 D. Coffey, *The Myth of Japanese Efficiency: The World Car Industry in a Globalising Age* (Cheltenham: Edward Elgar, 2006).
7 D. Coffey and P. R. Tomlinson, 'Globalisation, vertical relations, and the J-made firm', *Journal of Post Keynesian Economics*, 26(1) (Fall, 2003): 117–44.
8 M. A. Cusumano, *The Japanese Automobile Industry: Technology and Management at Nissan and Toyota* (Cambridge, MA and London: Harvard University Press, 1985).
9 A. A. Berle and G. C. Means, *The Modern Corporation and Private Property* (New York: Macmillan, 1932).
10 Womack *et al.*, *The Machine that Changed the World.*
11 National Association of Manufacturers, *How Structural Costs Imposed on US Manufacturers Harm Workers and Threaten Competitiveness* (Cambridge, MA: National Association of Manufacturers, 2003).

9 Offshoring to India

Human resource challenges

Bernard Arogyaswamy

The rapid, almost explosive, growth of East Asian economies in the short span of a little over two decades brought revolutionary economic change to a wide swathe of countries ranging from Japan and South Korea to Malaysia and Thailand. Exports were typically the drivers of growth that was most often launched from a base of imported technologies. While, no doubt, there were variations among the countries' strategies (the Japanese, for instance, often tested their products in the heat of intense local competition; South Korea's growth was fueled by the *chaebol* or large conglomerates; Taiwan drew on the energy of small and medium-sized enterprises; and so on), the model was faithfully implemented until domestic markets had expanded sufficiently.[1,2] Where foreign investments were needed to implement the new technology, by and large, multinational corporations (MNCs) provided both capital and technology with a view to exporting either the finished product, or components for assembly in the country of sale. Over time, as MNCs began to recognize the cost savings they could realize, and developed mechanisms to coordinate far-flung operations in regard to quality and delivery, outsourcing became one of the keys to success in many manufacturing industries. With the emergence of China as a player on the industrial stage in the 1980s, the race to outsource intensified even more.[3,4,5,6]

The impact of outsourcing on consumers in advanced countries (mainly in terms of product price and variety) has rarely been disputed.[7] Over the years, observers have, on occasion, been critical of companies shifting jobs abroad, the erosion of critical capabilities, and of foreign governments' implementation of industrial policy, by supporting local businesses. However, for various reasons, manufacturing outsourcing has proceeded apace and China has emerged as the dominant force as vender both in developed nations and among its neighbors in Asia.[8,9] The importing of products and the exporting of manufacturing jobs has generally been accepted in developed nations, in part due to the belief that routine manufacturing is best carried out in low-wage countries, while knowledge-intensive manufacturing (e.g. aircraft) would continue to be centered in countries like the US, Germany, Britain, and Japan. Even more strongly held was the belief that services requiring high-tech resources (human, equipment, informational, and organizational) would always remain the domain of firms in advanced nations.

In part, this confidence stemmed from the strong base in knowledge creation that these nations possess. The research and development (R&D) effort in countries like the US (around 2.5 percent on a gross domestic product (GDP) of over $11 trillion) dwarfs that in countries like China and India, whose GDPs are around $2 trillion and $800 billion with R&D efforts of the order of 1.2 percent and 1 percent respectively.[10] Investments in the US, and standards attained there in high-level technical education, are far ahead of what one would find in comparable institutions in large developing nations like China and India. The exciting developments in areas like chip design, high-speed computing, nanotechnology and biotechnology originate, in the main, from the triad (North America, Western Europe, and Japan), as one would expect.[11] Even when the manufacture of some of the products spawned in these areas (e.g. digital cameras, cell phones, advanced chips) is outsourced to China or Thailand, it doesn't seem to cause much concern among people in technologically advanced countries.[12] The explanation lies partly in the expectation and assurance that the knowledge driving these innovations resides firmly within their shores.[13] A similar sentiment prevailed, until recently, in the service industry as well. That is, it was expected that routine transaction processing, involving low-wage jobs, would be exported, and that the workforces in the triad countries would specialize in, and dominate, high-value-added services, such as system design, project management, engineering, consultancy services, and R&D for outsourced products. However, with the passage of time, as more and more jobs requiring progressively higher knowledge inputs are exported all over the world, a sense of disquiet has begun to infuse the debate on 'offshoring,' or outsourcing to foreign firms.[14,15]

Service offshoring has gained momentum over the past decade, and the reasons for its popularity are varied. To begin with, companies were drawn to offshore locations due to their lower wage rates, the cost advantage being as high as 60–70 percent for India and China (though set-up costs, infrastructure expenditure, etc. also need to be factored in.) Flexibility in ramping up or down also makes offshoring more attractive. An added bonus is that workers in countries like China and India are capable of delivering high-quality work, and are willing to work long hours. The time difference facilitates faster completion times, resulting in a combination of cost, quality, and cycle time that is difficult to resist. Experienced suppliers enhance the lure of specific offshoring locations. Other factors such as a competent educational system, a functioning infrastructure, cultural compatibility, language fluency (typically in English), and a supportive government are, so to speak, the icing on the offshoring 'cake.'[16] Overall, though countries like Canada and Ireland have an edge in language skills and cultural affinity, factors such as cost, depth of labor pool, time difference, and so on, have combined to make

India, despite some deficiencies that we will discuss later, the most favored destination for high-tech service work.

We now consider two firms: one Indian, and the other an American MNC. The former's core business is in various forms of service outsourcing, while the other specializes in a gamut of HR functions on behalf of its clients. The two firms, Infosys and Manpower, were selected to provide a deeper sense of the potential for, and challenges facing, the offshoring business in India.

Infosys is based in Bangalore, which, at an altitude of about 300 feet above sea level, is generally cool and dry most of the year, making it an attractive destination for foreign firms. Once known as the Garden City – it still is home to a range of beautiful trees and flowering plants – Bangalore is a teeming cosmopolitan city of over seven million people. Infosys has its sprawling campus in Electronics City, located about ten miles from the heart of the metropolitan area. My contact, Peeyush Dubey, Manager of Global Sourcing Marketing, met me at one of the many gates, all of which are heavily guarded. A management graduate in his mid to late twenties, Dubey exemplifies the breed of young, creative, energetic Infoscions (as Infosys employees are termed) who form the company's vital core. We drove to his office building in a modified golf cart, passing a few ultramodern glass and steel buildings along the way, including one that looked to be a recreation of the glass pyramid outside the Louvre in Paris, and that turned out to be the new multimedia auditorium. We walked over to meet with Aditya Jha, Head of Communications, and discussed the challenges the company faced in sustaining its meteoric growth. Founded in 1981, by a group of seven who contributed a total of $2,500, Infosys is now, by any standards, a bona fide success story. Its sales revenues doubled between 2002 and 2004, and again between 2004 and 2006, in which year it topped $2 billion. Revenues for the year ending March 2007 have passed the $3 billion mark, a jump of about 50 percent in a year! Net profits run at a cool 25 percent of sales, and the company (listed on NASDAQ) has a market value of the order of $20 billion, which is about the same as that of General Motors.[17]

How did a company based in India, a so-called developing country, scale such heights? As is true of most companies that experience rapid growth, Infosys, to begin with, was in the right place at the right time to take advantage of opportunities as they arose. Subsequently, it created its own opportunities, and new capabilities to match its strategies. In the late 1980s, there was an undeniable movement, in Indian policy circles, away from a strictly controlled economic regimen to a greater reliance on private enterprise. Reform was, so to speak, in the air. Matters came to a head in 1991, when the country almost defaulted on its foreign debt, and 'market reforms' were ushered in.

MNCs had discovered the cost savings involved in setting up IT-enabled services (ITeS) (also known as business process outsourcing (BPO)) businesses in the early 1990s, which included software and back-office processing. Back-office processing encompasses both voice and transaction-based activities, an example of the former being customer assistance, troubleshooting, etc.

over the phone, while transaction processing covers recording of used airline tickets, checking of insurance claims, preparing tax returns, and so on. Subsequently, offshoring has come to encompass other IT, such as developing software packages, application programming, engineering solutions, and so on.[18,19,20] We will return to these higher-value-added services later. Later, MNCs started scouting around for firms that could do more than process routine transactions or provide voice-based services. Enter Infosys and its competitors, Wipro and Tata Consulting Services (TCS). Drawing on engineers graduating from the many technical colleges and universities in India, and particularly those in the southern region, these firms set their sights on developing software for their foreign (mainly American) clients. While the premier Indian Institutes of Technology (IITs) were important sources for recruitment, the cream of the output from a proliferation of technical institutions as well as from training schools (described in greater detail later) also became a prime source of talent. As firms like Infosys started attracting more customers from the US, the Indian government introduced tax incentives, and state governments (particularly those in which the leading software cities like Bangalore, Hyderabad, and Chennai were located) got into the act as well, offering subsidies and improving upon, if not creating, the necessary infrastructure. While the cities concerned (and others like Mumbai, Pune, and Gurgaon, near Delhi) have succeeded all too well in attracting foreign and domestic investment in IT, the quality of infrastructure still leaves much to be desired. One marvels not so much that the IT and ITeS industries have grown in scale and scope so rapidly, but that they have done so in spite of having to cope with unreliable electricity supplies, diminishing water resources, apparently unremitting traffic congestion, and high levels of pollution in many of the cities hosting such industries. Even when certain essential elements are in place, complementary factors could prove to be stumbling blocks. Airline passenger traffic, for instance, is growing at 25 percent per year, spawning a whole host of new airlines, many with ambitious plans for expansion. The state of the country's airports is, however, nothing short of abysmal. Compared to China, the airports in India appear shabby and inefficient. (The author, and about two hundred passengers, on landing at Bangalore airport, could not find a single baggage cart and were asked to call a posted phone number to procure the carts!) The competition among various Indian states to attract foreign and domestic investments in knowledge-economy industries does, however, provide some grounds for optimism. Bangalore's gridlocked traffic, power failures, and inadequate airport (a modern facility at a new location has been nearly ten years under construction and is nowhere near completion) have caused companies to consider, if not actively pursue, alternative location strategies. IT centers in Hyderabad, Chennai, Pune, and other cities across the country are actively competing, indeed even bidding, against each other to attract IT, ITeS, and other knowledge firms.

Infosys's growth lay, and continues to be derived from, its genius at recognizing emerging opportunities among its multitude of foreign customers or, perhaps more importantly, working to create such opportunities. The company has progressively moved up the value ladder from staff augmentation through routine transaction processing and writing software to developing and customizing entire packages, diagnosing clients' needs (as partners where necessary), acting as problem solvers capable of delivering an integrated chain of products and services, functioning as consultants, participating in engineering and design in high-tech industries such as aerospace, and so on.[21,22] Though one of the firm's competitive advantages remains relatively low cost, Infosys has been undergoing a continuous metamorphosis over the past quarter-century. Not only has it made itself increasingly accessible and indispensable to its customers, it has also kept would-be rivals guessing and off-balance by its strategic flexibility (adaptive, anticipative, and proactive) based on developing new capabilities.

The progression of strategies adopted by firms such as Infosys is illustrated in Figure 9.1. In area 1, transactions are relatively structured and predictable (processing of credit card receipts, cancelled airline tickets, and so on), involving no personal contact with customers. Area 2 is characterized by equally programmable work, except that, in dealing with customers (customer service, troubleshooting, etc.), employees need a modicum of interpersonal and communication skills, and may have to adjust to diverse

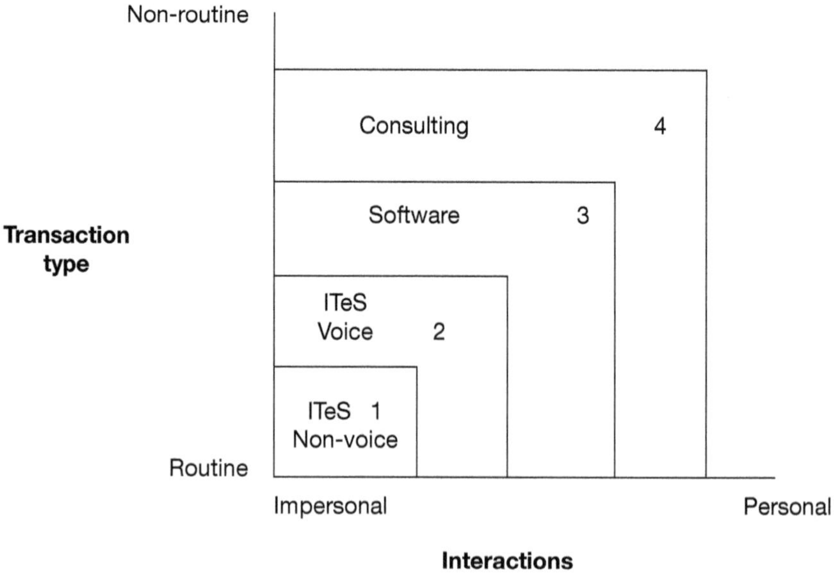

Figure 9.1 Strategic change at Infosys.

Source: Authors' own.

customers' needs. Software development (area 3), on the other hand, calls for higher levels of personal interaction to gauge customers' requirements, solve problems, and so on. Customization also makes for increasingly unstructured task performance. Clearly, employees of firms in area 4 have to demonstrate the highest levels of discretion, judgment and, perhaps, even spontaneity. Though these shifts in strategy – and concomitant transformations in capabilities – have served Infosys well, not all its clients are entirely pleased since Infosys has, by broadening its scope of operations, become their competitor. Though such firms (e.g. IBM, Accenture) still need to work with Infosys to facilitate the functioning of the other segments of their businesses, they are, as we shall see later, shifting their strategies and putting more pressure on Infosys to respond with a new strategic position.

Among the characteristics that define Infosys's approach to business success are what it refers to as 'scalability' and 'learnability.'[23] Scalability refers to the degree to which the service provided to any customer can be expanded in scope(range and depth) and scale, as well as replicated for other customers. The concept of scalability encompasses the capacity to fine-tune or transform organizational competences as needed across time, space, and client characteristics. Explicitly included is the attention paid to variations in client needs, adaptation to corporate and national cultures, and transferability across value chains. Scalability is put into action (and, indeed, even internalized) by fostering 'learnability' – a practice whereby employees are encouraged to exercise their powers of inductive reasoning, that is, of drawing general inferences from specific experiences. This quality is deemed critical to linking items of knowledge – technical, marketing, financial, etc. – together to improve existing businesses and to create new ones. Both scalability and learnability combine to make possible Infosys's Global Delivery Model (GDM) and its Knowledge Management (KM) System.[24] The GDM requires that project execution be carried out in less expensive locations in a different time zone, where, moreover, the leveraging of scalability and scope economies can be maximized. The KM system, as is often true of such technologies, attempts to collect and organize nuggets of experience. Sharing is encouraged, as is the publication of papers on the company's technical achievements in practitioner journals. Infosys is a dazzling example of a firm from a developing country going from strength to strength in a high-tech area. Along with Wipro and TCS, Infosys has blazed a trail of achievement that has both delighted its corporate customers, and alarmed citizens of some developed nations (in particular, the US and Britain) concerning the flight of jobs.[25] Employing over 70,000 people worldwide, with an increasing presence in North America, Europe, Japan, and China[26] Infosys is now truly an MNC in its own right. As long as it was involved in back-office work or executed projects on behalf of intermediate customers (such as Accenture) Infosys (and companies like it) were buffered, so to speak, from the uncertainty of dealing with the users of their services. Now that they are, more and more, dealing directly with the ultimate users, firms like Infosys have had to deploy more and varied resources at or near customer locations. In addition to hiring competent professionals abroad, Infosys has also hired over five hundred relatively inexperienced people in the US, and is providing them with extensive orientation into the company's systems, culture, and management style at its campuses in Bangalore and in nearby Mysore.

The challenges facing Infosys, as it attempts to position itself as a global competitor, should not be understated.[27] First, they need to confront the 'country of origin' problem. That is, customers associate companies with their home countries, which, if less developed, tag their firms with the same label. Though firms from India have received relatively favorable press in the IT and BPO industries, as Infosys attempts to cultivate end users (with whom it has hitherto not had face-to-face transactions), it has to present a reassuringly professional face to its clients, unlike its relatively experienced rivals with a reputation for dependability and interactive expertise. Second, the customer–IT vendor interface now goes well beyond users specifying their requirements and vendors meeting those needs. The expectation now is that IT firms will 'embed' themselves into their clients' businesses and devise effective strategies and business models to help improve their overall performance.[28] As American companies, for instance, turn to innovation to give them a clear competitive edge over their low-cost rivals abroad, it is indeed paradoxical that these same offshore competitors must demonstrate the ability to support this innovativeness! A third question that faces Infosys is that of security. Physically, it is equipped to resist a terrorist attempt to commandeer its facilities (strict electronic and personnel-based measures ensure that access to its campuses is closely monitored). The firm has bolstered system security as well and its Capability Maturity Model (CMM) level 5 certification signifies its attainment of the highest possible software credentials and also establishes its security capabilities. With the potential for possibly 30 percent of banking services being offshore in the next few years, Infosys, with its expertise in this area, stands to gain significantly.

A few days after my visit to Infosys in Bangalore, I flew to Chennai by Air Deccan, one of the slew of discount airlines that are criss-crossing India's skies. The fare at $20 for a distance of a little over two hundred miles seemed reasonable enough (even if the aircraft was a turboprop). I traveled across Chennai to meet Johann Pillai, a top executive with Manpower, Inc., a multinational out of Milwaukee, Wisconsin. Manpower is striving to achieve a strong, if not dominant, position in the booming recruitment market in India. (Chennai used to be known as Madras until a few local politicians decided that a British-given name just would not do – this notwithstanding the fact that Madras was founded by the British and numerous reminders of its British past, such as statues of Queen Victoria and Lord Minto, still stand in prominent places.) Johann Pillai lives in a recently developed part of Chennai, on the East Coast Road, which runs along the Bay of Bengal through formerly French Pondichery down to the southern tip of India.

Johann's career, over the past 15 years, reflects, in part, the changes that have taken place in India over the same period. After completing a bachelor's degree in Commerce at Loyola College (one of the many influential Jesuit institutions in India), he had worked for a few years for the National Institute for Information Technology (NIIT), a company whose mission was to bring increasingly sophisticated software and hardware skills within geographic and financial reach of young people seeking skills most needed in a modern economy. Arguably one of the early drivers of the 'software revolution' that was to sweep India, NIIT expanded rapidly through franchising. Johann's forte was to attract and select the most competent franchisees. The impact that the spread of computer instruction centers to the farthest corners of the country had on creating interest, and developing skills, in IT cannot be disputed. (NIIT, incidentally, continues to flourish and has, so to speak, taken its show on the road – to China, among other countries.[29])

As India shifted to an increasingly service-oriented economy (services comprise approximately 50 percent of GDP, the rest being evenly split between manufacturing and agriculture), the demand for professionals trained in ramping up operations nationwide expanded rapidly. After a stint of a few years in industries such as medical testing, Johann realized that IT had turned into a mammoth growth business in India (total revenues amount to around $30 billion today and are projected to touch $50 billion by 2010), and decided to accept an offer from Manpower, Inc. to take up a position as one of its two General Managers in India. Manpower has operations in over 40 countries, generating annual revenues of nearly $15 billion in 2004, almost 80 percent of which came from operations outside the US.[30] The scope of Manpower's activities includes recruitment – temporary, contract, and permanent – as well as assessment and training. If clients face declining demand, Manpower assists with employee transition and outplacement. Where needed, the firm undertakes managed services that take on complete business functions, such as help desks or call centers.[31,32]

Manpower forecasts that India will continue to be among its fastest-growing markets for at least the next decade. From rather modest beginnings in the early 1990s, offshoring of various services to India picked up considerable pace, subsequently reaching a total value of $30 billion in 2006. BPO exports totaled over $6 billion in 2005–06 and are expected to exceed $10 billion by 2010. Approximately 50 percent of all BPO services are provided by 'captive' units, that is, enterprises under the control of the client organization. For instance, General Electric and HSBC own and operate massive units in India to which they outsource most of their transaction processing.[33] The other 50 percent of the BPO business is split among 'pure' BPO providers based in India (about 20 percent), operations of IT multinationals (around 15 percent), and the so-called tier I Indian IT firms, which include Infosys, Wipro, and TCS, contributing no more than 5–10 percent of BPO revenues, focusing instead on higher-value-added (and revenue) services. The second tier among IT firms (e.g. Satyam) also prefers to devote attention to the more lucrative, increasingly knowledge-driven IT segment, and also provides about 5 percent of BPO output.

Since Manpower's operations in India are focused mainly on ITeS, we shall focus on this aspect of offshoring to India. Total BPO revenues in India, which stood at $3.4 billion in 2004, were expected to more than double to over $7 billion in 2006. Manpower's business has grown rapidly in India over the past five years.[34] Its headquarters are in New Delhi with two major branches based in Bangalore and Chennai. The latter is headed up by Johann, while the Bangalore office reports to Mr K. Subramaniam, an engineer by training, with whom I had the opportunity to meet. The demand for workers in the BPO segment has shifted up from about 25,000 in 2000 to about 415,000 in 2006, and is expected to touch one million before 2010.[35] Manpower's strategy has included spreading the net far and wide by opening offices all over the country in an attempt to capture as much of the talent as possible. Johann's proven ability to scale up operations of service businesses by establishing/franchising new offices has helped, particularly because the availability of skilled people, in the locations where they are most needed, is showing signs of drying up. Manpower's estimate of HR needs in India over the coming years is both optimistic and alarming. The recent forecasts indicate that the demand for skilled employees in the BPO segment is likely to continue its meteoric upward trajectory.[36] The company's quarter-by-quarter estimates during 2005 and 2006 projected that the growth rate is likely to remain at about 30–40 percent. Subramaniam added that BPO offshoring today is no more than the tip of the iceberg, in the sense that the potential demand is far greater, almost ten times of the present value. The CEO of Cognizant, an IT firm, echoes this view.[37]

The supply of qualified personnel has, by and large, kept pace with the demand until recently due, in part, to the proliferation of engineering colleges all over the country, but in particular near the major BPO centers, resulting in an output of over 200,000 engineering graduates every year. However, as Johann quickly pointed out, out of the roughly 1,200 engineering institutions in the country, no more than 50–100 are capable of meeting the skill requirements of BPO centers. He also indicated that, in his experience, only about 5 percent of those who applied to Manpower met the standards. Among the more common shortcomings are an inability to communicate clearly in English, orally and in writing, and a lack of basic social skills, encompassing both a general deficiency in relating to other people and, more specifically, severe problems with working in teams. More worryingly, many of those fresh out of engineering school are ill-equipped, where knowledge and analytical capabilities are concerned, to take up entry level positions without, in most cases, extensive training and orientation.

Compounding the HR recruitment problem posed by a potentially widening gap between availability and demand are the challenges BPO employers (captive and locally based) face, in retaining people, in most of whom they have invested considerable resources in terms of recruitment, training, relationships with customers, and so on. The attrition rate is beginning to climb steadily and at many BPO centers has reached almost 50 percent. The turnover is particularly high early on, touching about 30 percent in the first three months.[38] Part of the problem lies in the high expectations that incoming employees have of their jobs and of the firms hiring them. Wages have risen over the past four years by about 150 percent, making the compensation progressively a greater draw for recent graduates. However, the climbing salaries combined with all the publicity given to the 'booming' IT/ITeS industries, and the strong position that Indian firms have achieved in the global market, have served to raise employees' expectations, in particular those of the new recruits.[39] Many are unprepared for the rather routine, even repetitive tasks that they have to perform both in the voice and non-voice segments. The long working hours, mostly in shifts, are often a cause for dissatisfaction. For a while, after a woman working a late shift was kidnapped and raped by the driver of a company van, employee safety concerns came to the fore. The odd hours that employees worked (albeit in air-conditioned, comfortable offices – not sweat shops, by any means) and the safety of the employees, especially of women, were debated widely and critically in the press. BPO centers had to take prompt and effective actions, under the watchful eye of the media, to reassure employees and a concerned public. The need to sustain the recruitment of new employees at increasingly higher levels also no doubt induced a quick response.

In fact, when I had met Mr Subramaniam (Manpower's General Manager in Bangalore), he showed me a PowerPoint presentation he makes to engineering graduates in order to induce them to apply for a job with Manpower. The presentation, complete with facts, figures, and frills, is intended to reinforce the case that the demand for ITeS services is going through the roof, that it offers marvelous career prospects, and that they could do no better than apply for a job at Manpower. Subramaniam explained to me that he often took his show 'on the road' in order to sell the idea of a promising employment scenario, despite any reports to the contrary, to an increasingly skeptical college-age population.

However, there are clearly challenges facing BPO firms, Subramaniam's informative and upbeat presentation notwithstanding. The prospects for advancement/career progression are limited. The ratio of supervisors to line workers is about 15 percent, making promotions a rather remote prospect for the vast majority of new recruits. The escalation in wage rates and the high attrition rate have clearly brought pressure to bear on BPO firms to find ways to combat the upward movement in costs in the case of both captives and locals. Compounding the challenges posed by increasing turnover, rising wages, and falling productivity is the need to maintain a so-called 'minimum economic size,' which, in the BPO business is of the order of 3,000 employees. Dipping too far below this level typically results in the loss of scale economies. Making matters worse is the paradoxical fact that the employees who end up leaving are generally the best qualified. Many

BPO firms are now faced with the prospect that those who do not leave are the less productive ones who, moreover, have to be induced to stay so as not to make the attrition rate and replacement needs even more acute.

The cost advantage that India-based operations enjoyed has gradually dwindled, but the overall edge remains significant enough when considered in tandem with the other factors mentioned earlier. Other countries that are taking aggressive action to establish a foothold in the IT/ITeS industries have to confront hurdles of their own. For instance, while the Philippines boasts a fairly well-educated population which is fluent in English, the quantum of technical graduates and the intensity of clusters of similar and complementary businesses are still not sufficient to challenge the established order in the Indian BPO industry. China, on the other hand, is clearly adding considerably to its technical capabilities every year and is creating agglomerations of IT businesses so that they can feed off each other. However, the lack of widespread fluency in English is still somewhat of a hurdle, though one that is being addressed by schools and universities as well as by the scores of language institutes that have sprung up. Yet, as one executive at an Indian BPO firm pointed out, the difference between the general run of workers in China and India remains the ability to speak English as against being able to *think* in it as well. China enjoyed a head start of more than a decade over India, both in relaxing its laws governing foreign direct investment (FDI) and in achieving a low-cost position in manufacturing. India, even after 1991, has moved rather slowly in opening up to FDI, effectively putting it further behind China in manufacturing. However, India's forays into software and BPO, dating back to the mid 1990s have given it a substantial edge in high-tech-based services.

An additional brake on China's progress in playing catch-up is the shortage of competent supervisory personnel. A Manpower, Inc. study speaks to the apparent paradox of a country with a population of over 1.2 billion experiencing a talent scarcity. But the report paints a rather grim picture of the supervisory shortfall, estimating that it could affect not just China's ability to make inroads into the BPO market but also its continued dominance in efficient manufacturing. There is, however, a cadre of middle managers being created in China, partly by the multitude of management programs (many sponsored by foreign business schools) and partly by the training provided by MNCs over the past decade or so. Manpower's growth estimates for HR demand in China are also a fraction of the forecast for India, reinforcing the likelihood that, India's HR problems notwithstanding, its pre-eminence in the BPO field is not likely to be challenged anytime soon.

IT and BPO businesses in India have expanded rapidly in terms of revenues, employment, scope of services offered, range of customers targeted, and, in general, in terms of their impact on outsourcing worldwide. The prospects of the demand for IT offshoring continuing to rise sharply are undeniably bright. India is best placed, among the countries vying for this market, to capitalize on the diverse emerging opportunities. Manpower, Inc.'s highly optimistic forecasts, and strategies to implement them, indicate how seriously it takes the growth potential in the Indian BPO market. However, the looming HR challenges need to be addressed expeditiously if the lucrative IT and ITeS businesses are to continue growing without compromising on the quality they have hitherto maintained. The actions needed to deal with the problems of undereducated technical workers, the resistance to performing repetitive routine tasks, high turnover, a lack of social skills, and so on, are the responsibility of a variety of institutional actors.

Infosys and its rivals in the IT industry (e.g. Wipro and TCS), which have ambitions of succeeding in consultancy and other high-knowledge, customer-interactive businesses, are extremely concerned about the sputtering supply of qualified people. Infosys, anxious to sustain its GDM, is tackling the problem at the college level by offering support to technical institutions. In addition to scholarships, Infosys is also providing resources to faculty to upgrade their skills. Along with Infosys, other companies, such as IBM and Accenture, are also vying for Indian IT workers, and are engaged in an intensive effort to draw the best talent to them by paying highly publicized visits to the campuses of second-tier colleges. The intent is to encourage a spirit of competition among students with a view to lifting more of them above the threshold standards for recruitment.

Efforts are also under way in most BPO firms to not only provide employees with the skills and knowledge they need to perform tasks competently (and take on additional responsibilities as needed) but also to acculturate them into a modern organization. Verbal and written communication, teamwork, customer orientation, and cultural training are now standard fare. Infosys and other Indian firms are discovering that the transition from being a domestic firm to becoming an MNC with operations across the globe could be a difficult one. Faced with the need to hire local citizens in countries like the US and Germany, Infosys is being forced to confront the challenges of managing a workforce that may not be committed to its corporate culture. The well-known tension between corporate and national cultures[40] has to be addressed despite the fact that Infosys's management is relatively enlightened and decentralized. As critical as the cultural issue is for Infosys, the need for a constantly shifting strategy might well be even more significant. The expectation on the part of end customers, with whom Infosys increasingly deals directly, that their vendor will expand their scope of services to developing innovative strategies and business models, raises the stakes considerably.[41] Taking on such a challenge is indeed a far cry from the relatively 'insulated' operations that Infosys has been used to in the past. Coping with the demanding challenge of managing employees from diverse cultures, of articulating direction and detail for a range of customers, of hiring and retaining employees in an increasingly demanding labor market, and so on, might stretch Infosys's immense capabilities to the hilt. In fact, the firm will undoubtedly need to build new capabilities, and do it quickly – while dealing with an ever-changing cultural challenge.

Clearly, the big question that looms ahead of the Indian offshoring business as a whole is whether HR quality can be upgraded through collaborative efforts among the major players, such as the top-tier IT firms, interested MNCs, state and central governments, colleges and universities, banks offering educational loans, and so on. Thus far, the market has proved to be an effective mechanism for adjusting the flow of qualified personnel to match the demand. However, given the problems created, in a sense, by the industry's success, a coordinated 'innovation system' needs to be designed and operationalized at both the national and local levels. At the national level, the temptation to distribute resources (evenly across disciplines and regions) must be resisted. Capabilities are notoriously 'sticky,'[42] making them almost impossible to create from scratch or to transplant. While the efforts to replicate Bangalore's (and other such cities') success in other places is creditable (especially in view of the creaking infrastructure in some of today's IT centers), enhancing facilities at existing locations might produce far more rewarding results. By the same token, cooperation among contiguous regions (e.g. those to which Bangalore and Chennai belong) might prove more effective in addressing resources deficiencies than the present strategy of rivalry among them.

Notes

1 J. McCord, *The Dawn of the Pacific Century* (New Brunswick, NJ: Transaction, 1993).
2 World Bank, *The East Asian Miracle* (New York: Oxford University Press, 1993).
3 K. Ohmae, *The End of the Nation State* (New York: Free Press, 1995).
4 K. Ferdows, 'Making the most of foreign factories,' *Harvard Business Review*, 5(2) (1997): 73–91.
5 D. Drezner, 'The outsourcing bogeyman,' *Foreign Affairs* (May/June 2004): 22–34.
6 M. Isobe, S. Makino, and D. B. Montgomery, 'Resource commitment, entry timing, and market performance of foreign direct investments in emerging economies: the case of Japanese international joint ventures in China,' *Academy of Management Journal*, 43(3) (2000): 468–85.
7 *Business Week*, 'The future of outsourcing,' January 30, 2006. All *Business Week* articles cited in these notes are available online at: www.businessweek.com.
8 A. Ting, 'Outsourcing in China,' *Industrial Engineer*, 36(12) (December 2004): 46–50.
9 K. Bronfenbrenner and S. Luce, 'Offshoring,' *Multinational Monitor*, 25(12) (December 2004): 26–9.
10 National Science Foundation, *Science & Engineering Indicators, 2004* (Arlington, VA: NSF, Division of Science, Resources and Statistics, 2004).
11 Organization for Economic Cooperation and Development (OECD), www.oecd.com, 2005.
12 Ting, 'Outsourcing in China.'
13 *Business Week*, 'Innovation: outsourcing's second wave,' October 3, 2006.
14 *Business Week*, 'IBM's insider in outsourcing,' July 28, 2006.
15 Bronfenbrenner and Luce, 'Offshoring.'
16 A. Vashistha and A. Vashistha, *The Offshore Nation* (New Delhi: Tata/McGraw-Hill, 2005).
17 Infosys, www.infosys.com, 2006.

18 *Los Angeles Times*, 'Nation losing more than unskilled work,' October 20, 2003.
19 Forbes, 'The new HP way: world's cheapest consultants,' www.forbes.com, December 12, 2003.
20 *Business Week*, 'The future of outsourcing.'
21 S. Patel and M. Subramaniam, *From Outsourcing Projects to Strategic Relationships* (Bangalore: Infosys, 2006).
22 R. Puri, A. Saithu, and S. Singh, 'Global engineering: the new imperative for the aerospace industry,' *Infosys Viewpoint*, www.infosys.com/industries/aerospace-defense, December 2005.
23 R. Garud and A. Kumaraswamy, 'Infosys: architecture of a scalable corporation,' a case study, New York University, Stern School of Business, December 13, 2003.
24 R. Schmelzer, *Infosys: Global Consulting Powerhouse*, digital book, www.zapthink.com (Waltham, MA: ZapThink, October 19, 2004).
25 Patel and Subramaniam, *From Outsourcing Projects to Strategic Relationships.*
26 *The Economist*, 'If in doubt, farm it out,' June 2006.
27 *Business Week*, 'The future of outsourcing.'
28 *Business Week*, 'Innovation.'
29 *The Hindu*, 'NIIT plans more centers in China,' www.hinduonnet.com, February 1, 2002.
30 Manpower, *Annual Report 2004* (Milwaukee, WI: Manpower, 2005).
31 Manpower, *Offshoring to India: Managing Talent in a Transforming Environment* (Gurgaon, India: Manpower, 2006).
32 Manpower, *Manpower Employment Outlook Survey, Quarter 3* (Gurgaon, India: Manpower, 2006).
33 S. Subramaniam and B. Atri, 'Captives in India: a research study,' *Infosys Research*, www.infosys.com/global-sourcing/white-papers, February 2006.
34 Manpower, *Annual Report 2004.*
35 Manpower, *Manpower Employment Outlook Survey, Quarter 3.*
36 *Business Week*, 'Offshoring to India hasn't hit its peak,' February 17, 2006.
37 Ibid.
38 *Business India*, 'The war for talent,' August 13, 2006.
39 *The Economist*, 'If in doubt, farm it out.'
40 S. Schneider and J. L. Barsoux, *Managing Across Cultures* (London: Prentice-Hall, 1997).
41 *Business Week*, 'Innovation.'
42 A. Markusen, 'Sticky places in slippery space: a typology of industrial districts,' *Economic Geography*, 72(3) (1994): 293–313.

10 Information technology outsourcing in Korea

Hyun Jeong Kim and Wonchang Hur

Introduction

In 2000, Samsung Electro-Mechanics (SEM) had to withdraw from its memorandum of understanding with UPS Korea on outsourcing their logistics operation. While promoting the outsourcing contract, the two companies could not come to an agreement regarding the perception of the visible effects of outsourcing; for example, the point in time when profits could be taken, and the method of sharing the profits.[1] There were many other reasons for this failure, but the most significant one was probably a lack of lateral thinking and mutual understanding. The employees of SEM considered UPS as a subordinate service provider rather than their strategic partner. Because there was no confidence in each other, the SEM employees refused to cooperate with UPS employees and even resisted the outsourcing policies from the top management. Moreover, the fact that some companies misused outsourcing as a method of restructuring their organisations made the SEM employees afraid of losing their jobs.

Outsourcing can be described as commissioning part of the business operation to other company. According to Klepper, IT outsourcing can be defined as 'the provision of services by a vendor firm to a client'.[2] Similarly, Altinkemer *et al.* describe it as 'an act of subcontracting a part, or all, of an organisation's I.T. work to an external vendor(s), to manage on its behalf'.[3] Outsourcing is one of the major issues facing organisations in today's rapidly changing business environment and IT outsourcing in the Korean context is no exception, and is often carried out by external service provider(s) in order to acquire strategic, economic and technological advantages.

In general, a variety of factors has an impact on the successful performance of IT outsourcing. However, as shown above, the perceived significance of those factors can be different with regard to the area in which the business operates, the size of the organisation, and also the country that it operates in.[4] This chapter presents a current overview of recent developments in outsourcing issues and practices in Korea, attempting to explore whether there are country-specific patterns emerging rather than a global convergence of strategies and practices. By reviewing elements such as the types of outsourcing carried out by Korean organisations and diverse circumstances that prompt outsourcing decisions, this chapter will help readers to understand outsourcing in a country-specific context.

Market status

The need to invest in IT is decided by firms on the basis of strategic need. Large organisations invest in IT in order to improve current IT specifications, while medium-sized organisations focus their investment on developing the infrastructure. Regardless of the different IT investment purposes of individual organisations, a growth in overall IT investment is expected when compared to previous years. As a result, the Korean IT market in 2006 was forecast to grow 6.5 per cent from 2005 with a value of $13.6 billion.[5]

In the following sections, we are going to take a brief look at the current and future status of the IT outsourcing market in Korea. In addition, the competitiveness of corporate Korea as a global outsourcing provider will be examined.

IT outsourcing in Korea

IToutsourcing is a rapidly growing business practice in Korea. The Korean IT outsourcing market is dominated by several large, conglomerate-affiliated firms along with a couple of global IT firms such as IBM and Hewlett Packard. As shown in Table 10.1, the Korean IT outsourcing market in 2006 was forecast to amount to $1.44 billion, up 7.6 per cent from the previous year, and such growth is expected to continue. The anticipated rate of growth will be approximately 8.5 per cent over the next five years. Among various industrial sectors, IT outsourcing of manufacturing companies constitutes the largest portion (40.1 per cent) of the total IT outsourcing market, followed by telecommunications (18.8 per cent), finance (16.2 per cent) and public sectors (14.5 per cent).

Table 10.1 Korean domestic IT outsourcing market forecasts, 2005–10 (US$ billions)[6]

Area	*2005*	*2006*	*2007*	*2008*	*2009*	*2010*	*Rate of growth (2005–10) (%)*
Finance	2,032	2,207	2,414	2,661	2,922	3,189	9.4
Telecommunications	2,351	2,530	2,733	2,967	3,212	3,462	8.0
Manufacturing	5,089	5,473	5,913	6,419	6,975	7,561	8.2
Public sectors	1,810	1,948	2,113	2,323	2,563	2,796	9.1
Logistics	1,012	1,080	1,161	1,260	1,369	1,485	7.9
Education	177	188	202	219	238	258	7.8
Totals	1.34 (8.2%)	1.44 (7.6%)	1.56 (8.2%)	1.70 (9.0%)	1.85 (9.0%)	2.01 (8.5%)	8.5

It is also anticipated that those trends will centre on five areas within IT outsourcing: application management, information systems (IS) outsourcing, network and desktop outsourcing, system infrastructure service provision, and application service provision. Figure 10.1 shows the detailed proportions of these five areas of IT outsourcing from 2003 to 2008.

IS outsourcing has been expected to take most of the market share. In the midst of overall expected growth, this particular type of IT outsourcing is expected to grow further. Application service provision (ASP) is expected to have a high rate of increase (more than 20 per cent) due to the increasing demands of effective operations and in order to decrease IT costs. Also, expansion of enterprise resource planning (ERP) applications by medium-sized companies and governments' need to oversee and maintain IT infrastructure have been identified as main reasons.

According to the Gartner report,[8] another major area in IT outsourcing consists of networking outsourcing. This is due to the efforts of a large Korean telecommunications firms' market initiative, transferring the previous basic network service to a networking outsourcing service by introducing network managed service. Furthermore, data centre outsourcing is expected to grow as a result of an increased requirement from managed web hosting, storage management, and help desks.

According to the 2005 International Data Corporation (IDC) report,[9] the key market trends of Korean IT outsourcing market in 2006 centre around the following issues. First, the report forecast improvement of the overall market through the recognition of the value of IT outsourcing. Second, reinforcement of market entrance to the non-affiliate sectors and a more strengthened management relationship with the target of the affiliate market are expected. Third, expanded partnerships with specialised vendors in specific areas are anticipated. And, finally, exploring market opportunities by linking with project-based service offerings is considered likely.

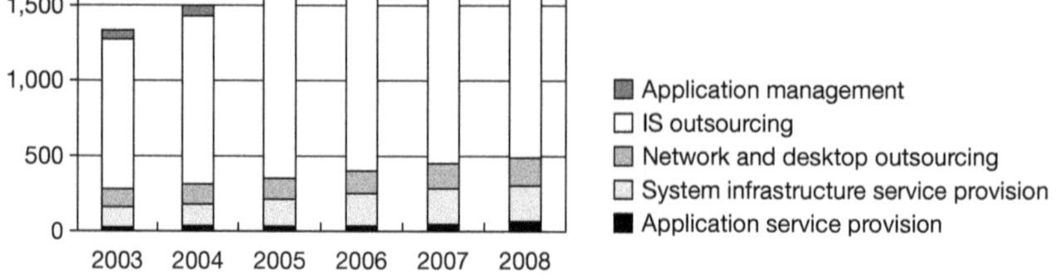

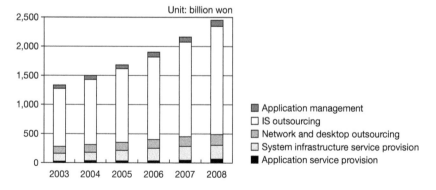

Figure 10.1 Korean IT outsourcing forecast, 2004–08.[7]

In the meantime, according to the report on a survey of Korean companies' outsourcing practices,[10] quality (42.8 per cent) was found to be the most important point when deciding on a contract, followed by the price (27 per cent). Other concerns, such as flexibility of the contract (8 per cent), similarity of corporate culture (6.6 per cent), trust (5.4 per cent), added value (4.8 per cent), previous contracts (2.4 per cent), and other issues (3 per cent) were included in the response. By analysing the survey, the report also emphasised that, in order to have successful outsourcing, the following issues should be carefully considered: continuous relationships; competitiveness of internal job competency; strategic vision and plan; cultural fit between two organisations; and deciding on a competitively priced outsourcing company (see Table 10.2).

Table 10.2 Criteria for the success of outsourcing[11]

Criteria for success	*Explanation*
Continuous relationships	Frequent change of outsourcing company may result in the ineffective management of the outsourcing process.
Competitiveness of internal job competency	Company needs to concentrate on its resources more effectively after the outsourcing.
Strategic vision and plan	Company is required to have a strategic plan that they want to accomplish through the outsourcing practice. In order to do this, thorough analysis is recommended.
Cultural fit between two organisations	Cultural fit between two companies is important because a different understanding could result in everyday miscommunication.
Deciding on a competitively priced outsourcing company	The high cost of outsourcing could result in internal resistance as well as having an effect on a company's profit and loss account.

Corporate Korea

According to a recent report of the Korea Trade Investment Promotion Agency,[12] Korean auto parts makers were picked as the most attractive outsourcing partners by the three biggest US auto manufacturers (General Motors, Ford and Chrysler) based on high quality and price competitiveness. In fact, for the first four months of 2006, Korean shipments of auto parts to the US stood at $2.7 billion, up 45 per cent from the same period of 2005. This amounts to about 3 per cent of Korea's total annual exports. Moreover, due to the recent bankruptcy of Delphi, the largest auto parts company in the US, the increasing global demand for auto parts made by Korean manufacturers is likely to continue.

Traditionally, many Western companies have considered Korea to be the most promising investment area for their manufacturing outsourcing. Despite the rising labour cost and militant labour unions, Korean manufacturing companies have been expected to provide many advantages, including competitiveness on price compared to quality, a good market access to neighbouring countries, a skilled workforce and high productivity.

However, in contrast to such bright prospects of Korean manufacturing outsourcing, many companies have seen that the traditional role of Korea has been gradually replaced by several new developing countries, such as India and China. In fact, Korean companies as IT outsourcing providers seem to be valued less highly among Western countries considering IT offshoring. As shown in Table 10.3, it has been reported that 'corporate Korea', as a possible IT outsourcing service provider, has relatively low competitiveness compared to other countries, such as China and India, in competing in the global IT outsourcing market. Even though corporate Korea holds a stronger position in the IT infrastructure than the other countries in the list, many other problems, such as high labour costs, low labour quality and language barriers have become big obstacles to overcome in achieving competitive advantages in IT outsourcing. Even more, the biggest headache for domestic small and medium-sized enterprises (SMEs) providing IT services is that the domestic IT outsourcing market is also being nibbled at by the above-mentioned countries as large Korean corporations are gradually turning to India or China for outsourcing.

One item of good news regarding corporate Korea in IT outsourcing is that many Japanese companies are looking for IT professionals in the Korean labour market because of a shortage of IT labour specialised in system/network maintenance, software engineering, programming and so on. This trend is expected to grow as the economic situation of Japan gradually recovers from a long period of recession. Moreover, geographical accessibility and cultural similarity can also be considered as positive factors.[14]

Table 10.3 Competitive IT service-providing countries, 2005[13]

Country	*Labour cost*	*Labour quality*	*IT infra-structure*	*Rank*
India	9.69	7.78	4.60	1
China	9.70	6.46	5.20	2
Czech Republic	8.50	5.62	6.20	3
Singapore	6.23	6.92	7.40	4
Canada	5.08	7.60	8.40	6
Philippines	9.80	5.18	5.00	9
Taiwan	6.80	5.79	7.80	16
Korea	**5.58 (41st)**	**6.09 (15th)**	**8.00 (4th)**	**25**
Ireland	3.80	6.37	7.40	27

Trends and features

IT outsourcing industries in the 1980s started focusing on supporting technology, which then later expanded into the application development area. In the middle of 1990s, systems integration (SI) companies came into the industry because of popular demand for database and network configurations. As the speed of IT rapidly expanded through the late 1990s, companies faced difficulties in managing IT resources and infrastructure effectively. Furthermore, IT equipment needed controlled environmental conditions in which to operate, thus increasing the necessary investment, and also organisations realised that there were strategic advantages to be gained from the use of IT. As a result of these changes in the industry context, companies recognised IT outsourcing not only from the economic perspective, as providing cost effective options, but also from the strategic perspective.[15]

In Korea, similar progress has been shown since the 1980s. Korean organisations started to outsource only specific application development projects in the beginning due to the security concerns of valuable information being uncovered. In addition, difficulties in contracting a reliable IT service provider caused the companies to limit their outsourcing.[16] Since 2001, the delay in IT investment has caused the organisations to face difficulties in the competitive business environment and they are at the stage where they cannot afford to delay investment any longer. Another positive movement in the market is the great demand for the progress of a flexible IT systems development to correspond with rapid business changes. Organisations need to cut costs and leverage highly available infrastructure in order to meet budget constraints and support more efficient business processes. In other words, there is an increased need for consolidation as an important step towards utility, a need to focus on the business value improvements (flexibility, security, service levels) with reduced IT costs, and increased interest in server virtualisation technologies such as partitioning and capacity on demand (COD). Already, large conglomerate-affiliated firms have made a plan to invest in IT for strategic management and the same interest has been expanded into the medium-sized firms.[17]

Conglomerate groups

In order to better understand the IT outsourcing practice of Korean companies, it is necessary to understand the features and issues found within the developmental process of large SI companies of Korean conglomerate groups. This is because the IT outsourcing market in Korea has been led by those large SI companies, and thus the features and problems of the early market of IT outsourcing have taken on the characteristics of those features found in the process of SI companies' development.

As the need for high-quality IT services expanded, conglomerate groups such as LG, Samsung, SK and Hyundai in Korea began to establish their own subsidiary companies to integrate IT departments and to create opportunities in the IT industry. Major examples are found in LG-CNS of the LG group, Samsung Data Systems (SDS) of the Samsung group, SK C&C of the SK group, and Hyundai Information Technology (HIT) of the Hyundai group. Table 10.4 lists the relevant information on the major conglomerate groups.

Increasingly, the SI companies of conglomerate groups expanded their IS services beyond their group boundaries into other sectors.[18] In the 2000s, SI companies of conglomerate groups continued to provide IS services to affiliate companies, advancing their contracts to the next level, providing a shared internet-based data centre and email services, and renting servers. According to a survey conducted by the Korean Information Technology Service Industry Association (KITSIA), the SI market expanded from $500 million in 1997 to $12.7 billion in 2006, which is approximately a 12.6 per cent increase compared to the previous year.[19] This figure amounts to 80 per cent of the total IT service market, which includes various IT-related services such as consulting, outsourcing, solutions, maintenance and training.

It has been said that the SI market in Korea has been growing along with the increasing IT service need from the public sector, but the market, in fact, has always shown a surplus supply rather than competition and thus the SI companies have taken on an aggressive low-price strategy to obtain contracts. This is believed to be the major cause of lowering the gross profits of SI companies and has weakened the technological competence of those companies. About half of the total SI market comes from the conglomerate-affiliated firms.[20]

The establishment of subsidiary SI companies has resulted in most of the IS services having to rely on these companies. This trend indicated the increasing realisation in the IT industry that the companies are in need of various IS services and also led to the outsourcing of their entire IS operations to their subsidiary companies. This practice also created entrance barriers

Table 10.4 List of group SI companies in Korean conglomerate groups (from the annual reports of each of the companies, 2006)

Group	*Group SI company*	*Year established*	*Assets (US$ m)*	*Employees*	*Sales (US$ m)*
Samsung	Samsung Data Systems (SDS)	1985	1,074.9	7,092	1,983.7
LG	LG-CNS	1987.1	597.3	6,000	1,676.1
SK	SK C&C	1990.10	1,495.3	2,028	1,060.8
Hyundai	Hyundai Information Technology (HIT)	1989.5	290.5	1,285	365.5
POSCO	POSDATA	1989.11	264.0	1,224	338.5
Daewoo	Daewoo Information Systems	1994	116.9	1,314	188.6

for other IS companies by forcing them to become competitive. These small IS companies usually participate in big contracts as subcontractors rather than win the whole contracts themselves, which is a common phenomenon in other industrial sectors in Korea. Consequently, such an imbalance in the market with regard to competition prohibited IT SMEs with big growth potential from expanding.

Organisational culture of Korean organisations

Korean organisations have their own distinctive characteristics due to the national culture based on Confucianism, which acts as a foundation in all areas of life. The influence of this belief is central to personal everyday life, but is also at the heart of Korean management style. Koreans perceive Confucianism as a form of collectivism, emphasising group benefits as a whole.[21] Therefore, such collectivism allows for a high degree of group harmony within Korean society. This has been pointed out in a study by Hofstede,[22] who shows that Korea features highly in power-distance (a national culture attribute describing the extent to which a society accepts that power in institutions and organisations is distributed unequally) and low in individualism, resulting in Korean organisations emphasising group togetherness as an important value.[23]

The uniqueness of Korean organisations also presents the following features. Authors such as Kim *et al.* and Lee[24] describe leadership in Korea as hierarchically authoritative and paternalistic, resulting in autocratic behaviour. The consciousness of authority and hierarchical values, together with group togetherness, has played a positive role in some aspects, for example in quick decision-making and the regulation of behaviour. However, unlike the general belief that a hierarchically authoritative and paternalistic leadership style presents a rather unfriendly organisational atmosphere, resulting in the loss of organisational commitment and motivation, the authoritarian style of the Korean manager is rarely despotic, is without excessive power abuse and is free from closed interaction.[25] In practice, paternalistic HR management emphasises the principle of reciprocity and collectivism through the ideas of trust, filial attachment, harmony and cooperation. Organisational members understand the rank and order, which has created a distinctive feeling of mutual commitment. This commitment, created both vertically and horizontally, has in turn created a sense of common objectives and a concern that results in a notion of filial attachment. In other words, in practice, in order to meet goals and produce results, filial attachment is emphasised, thus creating a collective team spirit, resulting in a network that encourages employees to commit to spontaneous cooperation in their work efforts.

Other characteristics that Korean organisations possess include the importance of personal relationships based on reputation and respect during business contracts. Personal relationships can be explained by the concept of social capital. Authors such as Adler and Kwon, and Oh *et al.*,[26] explain social capital as the goodwill that is stimulated by the fabric of social relations and that could be mobilised to facilitate action. In other words, group social capital can be described as the formation of social relationships within the social structure of the group itself, as well as the group within the whole organisation. Emphasising social relationships within the Korean organisation presents the importance of informal socialisation outside the workplace with other members of the group in forming group social ties within the organisation. This concept is translated in practice into social relationships appropriated for task-related advice, political support and strategic information.[27]

As we have described in the above section on the conglomerate groups, the management practice of SI companies particularly demonstrates the typical features of Korean organisational culture. SI companies among the big six (see Table 10.4), having to rely on the conglomerate subsidiary companies for investment and project contracts, are influenced by key values of Korean organisational culture, such as harmony, collectivism, filial attachment, leadership, and personal, group and corporate relationships. IT outsourcing practice is strongly networked and characterised by an emphasis on values, feelings and emotions, similar to, and an extension of, family ties.

Small and medium-sized enterprises

Meanwhile, as for the IT operations of SMEs, they relied totally on their internal IT departments, which were very small in size. Starting from the early 1990s, the introduction of the intranet, groupware and ERP packages has been booming among the SMEs, and they began to realise that the effective employment of an innovative IT infrastructure was a critical factor for successful operation of their businesses.

However, due to the lack of expertise in their own IT departments, SMEs recognised the need for outsourcing. IT departments within SMEs usually consisted only of IT professionals who usually lacked understanding of actual business processes and work experience. Even worse, they were not capable of responding immediately to the fast-changing IT environment, and it was not easy to keep their technological competence up to date. According to the National Computerization Agency (NCA), it has been reported that only 54 per cent of Korean SMEs have their own IT departments and 97 per cent of these employ no more than five people.

However, as mentioned earlier, the early market for IT outsourcing was dominated by several major conglomerate groups and their subsidiary IS companies and it was not easy to find vendors who were specialised in providing IS services to SMEs. As IT outsourcing was relatively new to those SMEs at that time, it was not easy to find good examples of success stories or best practices. In addition, they were concerned about disclosing their internal information to other companies, and they did not have sufficient experience and skills in determining details of an outsourcing contract and managing the outsourcing contract effectively.

This situation made them narrow their options in choosing a suitable outsourcing vendor. They tried to select their partner among the firms with which they had been in a close relationship for a long time. In many cases, they contracted their outsourcing services by partly owning a share of the partner firm, or sometimes a new company used to be established by a joint investment with the partner firm. Most SMEs thought that this method could reduce the cost and time required in the process of selecting the best IT outsourcing partner, and that it was possible to settle effectively the potential problems occurring during the outsourcing operation by cooperating with the partner firm over which they had direct control.

Pulmuone is known as the first SME that performed IT outsourcing by establishing a co-owned company with its partner firm. Pulmuone, which was established in 1984, started as a small food company and has grown to a medium-sized company having more than 1,500 employees. As of 2005, its annual revenues amounted to $360 million. By making a joint investment with CSG (Consulting Software Group), which had performed the various IT-related services for Pulmuone for many years, it established an outsourcing company called Linkware (now MetanetBTS). Then, in 1996, Pulmuone initiated a five-year IT outsourcing contract with Linkware. Based on the contract, about 20 employees of Pulmuone's IT department were transferred to Linkware.[28]

Pulmuone's initiative, occurring when there was no precedent for IT outsourcing among SMEs, provided many significant implications in understanding IT outsourcing practices in Korea. Its case has been considered as a reference model for the successful practice of IT outsourcing among SMEs at that time.

During the phase of preparing the outsourcing contract, Pulmuone did not set up any teams for designing the detailed items in the service level agreement (SLA). Instead of identifying all the possible service items and corresponding metrics and cost structures, the company preferred an imperfect contract, which meant that most future problems or unexpected situations were to be resolved mainly by cooperation and discussion between the parties. This reflects the distinctive features of IT outsourcing practice in a Korean context, which is different from that of Western companies, which prefer a more rigid and complete pre-arrangement for dealing with possible future disputes and contentions.

At an earlier stage, the outsourcing charge was computed on a monthly basis. Because there was no predefined framework for exact costing, the service charge was determined just by multiplying the number of input employees by their labour costs. The limitation of the imperfect contract was overcome by strengthening the relationship between Pulmuone and Linkware. They introduced a flexible facility called a help desk, which was designed to resolve various problems, especially any disagreement over charged costs. As the outsourcing operation became more stabilised, they could develop a more reasonable and effective costing scheme based on the data accumulated throughout the frequent meetings and discussions. The standardised costing scheme was incorporated into the SLA and the companies could compute the outsourcing service charge twice a year based on the actual level of service provided, in a more reasonable fashion than before.

The experience of the outsourcing contract has had a positive effect on both companies. For Pulmuone, it was able to understand that the outsourcing service cost could be raised by an excessive request for IS services, which was common in the past context. Now, before requesting a service from Linkware, it pre-investigates the necessity of the service thoroughly. This gave it an opportunity to increase its understanding of the nature of IS services. Linkware also perceived that it could charge the same for the services, as long as the services could be maintained at a certain level. So it tried to identify various types of inefficiency found in providing the IS services, and to remove them without lessening the level of services. These efforts resulted in a 20 per cent decrease in the total service cost.

Many SMEs in Korea at that time followed the example of Pulmuone's outsourcing contract. The primary reason for this type of outsourcing practice at that time can be described as the lack of experience in outsourcing to business and deficiencies in defining a systematic SLA and cost model. Arguably, however, it also might be the result of the distinctive characteristic of Korean companies, which prefer sustainable and reliable relationships based on trust and understanding between customer and supplier.

Challenges and opportunities

So far, we have examined the trends and features of Korean companies in terms of IT outsourcing practice. The twenty-first-century business model is to maximise synergy by networking with companies with complementary values and strengths. As outsourcing practice is expedited globally, Korean companies are facing challenges to survive in an increasingly competitive business environment.

Overcoming the limits – SMEs

Many SMEs are now trying to escape the limits of an exclusive outsourcing contract and are advancing to achieve more strategic success. For example, Maeil, a company that produces a dairy product, could successfully transform its outsourcing service to total outsourcing. Maeil, by benchmarking the success story of Pulmuone, established a joint venture, which was dubbed M&L, by making a 50:50 investment with Linkware.[29] It outsourced the implementation and management of ERP systems to the joint venture. After years of successful performance of outsourcing services, M&L was able to become independent by buying back all the shares that were initially owned by Maeil. This was a new opportunity for M&L, which could develop its capability as an independent IT outsourcing service provider. For Maeil, the fixed costs, such as labour and rent, required to manage the joint venture could be transformed into variable costs, such as operating costs. By doing so, they could focus more on finding a better way to remove overhead costs and gain excellence in outsourcing management.

Similar success stories can be found in the financial sector. The Korea Development Bank (KDB), for the first time in the banking industry, promoted a total outsourcing of their IT functions in 1999, thus creating the leading outsourcing system. At that time, most companies did not have much experience of total outsourcing and they were afraid of possible operational accidents and security issues. However, the KDB was determined to enter into the joint liability operation period after going through the outsourcing operation and cooperation period, and then it could accept the most up-to-date IT, concentrate internal manpower on core capabilities and secure the flexibility of manpower.[30]

Besides IT outsourcing, many other successful outsourcing cases relating to SMEs have been reported. One of the most famous concerns Reigncom, Korea's market leader in MP3 players. They focused on design, and strategically outsourced their design activities to INNO design, a Korean design consultancy firm located in Silicon Valley in the US. Humax is also a good example. The company is famous for developing, for the first time in Asia, digital satellite broadcast set-top boxes that comply with European standards. It could set up an outsourced production system, effectively combining its own production team with outsourcing providers. By doing that, it could focus its internal power more on research and development (R&D) activities, with all the other activities, such as procurement and inventory management, being performed by their outsourcing providers.

Growing competition – conglomerate companies

Large SI firms are facing growing competition with global IT service providers. In September 2006, Kyobo, one of the biggest insurance companies, signed an IT outsourcing contract with IBM Korea, which has been recorded as the largest IT outsourcing contract in Korea. Through this contract, IBM Korea is expanding its market in Korea, becoming the market leader in IT outsourcing services. Actually, several global IT companies are expanding their markets in Korea by accepting such big contracts from large companies.

As mentioned earlier, SI companies have occupied a major part of the IT outsourcing industry in the Korean market by contracting with their conglomerate-affiliated firms. Among them, however, affiliated firms with strong group positions or with high information intensity levels employed external service providers without worrying about group interference or the group SI company. In addition, even the affiliated firms with weak group positions or low information intensity levels were attempting to pick the best service providers for their information needs. As a result, it appears that there will be an increasing trend towards adopting a strategy of free competition for outsourcing.

Now, local IT outsourcing providers such as conglomerate SI firms have to compete with global IT firms to survive in the domestic market. They have to try their best to cut the subordinate relationship they have with their conglomerate-affiliated firms. They also need to try their best to become specialised outsourcing providers through the support of skilled manpower and manufacturing facilities. This will help to facilitate the growth and specialisation of domestic IT service providers. Meanwhile, as for the large conglomerate companies, they should identify their areas of core competence, so that they develop them to a global standard. They should cut the subordinate relationships they have with their subsidiary SI firms and let them develop their own business opportunities through free competition with global IT companies. Besides their affiliated SI firms, they must be prepared to accept outsourcing from other companies with advanced technology to increase their own strength.

Outsourcing to North Korea

Outsourcing to North Korea is considered much more price competitive than outsourcing to other countries, because it is not subject to tariffs. Also, it has both geographical and cultural advantages because of its proximity and language. The Gaeseong Industrial Complex, located just north of the border between North and South Korea, is one of achievements of the historic inter-Korean summit in 2000, and most of its manufacturing is operated and managed by the 'Gaeseong industrial district management committee'. Outsourcing to North Korea has been stable since the late 1990s, when some Korean companies outsourced certain manufacturing items to North Korea under inter-Korean economic cooperation projects. For instance, Kolon outsourced its production of knapsacks to North Korea in 1992; and general trading companies within the Daewoo, LG and Samsung groups began outsourcing garments and other labour-intensive products to North Korea under consignment manufacturing contracts. Similar deals with North Korea will become more active once the Gyeongui railway connecting Busan and Seoul with Pyongyang and Sinuiju is restored. Completion of the Gaeseong Industrial Complex and improvements in international relations will expedite the trend.[31]

Outsourcing to North Korea, however, has been mainly concentrated in the areas of product manufacturing, such as plastics, automobile parts, electronic parts, watches and garments. Fifteen companies have moved into the industrial park, but only 11 have launched operations, according to government officials.[32]

With regard to IT outsourcing, plans were set up in late 2005 to open an IT centre for the purpose of software and programming outsourcing in the near future. Also, Korea Telecom (KT), the largest fixed-line and broadband service provider in Korea, has announced plans to build a communications centre in an industrial complex in the North Korean border city of Gaeseong to provide both land-based and wireless communications services to companies operating in the industrial complex. Despite these efforts, the active operation of any business is still to come and the issue of IT outsourcing could be delayed for some time.[33]

In order to progress further, the government's role is very important in cooperating with North Korea, as well as with companies from other countries who have an interest in outsourcing to the country. At a national scale, the Korean government already has plans to make Korea into a northeast Asian hub for finance, logistics and IT. To facilitate these plans, outsourcing issues should be carefully addressed and linked up with strategies to make Korea into a global outsourcing centre.

Notes

1 W. M. Hur, S. C. Lee, E. K. Seo and H. K. Lee, 'A collaboration strategy for successful logistics outsourcing – a case study of Samsung Electro-Mechanics', paper presented at the domestic conference of KMIS (The Korean Society of Management Information Systems), May 2005.
2 R. J. Klepper, 'The management of partnering development in IS outsourcing', *Journal of Information Technology*, 10(4) (1995): 249–58.
3 K. Altinkemer, A. Chaturvedi and R. Gulati, 'Information systems outsourcing: issues and evidence', *International Journal of Information Management*, 14(4) (1994): 252–78
4 S. Samaddar and S. Kadiyala, 'Information systems outsourcing: replicating an existing framework in a different cultural context', *Journal of Operations Management*, 24(6) (2006): 910–31.
5 S. Han, *IT Outsourcing Services Outlook, 2005: Building a Dynamic IT Expertise*, International Data Corporation Report (Seoul: IDC Korea, 2005).
6 See IDC, *Korea IS Outsourcing 2006–2010 Forecast and Analysis*, International Data Corporation Report (Seoul: IDC Korea, 2006).
7 Han, *IT Outsourcing Services Outlook, 2005.*
8 Minjoo Chon, *Market Focus: IT Service Contracts Review, Asia/Pacific, 1999–2005*, Gartner Report, 14 November 2005 (ID Number: G00132778).
9 See Han, *IT Outsourcing Services Outlook, 2005.*
10 KCCI (Korea Chamber of Commerce and Industry), Press Release, March 2006.
11 Ibid.
12 KOTRA (Korea Trade Investment Promotion Agency), 'A change and opportunity in North American auto-part markets', government research paper (April 2006; available in Korean).
13 EIU (Economist Intelligence Unit), 'Corporate priorities for 2005, CEO briefing, 2005.
14 KITA (Korea International Trade Association), Press Release, May 2006.
15 V. Grover, M. J. Cheon and J. T. C. Teng, 'The effect of service quality and partnership on the outsourcing of information systems functions', *Journal of Management Information Systems*, 12(4) (1996): 89–116; V. Grover, M. J. Cheon and J. T. C. Teng, 'An evaluation of the impact of corporate strategy and the role of information technology on IS functional outsourcing', *European Journal of Information Systems*, 3(3) (1994): 179–90.

16 Jae-Nam Lee and Young-Gul Kim, 'Information systems outsourcing strategies for affiliated firms of the Korean conglomerate groups', *Journal of Strategic Information Systems*, 6 (1997): 203–29; J. Kang and J. K. Lee 'A case study –IT outsourcing of the Development Bank', *Information Systems Review* (December 2005): 229–55.
17 See Han, *IT Outsourcing Services Outlook, 2005.*
18 C. J. Park, D. Y. Moon and U. L. Jeon, 'Business analysis of IT companies' (in Korean), *High Tech Information* (20 December 1996): 36–7.
19 KITSIA (Korea IT Service Industry Association), 'A survey of the IT outsourcing market, Korea IT Service Industry Association' (February 2006); KITSIA, 'A survey of the IT service market, Korea IT Service Industry Association' (December 2005).
20 Kichan Nam, 'Comparative study of the business outcome of domestic SI companies', paper presented at the KMIS conference, Pusan, Korea, 29–30 May 1998.
21 J. K. Lee, 'A comparative study of leadership and ethical values in organisational culture revealed in the thoughts of Confucius and Aristotle: from the perspective of educational administration' (in Korean), *Journal of Educational Administration*, 16(2) (1998): 76–107.
22 Geert Hofstede, *Culture's Consequences: International Differences in Work-related Value* (Newbury Park, CA: Sage, 1980).
23 K. R. Gray and K. P. Marshall, 'Kenyan and Korean management orientations on Hofstede's cultural values', *Multinational Business Review*, 6(2) (1998): 79–88.
24 Nam-Hyeon Kim, Dong-Won Sohn and James A. Wall Jr, 'Korean leaders' (and subordinates') conflict management', *International Journal of Conflict Management*, 10(2) (April 1999): 130; S. H. Lee, *Argument of Asiatic Value and the Future of Confucian Culture in Korean Identity in the New Millennium* (Seongnam-si, Korea: The Academy of Korean Studies, 2000), pp. 12–27.
25 Kim, Sohn and Wall Jr, 'Korean leaders' (and subordinates') conflict management'.
26 Paul S. Adler and Seok-Woo Kwon, 'Social capital: prospects for a new concept', *Academy of Management Review*, 27(1) (2002): 17; Hongseok Oh, Myung-Ho Chung and Giuseppe Labianca, 'Group social capital and group effectiveness: the role of informal socializing ties', *Academy of Management Journal*, 47(6) (2004): 860.
27 Dong-Yeol Lee, 'Developmental relationships in the organisation: a social network perspective', *Academy of Management Proceedings* (2003): F1.
28 Kichan Nam and Wonjun Jung, 'Information systems outsourcing between Pulmuone and Linkware', *Information Systems Review*, 2(1) (2000): 85–99.
29 Eun-Han Moon, Hong Sang-Cheol and Yu-Jin, 'The beginning of new change: Maeil's outsourcing', *Yong Information Systems Review*, 7(2) (2005).
30 Kang and Lee, 'A case study –IT outsourcing of the Development Bank'.
31 Samsung Economic Research Institute (SERI), 'Profusion of outsourcing and implications for corporate Korea', *Korean Economic Trends* (Seoul, Korea), 8(16) (May 2004).
32 *The Korea Times*, 'KT to open communication center in Kaeson'. Available online at: http://search.hankooki.com/times/times_view.php?term=kaesong++&path=hankooki3/times/lpage/biz/200602/kt2006020621250111910.htm&media=kt (accessed 13 June 2007).
33 *The Korea Times*, 'Mushroom cloud on NK businesses'. Available online at: http://search.hankooki.com/times/times_view.php?term=kaesong++&path=hankooki3/times/lpage/200610/kt2006101618495453460.htm&media=kt (accessed 13 June 2007). Due to issues surrounding North Korea's test of a nuclear weapon in October 2006, the Gaeseong Industrial Complex is facing further uncertainty and the UN Security Council's resolution to sanction the communist state.

11 Outsourcing from the UK to the Far East

Ian Pogson

Outsourcing can be defined as subcontracting from a major company to a smaller one. It can also be defined as subcontracting to a lower-cost company, region or country.

Outsourcing has been a feature of business in the UK for many years. Based on 26 years of automotive industry experience, the author will cover:

- background;
- preparation;
- benchmarking;
- people – health and safety, in territory, and back at base;
- measures – interpretations of 'quality', delivery on time, costs, and liaison with current customer/user and with supplier;
- outsourcing as a quality improvement; and
- project management across cultures.

Outsourcing should save time and cost. Overseas, people generally work more hours per week with fewer breaks and for comparatively lower wages.

Background

Outsourcing is not to be taken lightly or without due consideration. It is unavoidable in the modern world of manufacturing. Some companies have been ploughing this furrow for many years now, some quite successfully.

The author's first brush with this was as a young engineer at Land Rover, when it was realised that the supply chain stretched from a small supplier's factory down the road from the main Solihull plant to Australia. In order to supply vehicles to the Australian Army, the company had to include a large component of the car, which was sourced locally, shipped to the UK and fitted; then the vehicle was exported as a whole. This was outsourcing driven by market demand for local content and a certain element of customer stipulation. There was no alternative or the contract would not have been secured, so this was outsourcing forced on the supplier, as perfectly serviceable units could have been sourced in the UK. It did enable vehicles to be sold to this particular customer and also meant that the unit in question could easily be serviced in the market.

Outsourcing can be applied to any product or service; we have all in the UK been faced with our bank or telephone company having offshore call centres. Even railway timetable enquiry services have been handed to companies not located in the UK. Sometimes this works and the experience is a satisfactory one; at other times it is infuriating and mistakes are made. Many of the companies involved have outsourced this activity to save money as labour and facility costs in the UK have risen. A good example of outsourcing concerns computer services, whereby the computer operator can be located anywhere there is a networked terminal and the keypad pressing is done by someone perfectly qualified, but paid at local rates.

Outsourcing in a manufacturing sense is just the same; a company could be perfectly capable of the work but decides for various financial and commercial reasons to farm it out. This has been the case in the clothing industry for many years, resulting in massive employment shifts from the original companies in the developed world to lower-cost countries or even lower-cost areas of the same, originating country. An example is UK books being typeset in India, thus saving two-thirds of the printing costs.

This chapter will cover the subject of outsourcing from an automotive manufacturing viewpoint, from personal experience of working in a UK plc and then over a one-year period in the Far East. The views are those of the author, derived from close observation in either country and will refer to very few other people's work.

Preparation

Outsourcing is a journey and, like any other, requires adequate planning and coordination. If there are any readers who are contemplating it, please stop now and consider your plans. This journey could be long, tortuous and painful. Although it feels like a simple thing to do – take a part or assembly made in one place and transfer it elsewhere – reality has a way of complicating apparent simplicities. Like extracting a stuck 4 × 4 vehicle from the mud, about five times the effort should go into the preparation than the extraction itself.

Some outsourcing activities are transplants, whereby complete facsimile copies of a facility are taken from the host company/country and transplanted abroad. There are many examples of this working well. It is arguably the easiest way to do it, especially if the original site continues to operate, supplying support, while the new one is brought up to speed. Everything can be copied and faithfully replicated until some smart individual suggests an improvement to the process, which may well be desirable, but then the gremlins come marching in.

The outsourcing with which the author is most recently familiar began at a component level, so this type of activity will form the basis for most of the chapter.

Benchmarking

As the author held the position of Benchmarking Manager for a large UK plc, the subject cannot pass without a mention, as it is a vital prerequisite of outsourcing.

Benchmarking is a useful study tool that enables comparison of one's own company processes with those of another on a like-for-like basis (see Figure 11.1). The first step of any benchmarking process is to review closely what one's own processes are. It may be prudent to pause following this activity, because the review may demonstrate the need for necessary change and improvement within. This needs to take place, or at least be under way before one has the right to go and look at others.

Benchmarking in its purest form involves deciding whether to use a competitive or non-competitive approach and then identifying the best in class, or the 'benchmark company', to measure oneself against. The activity can be conducted by trained in-house individuals or via an intermediary. It needs process, structure and discipline, and entails looking at how other

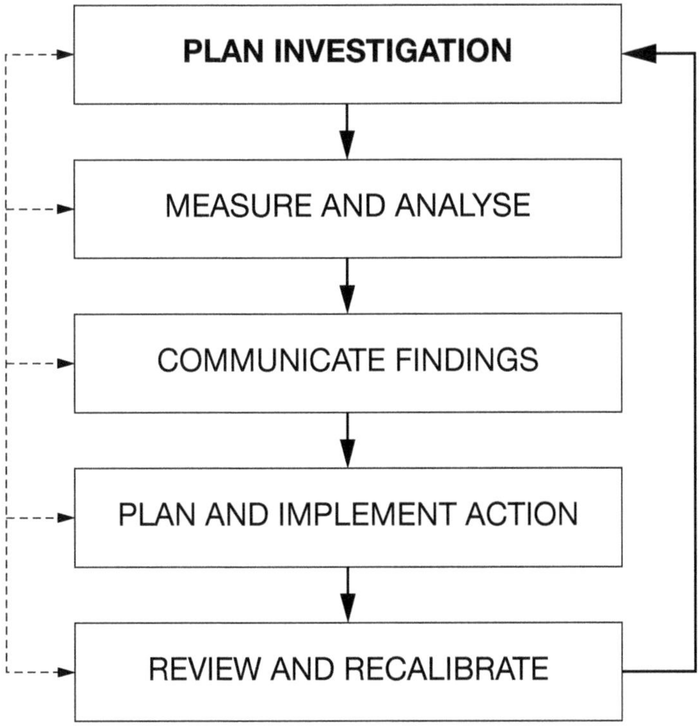

Figure 11.1 Benchmarking: five key stages.

Source: Authors' own.

companies have gone about their outsourcing project and at their successes or mistakes, which could save you a lot of time and money later.

Above all, it must be remembered:

- Benchmarking is: understanding the specific processes by which performance can be improved to world class.
- Benchmarking is not: a simple statement of a world-class performance target.

The benchmarking conducted prior to the most recent outsourcing work in the Far East with which the author was involved was preceded by a long, hard assessment in great detail of the company's then current product line-up. A high-level, experienced manager with a track-record in outsourcing was recruited from outside to head the purchasing team. He put in place the following actions:

- A room was set aside to display the components, with labels and part numbers.
- Parts were presented with weight and cost information.
- A coordinator for the work was appointed, who knew the components in detail.
- PC systems were devised to accurately store and clearly present the sourcing details.
- A series of multifunction meetings was held to assess the priority of parts to be outsourced. (This ensured that all functions 'bought in' to the process.)
- Risks of outsourcing, both technical and commercial, were assessed at the meetings.
- Parts were divided into short-, medium- and long-term priorities.
- Fixings were taken as a specialist subject.
- Regular progress meetings were held with the multifunctional team.
- Targets were set and reviewed at these meetings.
- Account was taken of any engineering or logistics costs resulting from the outsourcing plans.
- Some high-cost parts were taken as outsourcing pilot examples to prove out processes and also to convince the 'doubters' that the overall plan was workable.

The early pilot parts were deemed a success and were of high-quality Korean manufacture. The way ahead was thus clearly marked and the doubters silenced. The project then grew to outsource more complex, sensitive or expensive parts. At all stages checks were made on the real savings delivered to the assembly facility and not on some notional figure. Quality checks were rigorous, using in-house measuring equipment and skilled metrologists to verify dimensions claimed by the new suppliers.

In order to fully validate components from another supplier, it is most important to have access to calibrated metrology equipment or your own in-house team who are almost fanatical about the subject and will not entertain any dispute. There are accredited laboratories that will measure components if you do not have your own. Always ask to see their accreditation certificates and, in any case, whatever measurement is taken, the equipment used must be calibrated in five or fewer steps in accordance with UK National Physical Laboratory standards. This ensures accuracy and repeatability.

Material properties are to be checked as well. Do not rely upon a 'certificate' claiming to verify that the component is made of the correct material unless it is a certificate from a reliable source. The substitution of cheaper materials in place of those specified is a regular way of saving money for unscrupulous suppliers at home and abroad – beware. Always check yourself that the right material is being used. Go into 'Goods Inwards' and check the bulk stock of steel or plastic granules (or whatever the raw material is) and ensure that this matches the drawing specification exactly.

People

The author has also had some experience in the planning and delivery of a large and complex facility in the UK for the manufacture of major units to be consumed across three continents, which up until then had been made in mainland Europe – this was outsourcing *into* the UK. This country was chosen for many reasons, including:

- lower social costs than the originating country;
- the availability of skilled labour from a facility that was being run down;
- three UK locations that would consume the major units in high volumes; and
- the availability of a suitable site and grants to build thereon.

What made this successful was the 'quality of the people' recruited to do the job and the basing of the whole operation on a benchmarked existing facility and direct comparisons with others. It is still successful and has grown. Notably no corners were cut in its execution and appropriate funds were available to buy the best equipment and facilities.

To ensure the quality of employees, the author's recruiting department (Manufacturing Engineering) and Personnel worked closely together to create a job and person specification, with the recruiting project being wholly managed by the author. A standard tried and tested company process was employed and rigorously applied to the whole recruitment activity, with regular liaison between Personnel and the recruiter. Only the department with the need for people really knows what is required and must take a close and personal interest in the selection. It is easy to say 'people are our greatest asset', but, unless care is taken to select and nurture them, then the work, service or product will suffer.

In the end, the selection of 10 external applicants and the development of 26 from within the team produced some really top-class engineers and managers. The project was a great success and most of this was down to selecting the right quality of people.

The process of outsourcing is also going to need the right quality of people. If you do not have them, hire them. If they are, as is likely, to be heading east, then you will need people who can handle the new and different culture that they will find. It is no use following the stereotypical English behaviour abroad and expecting that, if you shout loudly enough, people will understand you. Like filling any job vacancy, it is often easy to find the person with the right qualifications, but not the right attitude, or vice versa. Pick someone who can handle frustration in a calm fashion, as this is the most widely felt emotion of any expat outsourcing worker while in the market. (Whatever industries were involved, chance meetings with other outsource professionals showed this to be the overriding experience.)

Outsourcing is going to need people:

- with due regard for health and safety;
- in territory working closely with the new supplier; and
- back at base, project managing the change.

And at each location, people will need to be focused upon the usual measures:

- quality;
- delivery on time;
- costs; and
- liaison with the current customer/user and with the current supplier.

Do not expect the new supplier to share the same idea of what these measures mean as you. European quality and that in other markets can be poles apart. Expect to have to redefine what you mean by 'quality'. Be *very* sure of what this means to you, and have the data ready to back up your case and photographs to prove it. Do not waver in the pursuit of quality. Find someone in the local team who shares your ideas and standards, so he or she can explain to the other locals. It is often better coming from a local to a local, rather than from an outsider.

People – health and safety

No modern Western writing would be complete without the standard health and safety (H&S) warning. Fortunately, the author has been sent out to the

Far East by two employers who were au fait with H&S requirements in the West. Efforts were made to ensure that employees were not going to be placed needlessly at risk, or, if there was a risk, that it was minimised and support was in place should the worst happen. The importance of this awareness and risk assessment cannot be overstated. Other countries are not protected by the same cottonwool style of H&S legislation that is gradually strangling our everyday activities in the UK.

This is one reason why other countries are often so much cheaper than Europe and the UK. They save money by not guarding machines, not issuing personal protection equipment (PPE) and allowing all sorts of nasty chemicals to be used. So the lesson here is 'protect yourself', for no one else will. Experience has seen factories where any lifting of equipment or parts is seemingly done to test the maximum capacity of the lifting machine to an overloaded state. Places exist where the air is filled with the foulest stench and is unwittingly being added to by workers unaware of what they are doing, because they do not know any better.

Do consider, it is only in the author's short quarter of a century of working that we in the West have really looked hard at hearing protection, for example. We have had dirty factories in the UK. Our beaches were so polluted that near the author's home it was too risky to swim in the grey sea. Let us not feel too superior here – smog warnings have been in operation as recently as in the summer of 2006 in London. Having said that, the standards you are used to back home are not necessarily going to be those you meet in developing economies. Be careful and look after your own body. Colleagues took their own steel toe-capped shoes out on overseas visits, as they were quality, British-made, comfortable items. One individual wore these on the aeroplane and could not work out why he was setting off the metal detector at Immigration – beware! PPE is not always widely available, so bring your own.

One contract my employer was involved with meant having engineers in engine test cells in the Far East. During one test, a local fitter tripped, fell and cut his head open. He was propped up in the corner with a rag and left until the end of the shift, because if they lost time their wages were docked. Things work differently outside the closeted confines of Europe and the US.

People – in territory working closely with the new supplier

Choose your people well, for your success or otherwise is entirely reliant upon them. Employees working in territory require access to basic health care when they need it, access to emergency services if required and, most importantly, a method of paying for the services at the point of consumption. In one posting, the author was working with Personnel officers quite unaware of even the daily risks we were taking in just accepting a taxi ride, despite the endless debates on health care providers/insurers.

Ensure that your people:

- Are covered by health care and have cards and membership numbers with contact details.
- Know where the hospitals are that will treat them, and that everyone has a card for these places in case of the need for treatment.
- Are advised on their appropriate tax liabilities. Remember – tax is between an individual and the tax authorities; but both the employer and employee have responsibilities.
- Are housed, fed and watered to their tastes and know how to make it to and from work. (It was months after we started in one job before HR told us about the cheap buses, which ran almost door-to-door from our apartments to work.)
- Are patient, skilled and robust. They may need many aspects to their characters in order to survive away from home comforts.
- Are balanced individuals who are likely to be reliable and not turn into the stereotypical 'Brits on holiday' as soon as they land in a foreign country.
- Can earn respect from those about them in the local team. In some cultures, this is guaranteed by advancing age, but not necessarily by ability. (This often applies to expats *and* locals.)

People – back at base, project managing the change

In the beginning, there will always be a larger 'home' than 'away' team, to use a sporting analogy. Lines of communication need to be established and recorded to avoid arguments later. Questions asked of the home side (which should have access to all the necessary information) need to be fed back to the team in territory quickly. If there is a significant time zone difference (the UK is seven hours GMT behind China, for instance), it may be necessary and prudent to change home start and finish times to best support the team in territory. Otherwise, whole days can be wasted just waiting for replies to questions or requests for data. It is wise to log any data transferred, and some packages that handle computer-aided design (CAD) data have this facility built in, then there are no arguments about who sent what and when.

Be prepared for the localising team to be data- and information-hungry. Some cultures view the only answer they trust as the one that comes directly from the originating plant. This may well be the same answer as that given by the team in territory, but they like to be sure. Many cultures ask the same question of several people, before deciding upon a consensus of their own choice from these replies; or they decide that so many people have said the same thing that it must be correct.

Measures

Quality

Quality is a metric that must be measured. It is vital that some measure is made to compare what was made in the originating location against that which is being localised. There are some markets where cost is far more of an issue than quality and customer expectations are also low. As long as this is true, any exports back to a more sophisticated market will be subject to possible rejection and even ridicule. Think back to Yugo cars sold in the US. They were cheap, yes, but nowhere near the quality standards of even the general US motoring public, and for that reason (along with others) they failed.

You will need to know how successful your outsourcing has been, and quality is an essential measure, however it is defined. Your local partner may also have its own ideas, and it is vital that these somehow coincide with yours. Do not accept without validating the results, methods and processes yourselves that the locally generated results are credible. In China, within the clothing trade, the market in Shanghai for fabric sells in inches as well as metric measures – there are, however 30 inches to a yard there. Similarly, a US gallon is not quite the same as an imperial one, so miles per gallon (mpg) fuel economy figures need careful consideration. Be careful with even the basics – assume nothing; check everything.

The author has been to factories in the Far East where there are rooms full of impressive, often new measuring equipment, carefully covered in the maker's dust cover. The machines may not be plugged in and in one case there were no sockets in the room into which to plug them! So check everything, dig for evidence, and use your eyes and ears, sense of smell and foul play – be alert and cynical even. Your directors will not thank you if the outsourcing fails. If you have the sort of experience that you should have, you should be able to sense a good factory or company within minutes of being on the shop floor. Always insist upon going there; impressive PowerPoint presentations just tell you that there is a good PowerPoint engineer in the area. Think of it this way: if a vehicle is indicating to turn, that just means that the circuit is working. The indicator could have been accidentally operated or broken in the 'on' position. Always dig deeper for what is really happening. Only believe your own senses.

A useful piece of equipment to take with you (or even buy in territory, but beware of calibration) is an appropriate measuring device. A simple vernier calliper is a wise investment, as no one, not even the Chinese (who, in my experience, can sometimes be a bit intransigent), can argue with a direct measurement. Only believe the evidence of your own eyes. Many engineers have seen falsified inspection reports in countries where corruption and backhanders are rife. Even in the UK this happens! In some markets there is so little understanding of real quality that fudging figures is accepted.

The important point for some is that an inspection report is available and the box for 'Inspection report' is ticked. This is clearly insufficient for the experienced outsourcing engineer; we need proof of quality.

Do beware of the 'tick-box' mentality. This was a feature of early 1970s' Japanese motorcycles and cars. In those days, their offerings were good, but just did the job. They handled poorly, as the manufacturers had little idea of the finer points of vehicle dynamics, or tyre technology. It took people like Lotus working with Toyota, for example, and Rover with Honda for the Japanese to learn the lessons and become proficient on their own. Many engineers in Rover and Lotus worked with early engineers from the East who did just tick boxes when a task was completed. It was black or white, but real engineering has many shades of grey and this is where real, personal experience of current components, assemblies and vehicles comes into play.

Delivery on time

This is a key issue. Time, in some cultures, is an illusion, brought on by a good lunch, and everything is '*demain*' (tomorrow) – even in some parts of France, particularly the furthest away from the outskirts of Paris and certainly down south. Agitated British engineers working across the Channel were told that they simply do not understand how things work in France. Other cultures may not have the same view of time and its passage as you do; they may not share your sense of urgency. Similarly, whilst through experience you know that some elements of a timing plan can be flexed, and others are set and rigid, your counterparts may not see it that way.

It you are working to a computer-generated timing plan, be sure to use the facility to identify local holidays. In some markets these are 'floating' and are only set just before the expected date by the central government. Some countries work weekends to 'earn' a full week's holiday. If you overlay holidays in the localising market, these mismatches can add up to significant 'lost' time. Also, beware of overcomplex project management tools; these may not be appropriate for the market. At least to start with, use the tools they use.

Costs

Cost is the main reason many companies start on the outsourcing route in the first place. Whether one is outsourcing canteen services, engineering programme management or parts manufacture, cost will be the driver.

It is vital to be aware of the true costs of one's own parts before starting the exercise. Consider the whole cost of a component, which includes delivery and associated expenditure. Also consider current warranty information, as this is something one should aim to improve or at least maintain after the resourcing.

As described in the earlier example, it is vital to know and make available to all concerned the true costs and the planned improvement following outsourcing. There are many tools for measuring cost, such as activity-based costing (ABC), and it does depend upon one's company as to which is preferred. The only stipulation that should be made is to ensure that the costs identified for the original component or assembly include all piece, delivery and service costs, that is, the real price for the part turning up at point of use. It is easy to miss out shipping and other logistical costs. When the outsourcing is in progress, it is vital that cost comparisons are made on a like-for-like basis; otherwise the main point of the exercise is lost. Be very careful with overseas quotes on supply: are they ex-works (and therefore has transport to be added) or are they via the supplier's own transport or your own carrier? Also, in either case, who insures the goods?

It is very easy to be carried away with the case for resourcing when just labour rates are shown. These can be different for regions of the same country, depending upon whether fully paid-up unionised labour is used or local, sometimes illegal, immigrant labour is employed. Different areas of even a small country such as the UK will show disparities depending upon local employment levels and general affluence. Regional variances can also occur as government and European initiatives favour one region or another.

It is vital to fix the precise costs of all aspects of the goods or services under review before making a recommendation and committing the company to a change. Beware of well-meaning but misguided individuals with a personal agenda; ensure that they are considering the product, service or company's best interests. Firm, agreed, quoted and written costs from new suppliers as well as logistics issues must be the information on which a decision is made.

Cost saving example: the links between manufacturers and major unit sharing and supply

In the automotive industry, it is quite common for some major units to be made in one country and exported for final assembly into the vehicle in another. Some companies have set up, for example, engine manufacturing plants in South America, when the 'consuming' vehicle assembly plants are in the US and Europe. Some local governments are so desperate for employment in their areas that they offer irresistibly low operating costs and massive infrastructure support to tempt major manufacturers to settle in their area. Local labour often has no automotive manufacturing experience and so the new workers can be trained as the manufacturer wants them to be.

It seems hardly worthwhile to manufacture major units and then have to pay to ship them around the world, but there are many leading names in the industry that have chosen this outsourcing path. What the major unit plant does achieve though is economies of scale; they become the worldwide centre for that unit and many different cars are designed to use it, so up goes the volume and down should come costs. Toyota once observed that there is no point in planning to manufacture less than half a million units; that there were not the economies in any lower volume. As the richest player in the business, they should know.

If one tours the factory of a particular leading UK specialist vehicle manufacturer, nearly all the parts supplied to the line arrive with Eastern characters on the box, as many parts of the final product arrive from the Orient. The manufacturer used to make its own frames and exhausts in their Midlands plant, using specialist machines developed in-house, but now these are made at a wholly-owned outsourced facility in Thailand. Quality has been maintained and the price has tumbled.

Liaison with the current customer/user

If one is outsourcing a component or assembly, it is important to consider how much to involve or inform the current customer or user if they are a third party. Agreements may already be in place to cover this. It is best to be honest, but occasionally wise to remain quiet until things are clearer, so this must be considered. The sort of conversation one has will depend upon the relationship with the current customer. Some customers will not be happy that outsourcing is taking place and, unless they are fed facts on time and with suitable evidence, with cast-iron guarantees that their parts will be unaffected, they will remain unhappy. An important job is to manage that relationship.

Liaison with the current supplier

It is a company decision as to how the news of a contract cessation is broken to the current supplier. Indeed the whole issue of supplier relations and partnership details should be carefully considered before any outsourcing is attempted. No matter how confidential one tries to keep the project, someone somewhere, even unwittingly, may alert the current supplier. There is a choice here: either keep the whole subject totally confidential and, when all facts are known and verified, inform the supplier; or enrol them at some earlier stage.

As for any considered supplier change, if one enrols the supplier at the start, it could be argued that they will respond with cost savings themselves. If they cannot, supply could be interrupted as they consider their own options, but this depends upon the type of contract one has in place for continuity of supply once notice of termination is given. What is always possible is that, as soon as the notice is given, quality could well take a downturn as the human emotion of ‘Why should we bother?’ takes root. Guard against this in contract details at the very beginning and with your own quality processes. The only sure thing is that it will happen. Acrimony may creep in too, so be alert for this.

Not involving the current supplier could be the only course of action if one definitely does not wish to remain one of their customers – for example, if they are a 'bad supplier' by any measure or if they themselves show any signs of instability or of not planning for a long-term future relationship. There are many reasons for wishing to change supplier, not just to realise lower costs.

There is the possibility of the current supplier being encouraged to set up overseas joint ventures themselves and for them to realise savings, which could be passed on to you, the customer. This could be a positive move for both sides and achieve the cost savings you are after; it could also grow their business. Keep your mind open to the wider possibilities. If this happens, also keep your eyes on the quality control of any subcontractors.

Outsourcing as quality improvement

There are opportunities to use outsourcing as a quality improvement and not necessarily to save money on the piece price. This is a normal business activity – changing supplier to remove a quality issue – but the outsourcing project can itself be a catalyst for reviewing all suppliers.

The benchmarking activity forces one to look hard at current parts and costs, which should include costs of quality, such as warranties and failures. Outsourcing may be the only way to break a long-running series of 'poor quality' issues.

It is essential to keep a keen eye on the product quality and any variation from the specification should be tracked and hunted down with vigour. As mentioned before, it is vital to measure and check parts via a process and people one trusts, in order to be happy oneself that standards are maintained or improved. It is also possible that, by moving manufacture to somewhere with little or no manufacturing or even employment, one can have the pick of a new workforce and train them to work to a process – your process. Assuming the process is sound, this can be the key to quality products or services – consistency. These issues go a long way to understanding the success in the UK of Japanese motor manufacturers.

Project management across cultures

In the author's experience, project management is the key weakness of many Chinese engineers. Although simply stunning building and civil engineering projects in China (such as the Three Gorges Dam and the new North–South Canal) are there for all to see, at a working engineer level the reality is different. Planning does not appear to be on the curriculum of any Chinese engineering course. This will be a real test for any outsourcing in that country. Locally generated timing plans can be very misleading and many dates regarded as simply idealistic or 'hopeful'. An engineer with the ability to plan and convey this to the local engineers will be an absolute necessity to the team.

In terms of project management tools, it is highly likely that the local tool of choice will be a very simple one, perhaps just a series of block diagrams on Microsoft Excel. This is perfectly fine for most, and use of the same software company's Project tool may well be 'overkill'.

Other pitfalls to avoid include assuming that people will *want* to come to project meetings or will even organise them. Assume nothing and always check for understanding. The author and his UK colleagues have attended many meetings in the Orient where no local took any notes at all on the project. Unless these people all have a greater memory capacity than us or think differently, then some facts are going to be forgotten or lost. The advice is to keep your own notes and circulate them among the team, so that facts are recorded and shared. Accurate records will not themselves ensure that a project succeeds, but can be useful later to resolve disagreements over what was said.

Case study: Outsourcing a large casting

The following example has been simplified for brevity and to disguise the identities of any parties involved. Nevertheless, the principles outlined in this chapter remain valid and are highlighted where necessary.

The following parties were involved, and are identified later in the script from the numbers below:

1 The author's employer, an engine manufacturer, had an unhealthy reliance upon one unstable volume customer. It was therefore actively searching for new business opportunities.
2 Such a customer had been identified in the Middle East. It was looking for engines to power two commercial vehicles.
3 The casting in question was cast in the UK, but the foundry was to be closed and therefore supply would cease, with no alternative founder offered.
4 The casting was machined on a line shared with another engine. The machining line was on the site of another vehicle manufacturer. This engine was coming to the end of its life.
5 There was no opportunity to buy this machining line and drawings were deemed as the property of the manufacturer (4) above.
6 As luck would have it, the Middle East customer had access to foundry and machining suppliers in the local market.

These points presented a clear choice: outsource casting and machining or stop production of the engine. As the engine was still required by (1) well into the future, any notion of building up a stockpile of castings or engines was out of the question for cost reasons, so the search began for an overseas supplier. The opportunity was taken to use the local foundry and machinist in the Middle East mentioned in (6).

As stated in the main text, it is vital to have an indigenous engineer to support localisation projects. A suitable UK resident was hired locally who spoke and also understood the language and the culture of the customer's country. This engineer was to be key for the engine supplier (1) in the whole process and could immediately work in territory.

Drawings and specifications for the casting were made available by the old foundry to the new supplier, moulds and cores were made by the foundry mentioned in (6) and castings were created. Having our local engineer on the ground meant that regular telephone calls to the UK could speed up communications with this supplier, involving the Engineering department and the original foundry.

Machining details were a lot more troublesome. These were regarded as part of the intellectual property rights (IPR) of the other engine (4) machined on the same line, so this presented a new challenge.

This was the engine manufacturer's first experience of 'reverse-engineering'. Drawings of the machined component had to be created from scratch by measuring the finished job. Again this was a new outsourcing opportunity. This sort of work could be undertaken in the UK, but could also be conducted far cheaper abroad. The result is on the face of it quite clear-cut: drawings were to be made and could be checked in the UK by a team in company (1) against a current component. Two-dimensional paper drawings and CAD output in an approved package could be scrutinised and checked. Although this was achieved in a cost-effective manner, it was an *additional* cost to the project.

All the above was put in place and seemed to be progressing well – until the first machined components arrived in the UK. The almost gleeful call from the manufacturing assembly area to Engineering asked for advice on how to seal the component to its neighbour, as there was a clear, pronounced step running the length of the joint face. To add insult to injury, someone at the machining facility had spotted this grave error and attempted by hand to use a stone to take the sharpness off the step! At least no one would cut themselves.

The local engineer had not passed them off before transport back to the UK (as his visit was cut short by the Finance department), but one had to ask how *any* machinist could possibly consider such product as fit for service. The incident not only called for the UK toolroom to mill the face flat and to fit a suitably thick gasket to take up the difference, but also called into question every other dimension on the component.

Fortunately, full coordinate measuring machines (CMMs) were available, with skilled metrologists to operate them and the ability to conduct a complete dimensional assessment. Fortunately, these programs had already been installed in the CMM software. This saved a huge amount of time and expense, as the component was arguably the most complex on the engine.

There were many lessons to be learned from this exercise, which did finally result in a quality component being supplied:

- The value of the local engineer was huge, but it clearly needed some closer management and process improvement training.
- The reverse engineering experience would later help us all when applied to other components.
- The value of having one's own in-house, experienced metrology facility was demonstrated.
- Do not lose control of the way in which major components or assemblies are drawn and the details retained in an up-to-date fashion. This can cost dearly when supply changes.
- Do not overestimate the savings that can be made by simply outsourcing. These can be eroded by additional costs, such as the need to reverse-engineer to create drawings.
- Supplier management over continental and cultural boundaries is not easy. It soaks up huge amounts of time in just communicating. These costs need to be recognised at the start.
- Bean-counters trying to save on travel costs must realise the importance of regular visits to the outsourcing location. There is a need to monitor progress, educate the new supplier and share in the project's success. Saving £100 on travel against the loss of several £1,500 engines is not a real business saving.
- Quality can be seen, touched and measured. Cover all these aspects diligently. Improve continually and never say 'That will do'. Measure it and be sure.

Conclusion

In conclusion, enjoy your experience, but keep all your senses keen and alert. Believe nothing you are told. Always check facts and details and ensure that you know the true status of your parts.

Take care over the make-up of the outsourcing team – there is certainly the need for a person who is skilled in everyday language and technical skills. As usual, most of the problems are created by humans and need suitable people to solve them.

Although the overriding reason to outsource is cost reduction, if the quality of the product or service declines, you risk losing customers and that could wipe out any savings generated.

12 Employee engagement in IT outsourcing

A South African case study

Sean S. Stuttaford and Stephanie J. Morgan

Introduction

As discussed in Chapter 2, the decision to outsource IT frequently does not consider the needs of the employee in the IT department of the organisation. However, the delivery of IT services is a people-based service function[1] and the success of outsource engagements can for the most part be attributed to the commitment of those people staffing the outsourcing contract. Outsource vendors therefore should recognise the importance of ensuring a smooth transition of employees from the old company (referred to in the text as Oldco), to the new outsourcing vendor (referred to in the text as Newco). Research on the employee perspective in outsourcing is limited, and samples restricted to Western European (particularly UK) organisations. Cultural differences may influence the responses of staff. For example, under Hofstede's dimensions there are differences in power-distance, individualism and long-term orientation between the UK and South Africa.[2] We cannot therefore assume that staff in different countries will react in the same manner.

Historical studies of organisations in South Africa suggest that management styles have been more autocratic than participative. A more recent study by Jackson[3] found that, even though organisations were seen as hierarchal, centralised and fairly rule bound, they showed elements of consultative management but not participative management.[4] This legacy from the apartheid and sanctions in the past means that full participation in decision-making of all members of the stakeholder populations of organisations may be some way off. This historical organisational behaviour with respect to decision-making may have influenced the way that affected employees accepted and verbalised their understanding of the reason for the organisation taking the decision to outsource. Since 1994, South Africa has been launched into a competitive global marketplace when mainly Western organisations internationally are becoming leaner and meaner,[5] – this has resulted in South African organisations having to observe and implement similar strategies, such as outsourcing non-core functions, including IT. IT workers in South Africa have been thrust into this environment and it is likely that the affected employees in outsource engagements are aware of and understand these strategies, which are driven by international market pressures.

The Labour Relations Act (LRA) in South Africa secures the rights of the employees being transferred, so that they do not lose the conditions of employment they enjoyed with their previous employer. The Act, with the enforcement of Section 197 and section 187(1)(g) makes any retrenchment of jobs, when only a portion of a business is outsourced, illegal.[6] Employees are mostly aware of their rights with respect to this Act and therefore concern for their job security during the initial outsource transition period is reduced. There are no IT industry unions, bargaining councils or collective agreements and, due to the history of the trade union movement in South Africa, most knowledge workers are not unionised. This chapter discusses a case study based on a small sample of people transferred to an IT outsourcing company in South Africa.

Prior to the un-banning of the ANC in 1990, followed by the first non-racial and democratic elections in April 1994, South Africa had been faced with the withdrawal of multinational IT organisations – for example, IBM finally divested in 1987 after intense pressure. This resulted in South Africa being isolated from international thinking in respect of IT outsourcing and, although there were South African companies who entered the IT outsourcing market, this was on a small scale with little or no international support. Since 1994 and the readmittance of South Africa to the international community, there has been a marked increase in outsourcing. IBM returned in 1994 through the acquisition of 51 per cent of Information Services Management. EDS South Africa was formed through the merger of three local IT companies in 1995. T-Systems South Africa was formed in 1997 and engaged in outsource contracts, initially with organisations with which its German parent had existing contracts. CSC entered South Africa with an outsource agreement at Old Mutual in 1998 – its first in South Africa. Edcon, one of South Africa's largest retail groups, turned to Accenture in 1998 when it was looking for an IT outsourcing partner. By this time IT outsourcing was seen as an option for South African organisations that realised that they needed to concentrate on their core business and leverage IT knowledge and skills from organisations who were best placed to provide these services. South African organisations rapidly had to compete on the world stage in order to ensure their long-term success and IT outsourcing was seen as one such strategy available to achieve this objective. Recent surveys in the IT outsourcing sector have revealed a general maturation in the outsourcing market, with outsourcing moving away from being an option only for large organisations to also being an accepted strategy for medium-sized companies. There has been a shift towards the multi-vendor outsourcing model in larger organisations, as the latter have gained experience of outsourcing as well as a better understanding of their business requirements.

Outsourcing engagements can be considered similar to a merger in which employees are transferred to a new organisation.[7] The employee is transferred to the employ of the new outsource vendor but is still required to continue doing the same job at the same location, but often with increased expectations of the level of service delivery. The transfer results in a change in the psychological contract with Oldco and the development of a new contract with Newco. The trust relationship will need to be redefined, as the employee will not be sure of the intention of either party, particularly if he or she has not been party to the negotiations prior to the outsourcing engagement. For the outsource engagement to succeed, both the outsourcer and the outsource vendor should place a great deal of emphasis on ensuring that the affected employees retain a commitment towards their old organisation, while at the same time developing a positive experience with their new employer. How well this process is managed may be crucial for long-term relationships.

Organisations whose core competency is the delivery of IT services and who are engaged as outsource vendors, should recognise that the success of the engagement is dependent on the well-being of employees assigned to the outsource contract. The initial cost to Newco of engaging in an outsource contract is high, therefore Newco would want to be able to extend the outsource contract beyond the initial term. Should the employees of the outsource vendor feel that there has been a breach of the psychological contract and that the trust relationship has been broken, this could result in the reduction of organisational commitment, which in turn may result in the outsource engagement being terminated. The management of Newco needs to understand what change-management processes should be implemented to secure the trust and commitment of their employees engaged in outsource contracts. This case has identified four phases of the outsource engagement and recommends a number of interventions that outsourcing organisations, particularly in this type of culture, should consider throughout the outsource contract period. First, we will outline the research purpose and design, then we will discuss findings from the study, and finally we will offer practical guidelines based on these phases.

Objectives of the research

This study investigates the organisational commitment of a sample of South African employees who have been outsourced to the outsource vendor, and considers how well these employees have adapted to their new environment since the initial outsource engagement. It is important for both Oldco and Newco to ensure that the long-term commitment of affected employees is obtained.

Affected employees experience a period of uncertainty and upheaval[8] and, if this is not properly addressed, a breakdown of the trust relationship and a low level of organisational commitment can manifest throughout the duration of the outsource contract. This may ultimately contribute to the outsource contract not being renewed due to a breakdown of the business and trust relationship between the organisations.

Research question

The literature revealed that some employees experience the outsourcing process and environment to be challenging and motivating. However, the majority of outsourced employees are not comfortable with the outsourcing process and, even after more than half of the contracted period had passed, still yearn to rejoin their original employer.[9] From the perspective of industry, it is important that transferred employees are able to make the transition to the new organisation successfully and to develop a sense of belonging to the new outsource vendor organisation. If outsource organisations are unable to manage this process successfully, they will be at risk of having a very difficult outsource contract to manage.

Organisations are now beginning to engage in transformational outsourcing, where the motivation to outsource is to facilitate rapid organisational change, to launch new strategies and to reshape company boundaries.[10] This expectation of organisations could result in the affected employees experiencing even further anxiety in their work environment.

Research indicates that the elements of trust, psychological contract and organisational commitment, along with leadership's ability in the management of employees, will influence the level of the employee's commitment. Perceptions of the processes implemented, the outcomes and the treatment of the affected employees are likely to influence whether employees feel trusting or mistrustful.[11] Perceived lack of procedural fairness is likely to elicit lower levels of trust in the affected employee.[12] In the context of an outsourcing engagement, the consequences of poor fairness perceptions can have a detrimental impact on the success of the contract – as highlighted in Chapter 2.

When employees are forced to transfer to the new organisation in an outsourcing engagement, their commitment to their old organisation needs to remain intact while, at the same time, a commitment to their new organisation needs to be developed. However, little is understood about the impact of dual commitment on staff, or indeed about the impact of the original outsourcing decision on psychological contract perceptions. Parker and Russell[13] contend that many outsourcing engagements have been unsuccessful because of a neglect of organisational and staff issues, and where employees perceive that the psychological contract between the employee and employer has been broken.

When the outsourcing process commences, employees start developing feelings of anxiety, resistance to change, feelings of isolation and downright anger,[14] which could have a bearing on the eventual long-term success of the outsourcing contract. Employees affected by outsourcing need to maintain their commitment levels towards their old organisation as well as their new employer, the outsourcing vendor. Both organisations in an engagement of this nature require that the affected employees deliver a high-level service to ensure a successful outcome.

The research questions therefore focused on investigating how those employees who are transferred to the outsource vendor during the initial outsource engagement experience their working environment in the longer term, and assessed whether there is a relationship between employee satisfaction and employee perceptions of change processes related to outsourcing engagements.

Research strategy

The research methodology used was a qualitative study of a small group of employees who are employed in outsource engagements with a South African outsource vendor. Affected employees who transferred to outsource engagements in successful contracts of four years' duration or longer, as well as employees who were employed on an outsource contract that was not renewed, were interviewed. This allowed us to assess the impact of outsourcing over long timescales.

The study focused on understanding the organisational behaviour of employees engaged in an outsource contract. The first author, through depth interviews, attempted to gain an insight into the thoughts and feelings of the participants, including their perception of the success of the outsource engagement. The interview guideline[15] focused on topics including the participant's background and their relationship with their new and old employing organisations. The interview guide assisted the researcher to investigate the relationship between outsourcing and its impact on satisfaction, commitment, fairness and justice in the work place.

The researcher randomly selected participants from two outsource contracts that were currently still successful (as defined by continuation of the contract for more than four years), and participants who were engaged in a third, terminated outsource contract with the same outsource vendor. A total of nine participants, six from successful contracts and three from the terminated contract, took part in the study. Of these only one was female. Six of the participants were white South Africans; one was African, one coloured and one Indian. All had been outsourced between four and ten years previously. The sample came from the Gauteng and Western Cape regions of South Africa.

A number of employees who were part of the affected group who transferred during the initial outsource engagement had left Newco and this research did not consider the experience of those employees nor the reasons for the attrition. The interviews covered each participant's recollection of the original employer and the outsourcing transfer process. The participants were then questioned about their perception of the success of the outsource engagement, both on a personal and organisational level. Analysis of the interview transcripts was based on thematic techniques[16] to identify main themes.

Research results

The analysis highlighted a number of themes, which will be discussed below. These included views on job satisfaction, stress and worry, the organisational commitment to employees, the employee commitment to the organisation, emotions and job security, communication levels, work relationships with Oldco colleagues, and views of the future. Each of these themes was discussed in different ways depending on four distinct 'phases' of the outsourcing contract. These we have referred to as implementation, honeymoon, stabilisation and maturity. Differences during these phases will be highlighted, and at the end of this chapter we will make recommendations based on these phases. References to participant views are reflected in the following way: A quote is shown in inverted commas, with the participant who made the statement indicated, for example, as (C1P1), which indicates Contract 1 and Participant 1. Contracts 1 and 2 were ongoing, while Contract 3 had been terminated.

Job satisfaction, stress and worry

There was a distinct difference in job satisfaction levels identified between participants in the renewed contracts and participants who were engaged in the contract that was terminated. Participants who were engaged in the terminated contract found the environment extremely stressful and perceived that support within Newco was inadequate.

Participants did not show any remaining levels of stress or worry related to the outsource transition; in all cases this took place so long ago that it was no longer of concern to them. Participants referred to Oldco as the customer: 'we were told at the beginning that Oldco is now the customer' (C2P1). The outsource contract had been renewed in two of these cases, and participants felt a slightly varied lack of concern as the initial term came to an end.

The participants engaged in C1 believed that they had no reason to be concerned that the outsource contract would not be renewed: 'I don't think that Oldco will think of any other company other than Newco' (C1P3). They had served Oldco for a second term and were confident that they would continue to deliver an above-expected service level, and that Oldco would continue to be satisfied with their performance. The participants who are engaged in successful outsource contracts described their work experience in terms of a single period: 'I feel comfortable looking down eight years and say to myself I could not see myself with another company other than Newco' (C1P1).

Experiences described related to everyday stresses of supporting an IT environment in a medium-sized to large organisation, and in the minds of the participants were not linked to being an outsource partner of Oldco. The most stressful part of the job, most frequently raised by participants, was that they were a supplier to Oldco and therefore needed to treat Oldco as the customer. Thus, 'the customer is king' (C1P4). The attitude correlated with the participants' belief that Oldco had benefited from the outsource contract. Participants expressed a belief that their opportunities at Newco as opposed to Oldco would naturally be greater: 'I don't think that I would have grown at Oldco, we would have got up to a level and got stuck' (C1P1), as Newco is a specialist IT organisation. Yet they were most concerned about their day-to-day functions. One remarked that he sometimes was not motivated to go to work because the job could get mundane: 'same stuff different day' (C2P1).

Participants who were engaged in the outsource contract that was terminated at the end of the initial term, in all cases, saw the contract go through three phases that impacted on their job satisfaction, stress and worry. Once Newco was appointed and met with the affected employees, they began to feel less concerned – Newco made promises relating to how the outsource would benefit the affected employees and the Newco HR department became intensively involved in the process. The period prior to Newco being selected as the outsource partner was lengthy and uncertain. However, once Newco was announced the process was rapidly finalised. Participants reflected on their emotions relating to having to work overtime and change to a night shift system, and the very high expectations of the Oldco IT management regarding their service delivery during this period. Oldco was growing and the Newco outsource team became short-staffed. Oldco also became very cost-conscious and questioned the value that each member of the outsourced team contributed. Despite this, most participants commented that they felt committed to the job that they were doing and knew that they 'just had to carry on' (C3P1). These participants generally did not delve deeply into this middle period of the outsource contract but focused their discussions on the beginning and end periods.

Participants in the terminated contract experienced lower job satisfaction levels towards the end of the initial term of the contract. One participant said, 'about a year before the end, the contract started deteriorating' (C3P2). Oldco IT management was making huge demands of the Newco outsource team, which required the staffing levels to be addressed, but, at the same time, Oldco was not prepared to discuss adjusting the contract fee. Although the outsource contract was moving towards the end of the initial outsource period and contract renegotiations would have been expected to take place, none of the participants raised this as affecting their stress, worry or job satisfaction levels.

The contract in fact went out on a closed tender, and Newco bid for the business, according to the senior outsource manager of Newco. Participants explained the termination of the contract by suggesting that Oldco had unrealistic expectations of the deliverables, and that Newco probably did not want to renew the contract anyway: 'Oldco believed that we did not meet their service level agreement because their expectations were too high' (C3P2).

Another contended, 'if I was Newco "management" I would not have wanted to renew the contract' (C3P1).

Organisational commitment to employees

Participants' perception of the organisational commitment of Newco was based on their experience of the Newco manager assigned to the outsource contract. Where the Newco manager was either absent or ineffective, participants believed that the organisational commitment of Newco was insufficient. Participants did not feel that their relationship with Oldco had been tarnished through Oldco outsourcing them: 'We actually retained a good relationship with Oldco' (C1P2). No participant expressed a feeling that Oldco had reneged on their contract with them; most expressed an understanding of the outsourcing concept and said that they understood why Oldco had made this strategic move. However, one participant from C2 did express a concern that Oldco was not benefiting from the outsource contract and he did not see why Oldco would want to continue with the contract – to the point of questioning a senior manager at Oldco as to why Oldco had outsourced the IT function.

Participants found it difficult to connect with the broader Newco organisation and, therefore, although they generally did not express negativity towards Newco, they were not able to relate easily with the Newco organisational values and culture. Most participants considered the management of Newco who were directly involved on their outsource engagement as the Newco organisation. The exception were the participants of the Western Cape outsource team, who felt that they were closer to the organisational activities of Newco due only to the fact that the Newco office in that region is in the same office complex as that of Oldco: 'I probably feel more a part of Newco here than my colleagues do in Johannesburg; I generally hear about Newco activities through the Newco branch office rather than through my outsource team' (C1P2).

Some participants expressed a lack of delivery of their expectations by Newco, although these were not *promises* made by Newco. Expectations were raised during the initial outsource engagement that the affected employees would benefit by being given exposure to other organisations and people in Newco. There were further expectations that developed after the initial outsource engagement in C1 that, if the participant worked very hard and kept the client very happy, that is 'if more than a reasonable job has been done' (C1P3) through exceptional service delivery, he would be rewarded. The contract had been renewed, Newco was successful and therefore the expectation was that the participant should have been rewarded by now.

Most of the participants expressed disappointment that Newco also did not meet the promises they made at the outset of the outsource engagement. The promises were seen to have come from Newco, 'however these expectations were not met by Newco' (C3P1). The participants all expressed the opinion that Newco had not fulfilled any of their expectations: 'I applied for three different positions in Newco and I am still waiting for a response' (C3P2), even though the participant knew that the positions had been filled. This participant rationalised that the outsource contract on which he was engaged required the people to stay because the contract was so complex: 'the outsourcing director of Newco was not prepared to move people off the Oldco site due to the difficulties of the outsource contract' (C3P2).

There was a perception that outsourced employees were prejudiced against because their permanent home base was at the Oldco premises and not at Newco. The impression was created that they were excluded from Newco mainstream operations: 'out of sight out of mind'; 'You can motivate to your heart's content but you get stuck' (C1P2). Participants engaged in the terminated contract saw organisational commitment from a limited perspective, as they related their experiences of such commitment from Newco in terms of the management of Newco that was directly involved in the Oldco contract.

Most of the participants believed that the IT management of Oldco had changed their attitude towards the outsourced staff almost as soon as the contract commenced. It was felt that the Oldco IT manager specifically did not want to manage IT people and this was why they were outsourced. The feeling was that Oldco had shown no commitment towards their employees: 'Oldco became a finance-driven organisation where they don't care about people' (C3P2); 'The new IT manager was not a pleasant person' (C3P1).

The anger was directed towards the Oldco IT manager who had initiated the outsource contract and had structured it in such a way that he was not outsourced. Instead, he became the Oldco person who would manage the outsource contract on behalf of Oldco. Some participants recalled that they had been angry at the time when they were initially outsourced: 'When you join a big company like that, you don't expect to be outsourced and forced to work for another company' (C3P3). An incident described by one participant illustrated this: the result was that a third-party supplier was found to be in the right and the Oldco IT manager in the wrong, which made the Oldco manager appear foolish. The participant said that he and the Oldco IT manager did not talk for three months thereafter.

Employee commitment to the organisations

Most participants believed that they were committed fairly equally to Oldco and Newco, and they were clear about the differences in the relationship between the two. Oldco was very clearly understood to be the customer and participants knew that Newco was their employer. However, their relationship was not perceived to be as strong as it may have been had they worked within the Newco environment, and was linked to how well they were managed. Participants showed commitment towards Newco and were in no doubt that Newco was the organisation for whom they worked. Most participants expressed pride in the achievements of Newco, as they had seen the organisation grow since they were transferred: 'I am fully behind Newco' (C1P1). Newco is a growing organisation and is viewed as well managed and strong. For this reason the participants employed on the oldest Newco outsource contract expressed satisfaction with the organisation and were positive about their decision to move to Newco: 'The feeling is good, I made the right decision' (C1P1). Once they had made their decision, the participants were committed to making the outsource engagement a success and, therefore, felt closely aligned to Newco.

However, one participant (from C1) expressed a concern that there had been a turning point in the last year or two, which resulted in the outsource team losing the personal interaction with senior management in Newco with whom they had initiated the outsourcing contract; the communication that they had was no longer there. The concern was that Newco had grown, but the original outsourced employees had not grown and had not been afforded opportunities to develop and grow with Newco: 'I have a feeling that we have lost out' (C1P2). C2 participants felt that their commitment towards Newco had only recently improved: 'Much better in the last four months, purely from a management perspective; you know who the person is' (referring to a Newco manager now responsible for the outsource contract); 'you see him here more often' (C2P2). The improvement was a direct result of a recent management intervention from Newco. When C2P1 was asked if he felt like he was a part of Newco, his response was, 'I do now, I didn't previously' (C2P1). The participants of C2 said that they had previously felt that Newco had ignored them: 'It kinda felt like we were put on the back burner but now "the manager" has stepped in' (C2P1).

One participant was adamant that, prior to this change, he did not feel a commitment towards Newco: 'There was a point when I had a bit of a negative outlook as to Newco' (C2P1). However, his attitude changed when Newco introduced a part-time, hands-on, people-orientated Newco manager into their environment. The participant stated that he now feels that he is equally committed to both Oldco and Newco. Another participant did not envisage that Newco would facilitate career planning and advancement: 'Currently I don't see it, "my career", going anywhere' (C2P1).

Participants were very focused on ensuring that they delivered an exceptional service to their customer. Comparing their degree of loyalty, some felt more loyal towards Oldco, due mainly to the customer relationship and the fact that Oldco was where they spent most of their time: 'My loyalty is to both but probably to Oldco more so because I am with these people all day and have working relationships with the people here' (C2P1).

The general consensus across all the participants was that the regular staff at Oldco did not treat them any differently to the way they were treated prior to being outsourced to Newco.

Participants did not express negativity towards either Oldco or Newco with regard to the outsource process, which was recalled in an emotionally detached way. Participants said that they had been concerned about the effect the outsourcing decision would have on them, but the apprehension was dispelled very quickly once the decision had been taken by Oldco and they were introduced to Newco. The participants did not express resentment towards Oldco for outsourcing them, mainly because the outsourced employees found that their day-to-day functions and working environment remained unchanged.

Participants from the terminated contract reported that initially it was difficult to align their commitment to either party. First, there was anger towards Oldco for outsourcing them, but, at the same time, 'we are professionals and as Oldco is the customer we must be fully committed to Oldco' (C3P2). However, these participants primarily felt commitment towards the Newco service delivery manager, 'because he had promised that if we worked hard we would get time off and good increases' (C3P2). However, when the first round of pay increases came they received 'perhaps a third less than at Oldco' (C3P3).

As promises were not kept by Newco and expectations were not met, so the levels of commitment towards Newco waned. One of the participants, now employed elsewhere, commented that he now felt that he was appreciated, whereas, when he was employed on the Oldco outsource contract, 'we were severely reprimanded in an unpleasant way every time something went wrong because we were considered useless' (C3P1).

Emotions and job security

Once participants had been engaged in the outsource contract for two years or more, their awareness of the outsource environment had diminished and their emotional and job security concerns began to focus on their career and personal needs.

Participants did not consider that the outsource contracts needed to be renewed every few years. Most considered themselves to be the incumbents and rated as slim the possibility of the outsource contract not being renewed with Newco. None of the participants expressed any strong emotions about the initial outsource engagement. An outsource contract has a term, typically between three and five years. Employees of the outsource vendor on a contract understand that their own employment term is linked to the duration of the contract. In South Africa, the affected employees are afforded some protection in terms of the LRA.

Participants believed that they had the power to ensure the longevity of the outsource contract with Oldco. In most instances, the participants were firmly of the belief that they were doing such a good job that it would be inconceivable for Oldco to want to change outsource partners. Because Newco did not move staff between outsource contracts, participants did not consider job security in terms of their employment contract with Newco as a concern. However, participants were concerned that they were not afforded the opportunity to move within the Newco group and more specifically between outsource contracts.

There was a clear message from all the participants who were engaged on the terminated contract that there was a general dislike for the Oldco IT manager and the way he handled people. There was criticism that Newco did not support the outsource team when they needed support. Participants indicated that they had experienced a negative emotionally charged environment, reflected in one participant's view of whether Oldco had benefited from the outsource contract: 'Oldco did benefit in a way as they were able to make huge demands on us which had to be met because we were now a supplier, they had someone to blame when things went wrong' (C3P1). Participants related concerns regarding job security, particularly during the period of turmoil towards the end of the contract period. Some expressed relief that this period of their lives was over. All the participants were not happy at that time, expressed by one participant who said that 'the ending of the outsource contract with Oldco was the best thing that happened to me, I feel like a person again, there is more structure in my current working environment and this makes the job much more rewarding' (C3P1).

Communication levels

Participants were positively affected by the intensive communication between themselves and Newco during the initial outsource engagement period. However, some participants' perception of communication with Newco in the latter stages of the contract was that it had been neglected, to their detriment.

The C1 contract is the longest contract that Newco has operated. The participants have seen Newco grow exponentially during this period, which has resulted in certain senior managers of Newco being unable to spend as much time with the Newco employees engaged on this contract as they had done previously. The perception was that the communication with Oldco had therefore deteriorated.

The participants of C2 said that they had recently seen an improvement in communication between Newco and themselves. The improvement was a result of Newco appointing a new external manager to the contract. He had arranged regular weekly meetings with the outsource team and had set about recognising individual team members for their contributions: '"Old manager" did not have the control and keep the control that "new manager" has over the whole thing' (C2P2). The lack of involvement of the first Newco external manager made the team feel that they were a part of neither Oldco nor Newco: 'So you sorta feel like you're out there and Newco management sorta feels like we don't hear from Newco, so where are we?' (C2P2). Once Oldco management saw more regular involvement of Newco external management, the perception of the participants was that the Oldco management therefore felt that things were more under control.

One of the participants related their experience of the impact that lack of communication had on the perceived stability of the contract. The perception was that the Newco manager did not have control of the contract, and the participants perceived that the Oldco management sensed this and were equally unhappy with the situation. Newco had recently instituted an internal marketing function to focus on the staff of Newco. C2 participants were not aware of this function and had not all received the internal marketing material. The participants expressed a concern that they were not aware of what the broader Newco group offered, particularly in the way of skills and knowledge that would assist them to enhance the service that they provided to Oldco.

In the terminated contract, communication from Oldco was tainted when the Oldco IT department was abruptly informed that they were to be outsourced. Oldco became the bad guys and exacerbated the situation by immediately changing the way they treated the outsourced staff. A participant who was second-in-command of the Oldco IT department before the outsource engagement was not informed of the process by Oldco. This participant felt that Oldco should have been honest about the process and not done things behind closed doors. Shortly after the first meeting with Newco, Oldco informed their IT staff that the decision to outsource had been made, and introduced them to the Newco manager. Some participants were equally critical of Newco, who also focused on operational issues: 'We were told how the salary structure would work via email' (C3P1). Another participant stated that Newco was very involved for the first three months, but thereafter they did not see anybody from Newco other than the Newco management directly involved in the project. When the relationship became strained with Oldco, towards the end of the contract, the Newco director had weekly meetings with the outsourced staff and listened to their concerns and had feasible explanations for the problems they were experiencing.

Work relationships with colleagues

While relationships with the broader body of Newco colleagues were perceived as being largely non-existent, participants experienced little change in their relationships with Oldco colleagues. They did, however, find that their relationships with the Oldco management had become more formalised. Relationships with Oldco colleagues were expressed as good, particularly with the staff below management level. Participants believed that, even though their Oldco colleagues are aware that they were no longer employees of Oldco and were outsourced to Newco, they were treated no differently from the way they had been previously. On the whole, Oldco management treated the Newco outsourced staff with respect, and, other than the participants referring to the need to deliver an exceptional service, there was no indication of friction between the Oldco employees and the Newco outsourced staff.

Relationships reported by participants from the terminated contract were, in the main, not good. They did, however, consider as good their relationships with their Oldco colleagues below management level and did not recall any hostilities among them. It appeared that the manager who was the individual who initiated the outsource process on behalf of Oldco did not relinquish his responsibilities for managing and directing the outsource team. This observation arises from statements by participants that the manager was instrumental in moving the first Newco outsource manager out of the contract, as well as dealing directly with outsourced staff to the extent that he had an argument with one of the outsourced team, resulting in that person resigning. The relationship with Newco was very weak, brought on by the fact that, although initially Newco installed their own manager at Oldco, the Oldco IT manager rejected this person and Newco then promoted one of the outsourced employees to the Newco managerial position.

Looking to the future

Participants were not generally concerned about the contract renewal period, but were motivated by having their immediate needs addressed. Work opportunities, training and opportunities to advance their careers in the IT field were the most common expectations participants had for their futures. One of the participants believed that, if employees were to be assured of secure contracts, Newco had to ensure that there was a 'motivated, dedicated and enthusiastic team' (C1P2). The participant had explained that, as a result of their expectations not being met, Newco was in danger of putting its outsource contracts at risk.

To summarise, participants discussed their views on job satisfaction, commitment, communications and work relationships. The responses did vary, particularly for those who were involved in the terminated contract. Although participants discussed positive aspects of commitment, the physical closeness to Newco did make a difference to responses. There was discussion of raised expectations and unmet promises. The role of the line manager in communications and gaining commitment was viewed as extremely important. Although some did speak of anger during the transition, on the whole there were good levels of job satisfaction and the nature of the outsourcing relationships.

Discussion

We have considered the results of the study in terms of the participants' recollection of the initial outsource engagement, through to the current reality. The findings can be classified into four phases of the outsource engagement (implementation, honeymoon, stabilisation and maturity) in which the experiences of the affected employees are grouped and discussed.

Many participants recollected an uncertain period during the initial 'implementation' stage of the outsource engagement. However, the period of uncertainty was mostly recalled as being that prior to the announcement of Newco's selection as the chosen outsource partner. The literature dealing with mergers shows that, after a merger, the morale of employees may improve.[17] The finding was reflected by participants who recalled that their anxiety levels were reduced after Newco was introduced to the outsource process.

In each outsource engagement Newco immediately introduced senior managers into the process who focused on the softer HR issues. Newco communications with affected employees during that period were specifically face to face – as postulated in the literature,[18] good communication during the initial outsource process will result in a perception that the outsource transition is a success. The participants recalled that Newco reassured them about being outsourced; they believed that Newco would consider their needs and ensure that they would be no worse off than before. Participants were aware of their rights in terms of the LRA and, when Newco made these assurances, this was in terms of the legal obligation and, therefore, the participants had no reason not to believe that Newco was acting with integrity. One participant recalled that a concern arose about their benefits after being outsourced. This resulted in Newco renegotiating that aspect of the contract, thereby resolving the problem. This reflects the understanding that the participant had of their right to no loss of benefits during the outsource transfer process as prescribed by the LRA. This finding is in line with that of Saunders and Thornhill,[19] that communication, especially face-to-face communication, improves the trust of affected employees.

Participants then experienced a 'honeymoon' period, during which their day-to-day functions returned to normal and they continued performing the functions that they did prior to being outsourced to Newco. Their work environment remained unchanged, their colleagues treated them the same as before, and they did not have much contact with Oldco management. During this period, Newco management were engaging with the management of Oldco and thus buffering the affected employees from Oldco.

The honeymoon period had very different time-frames for the participants, which resulted in some participants experiencing a longer period during which their work environment remained unchanged. The research found that it was during this period that the affected employees formed their expectations of what benefits they would derive from being outsourced to a specialist IT organisation. In an attempt to build a relationship with the affected employees, Newco managers assigned to the outsource contract sometimes created the expectations themselves by making promises to the affected employees that may have been difficult to fulfil.

Participants also redefined their relationship with Oldco during this period. In each outsource contract the participants felt that Oldco had altered their expectations of what the IT department, now outsourced to Newco, should deliver. In some instances, the participants did not understand Oldco's motives and intentions, and this caused the trust relationship with Oldco to be damaged. Organisations are no longer outsourcing to simply offload non-core businesses,[20] but are beginning to engage in transformational outsourcing to facilitate rapid organisational change.[21] Outourcing in South Africa is relatively new and the expectations of Oldco are developing as they learn more about this strategy as well as their own business needs.

Employees may often not be privy to the strategic intent of the organisation when embarking on an outsourcing approach. Not necessarily understanding the underlying reasons why Oldco had outsourced the IT function, some participants expressed a concern that they were not delivering the level of services that Oldco expected and this resulted in them questioning their own competencies and roles.

The demands placed on the participants in the terminated outsource contract resulted in the outsource team believing that Oldco no longer cared about them. This may have been a symptom of the expectation of Oldco – that the outsourcing engagement would transform the IT environment – which resulted in a mismatch between the objectives of Oldco and those of the Newco outsource team. There was severe conflict between Oldco and Newco because Oldco did not believe that its requirements had been met by Newco, and because the management of Newco was sidelined by the Oldco IT manager.

Once the 'stabilisation' phase had been reached, participants became more focused on themselves and their own needs in the outsource environment. Participants were no longer concerned about the fact that they were employed in an environment that had a contract period, as they believed that Oldco would not consider terminating the contract and would continue to renew the contract with Newco. Their relationships with both Newco and Oldco had stabilised, and the participants were comfortable in the knowledge that they worked for Newco, while at the same time providing services to Oldco exclusively, who they accepted was now their customer.

In this phase of the outsourcing engagement a new psychological contract with Oldco had been formed. The participants had come to understand what was expected of them in the new role, and they understood the form of the relationship they had with Oldco. A psychological contract with Newco by this phase had also been formed, specifically through the interaction with Newco management during the honeymoon phase. The ability of the Newco manager assigned to the outsourcing contract to provide vision, guidance and leadership to the outsourced team played a significant role in the organisational commitment that the participants had towards Newco, and in the perception that the participants had of the satisfaction levels of Oldco.[22] When Newco introduced a manager who was external to the outsourced team, there was a perception that Newco was in control of the outsource contract. The Newco manager was seen to provide direction and vision for the outsource team, which gave the participants the comforting feeling that Newco would support them in this new (to the transferred employees) endeavour. In those instances where the original outsourced team was being managed by one of the original outsourced staff or the Newco manager was not seen or heard from, there was a perception that Newco was not in control of the contract and a breach of the psychological contract had occurred. This was the finding of Parker and Russell[23] – that many outsourcing engagements are unsuccessful due to affected employees being neglected. This situation becomes even worse during the 'maturity' stage, where complacency by the outsourcing organisation can also leave employees feeling neglected.

The research revealed that participants were settled in their work environment only when they felt that Newco was doing a good job of managing the outsourcing contract. The involvement of the Newco manager was seen as important to ensuring that Oldco's requirements were understood and were being properly managed. Some of the participants' levels of job satisfaction correlated with their perception of Oldco's satisfaction with the outsourcing contract. This research supports the literature in that the job satisfaction levels of participants are reduced when there is low management support shown by Newco. The research indicates that participants also believe that Oldco is affected in the same way – if they feel communication is poor, so will Oldco management. This research shares many of the findings from studies with Western European samples, including the feelings of remoteness from Newco, the change in attitude of Oldco to the staff, the importance of line management and good communications, unmet expectations, and the short-term nature of contact with Newco managers in some cases. There is also some evidence of anger and insecurity during the initial transfer, although this memory was only discussed by a small number (and may, in turn, have been influenced by the long timescales since the transition). A key difference from research by Morgan[24] is that most of the participants in this sample seemed to understand the outsourcing concept and the strategic nature of the move for Oldco. This may be due to sampling differences, the timescales involved in this research (minimum four years compared to Morgan's maximum of two years since transfer), or to differences in culture between South Africa and the UK. The IT industry in South Africa has seen a large amount of change since 1994, when the country was welcomed back onto the international stage and many foreign IT organisations introduced operations into the country. Participants may be aware of the need for South African organisations to follow international trends, outsourcing being one such trend, thus they are more understanding of the move.

This study has a number of limitations, including the small sample size and the reliance on a single method of data collection. The weaknesses of interviews when discussing experiences over many years must also be considered. However, in-depth interviews do allow a full exploration of experience and offer rich information regarding process. We therefore feel it is acceptable to make a number of recommendations based on these findings.

Recommendations

Four phases were identified during which participants revealed different degrees of concern with their involvement in the IT outsourcing contract. The research identified specific interventions that outsource vendors should plan for during the implementation of IT outsourcing as well as ongoing interventions that will increase the prospect of the IT outsourcing contract remaining successful.

The implementation phase is a traumatic period for the affected employees. The IT outsource vendor is often not involved until a final decision has been made by Oldco to outsource its IT department. This is particularly the case if the organisation has followed a tender approach to selecting the outsource vendor. By the time the successful outsource vendor is introduced to the affected employees, it is likely that they have become very concerned about their futures.

From this point forward, the outsource vendor is in full control of the process and the research has shown that it is imperative that the outsource vendor moves quickly to allay the fears of the affected employees. The outsource vendor should immediately involve the HR department of Newco to deal with concerns that relate to the affected employees' packages. Also, senior management from Newco should be involved to provide the affected employees with a sense of the new vendor organisation. A Newco manager should immediately be appointed and the manager should have the time available to engage in face-to-face interactions with the affected employees as well as the authority to make decisions that relate to the their well-being.

The honeymoon phase is an important period because it is during this period that the outsourced employees could incorrectly interpret the nature and reason for Oldco outsourcing their department. Expectations should be built on reality during this period and the affected employees should be reassured about their role in the outsource contract. The outsourced team is now operating like a small business and therefore Newco management needs to define the objectives for the contract. The affected employees should be included in this process and should be involved in defining the vision and objectives for the IT outsource contract, which should be in line with the requirements of Oldco. Through this process, the affected employees should be encouraged to build a sense of ownership of their role in Newco. Newco should transfer at least one or more employees from other outsource contracts into the new contract to provide the newly outsourced employees with a support system.

During the stabilisation phase, the Newco manager needs to ensure that the Oldco objectives are being achieved and that the outsourced employees are meeting the needs of Oldco. The Newco manager should meet regularly with Oldco, preferably monthly, to discuss issues, as well as with the outsourced employees, preferably weekly, to provide support and guidance. The Newco manager should ensure that the outsourced employees are up to date with the requirements of Oldco and provide positive feedback on the satisfaction levels of Oldco.

During the maturity phase the Newco manager should be conscious of the dangers of complacency. Newco should ensure that a strong managerial function and presence is maintained over the outsource contract. The Newco manager should be aware of the dynamics of the outsource environment and the interventions needed to ensure happy and motivated employees. Outsourced employees should be stretched and given new learning opportunities and challenges. Personal goals and objectives should be taken into account and reviewed according to the Newco performance review mechanisms. Future expectations of individuals should be discussed and managed. Outsourced employees should be recognised and rewarded for their efforts. This will often require a special effort from the Newco management as the outsourced employees' place of work may be far from the Newco corporate offices. Extraordinary efforts should be made by Newco to ensure that all the outsourced employees are included in all initiatives aimed at the employees of Newco. Outsourced employees should not be excluded either intentionally or unintentionally.[25]

Notes

1 M. Hurley, 'IT outsourcing – managing the key asset', *Information Management & Computer Security*, 9(5) (2001): 243–9.
2 See www.geert-hofstede.com.
3 T. Jackson, 'Managing change in South Africa: developing people and organisations', *International Journal of Human Resource Management*, 10(2) (1999), 306–26.
4 T. Jackson, *Management and Change in Africa* (London: Routledge, 2004).
5 Ibid.
6 Labour Relations Act 66 of 1995 (Lansdowne, SA: Juta Law, 2000).
7 S. J. Morgan and G. Symon, 'The experience of outsourcing transfer: implications for guidance and counselling', *British Journal of Guidance & Counselling*, 34(2) (2006): 191–208; M. K. O. Lee, 'IT outsourcing contracts: practical issues for management', *Industrial Management & Data Systems*, 96(1) (1996): 15–19.
8 Morgan and Symon, 'The experience of outsourcing transfer'.
9 Ibid.
10 J. C. Linder, 'Transformational outsourcing', *MIT Sloan Management Review* (Spring, 2004): 52–8.
11 M. N. K. Saunders and A. Thornhill, 'Organisational justice, trust and the management of change: an exploration', *Personnel Review*, 32(3) (2003): 360–75.
12 Ibid.
13 D. W. Parker and K. A. Russell, 'Outsourcing and inter/intra supply chain dynamics: strategic management issues', *The Journal of Supply Chain Management*, 40(4) (2004): 56–68.
14 S. J. Morgan, 'How to: Manage the human side of outsourcing', *People Management* (May 2001): 44–5.
15 S. J. Morgan, 'Organisational attachments in IT outsourcing', unpublished Ph.D. thesis (Birkbeck College, University of London, 2003).
16 M. B. Miles and A. M. Huberman, *Qualitative Data Analysis: An Expanded Sourcebook*, 2nd edn (Thousand Oaks, CA: Sage, 1994).
17 R. Shield, R. Thorpe and A. Nelson, 'Hospital mergers and psychological contracts', *Strategic Change*, 11(7) (2002): 357–67.
18 M. Butcher and C. Hind, 'Communicating a major outsourcing deal at Barclays, *Strategic Communication Management*, 9(1) (2005): 22–5; Morgan and Symon, 'The experience of outsourcing transfer'.

19 Saunders and Thornhill, 'Organisational justice, trust and the management of change'.
20 See R. Hircheim and M. Lacity, 'The myths and realities of information technology insourcing', *Communications of the ACM*, 42(2) (2000): 99–107.
21 Linder, 'Transformational outsourcing'.
22 D. Asch and G. Salaman, 'The challenge of change', *European Business Journal*, 14(3) (2002): 133–44.
23 Parker and Russell, 'Outsourcing and inter/intra supply chain dynamics'.
24 Morgan, 'Organisational attachments in IT outsourcing'.
25 Some of the issues dealt with in this chapter are referred to in my recently published book, which is written in the form of a diary. *Carry on Car-Making – Life in China after Longbridge* is published by Brewin Books, Studley, Warwickshire, ISBN 1 85858 4094.

Index

For Product Safety Concerns and Information please contact our EU
representative GPSR@taylorandfrancis.com
Taylor & Francis Verlag GmbH, Kaufingerstraße 24, 80331 München, Germany

www.ingramcontent.com/pod-product-compliance
Ingram Content Group UK Ltd.
Pitfield, Milton Keynes, MK11 3LW, UK
UKHW021118180425
457613UK00005B/143
9780415428910